Deconstructive Constitutionalism

SUNY series in Contemporary Continental Philosophy
―――――――
Dennis J. Schmidt, editor

Deconstructive Constitutionalism
Derrida Reading Kant

JACQUES DE VILLE

Cover painting reproduced by courtesy of the artist, Ludovic Mercher, SPLIT (diptyque), 2022

Published by State University of New York Press, Albany

© 2023 State University of New York

All rights reserved

Printed in the United States of America

No part of this book may be used or reproduced in any manner whatsoever without written permission. No part of this book may be stored in a retrieval system or transmitted in any form or by any means including electronic, electrostatic, magnetic tape, mechanical, photocopying, recording, or otherwise without the prior permission in writing of the publisher.

For information, contact State University of New York Press, Albany, NY
www.sunypress.edu

Library of Congress Cataloging-in-Publication Data

Name: De Ville, Jacques, author.
Title: Deconstructive constitutionalism : Derrida reading Kant / Jacques de Ville.
Description: Albany, NY : State University of New York Press, [2023] | Series: SUNY series in contemporary continental philosophy | Includes bibliographical references and index.
Identifiers: LCCN 2022023023 | ISBN 9781438491714 (hardcover : alk. paper) | ISBN 9781438491738 (ebook) | ISBN 9781438491721 (pbk. : alk. paper)
Subjects: LCSH: Constitutional law—Philosophy. | Constitution (Philosophy) | Deconstruction. | Kant, Immanuel, 1724–1804—Influence. | Derrida, Jacques—Influence.
Classification: LCC K3165 .D4793 2023 | DDC 342—dc23/eng/20220924
LC record available at https://lccn.loc.gov/2022023023

10 9 8 7 6 5 4 3 2 1

For my dad: August 19, 1937–May 10, 2021

It can be said that establishing universal and lasting peace constitutes not merely a part of the doctrine of right but rather the entire final end of the doctrine of right within the limits of mere reason.

—Kant 1996b, 6:355

For philosophy, science, morals, law, politics, what does it mean to *render*, to render reason, render this reason which is not some thing, render this not-some-thing, this non-thing that is a reason and a cause, render an account and reply to the responsibility when the unconscious is in on the act?

—Derrida 1990, 7

I am ultra-Kantian. I am Kantian, but I am more than Kantian.

—Derrida 2001d, 66

Contents

Acknowledgments		xi
Introduction		1
Chapter 1	The Moral Law	19
Chapter 2	The Principle of Reason	37
Chapter 3	Freedom and Democracy	61
Chapter 4	Animal, Subject, Constitution	83
Chapter 5	Crime, Punishment, and Forgiveness	101
Chapter 6	Perpetual Peace	125
Kant after Derrida		145
Notes		155
Bibliography		183
Index		201

Acknowledgments

The first phase of this manuscript was made possible by funding from the Humboldt Foundation for a three-month visit to Berlin in 2017. I would like to extend my gratitude to Prof. Dr. Heike Krieger who acted as my hostess and to Ms. Bozena Sikora for her administrative assistance. Henk Botha provided valuable support and insights. Wessel le Roux and Derek Powell over the last months shared many fruitful sources and ideas for which I am grateful. The anonymous reviewers of the manuscript further provided many helpful suggestions for improvement. I would also like to express my gratitude to the National Research Foundation and to University of the Western Cape for financial support.

Earlier versions of some of the chapters in this manuscript have been published previously. Chapter 1 was originally published as "The Moral Law: Derrida Reading Kant," *Derrida Today* 12, no. 1 (2019): 1–19; chapter 3 as "Freedom and Democracy: From Kant to Derrida," *Law, Culture and the Humanities* (October 2020), https://doi.org/10.1177/1743872120956557; chapter 4 as "Animal, Subject, Constitution," *Mosaic: An Interdisciplinary Critical Journal* 51, no. 4 (2021): 113–28; chapter 5 as "On Crime and Punishment: Derrida Reading Kant," *Law and Critique* 31, no. 1 (2020): 93–111; and chapter 6 as "Perpetual Peace: Derrida Reading Kant," *International Journal for the Semiotics of Law* 32, no. 2 (2019): 335–57. My thanks to the publishers for allowing subsequent publication.

Introduction

As appears from the title, *Deconstructive Constitutionalism: Derrida Reading Kant* seeks to explore the relationship between the thinking of Immanuel Kant (1724–1804) and Jacques Derrida (1930–2004) with respect to constitutionalism. In what follows, the elements of the title are briefly unpacked to show their interrelation and significance. *Constitutionalism* at its most basic level refers to the definition and limitation of state powers through a constitution (Currie and De Waal 2013, 8; De Vos 2021, 42–3). *Kant* is widely recognized as one of the philosophical forebears of this idea, together with John Locke (1632–1704), Montesquieu (1689–1755), and Jean-Jacques Rousseau (1712–1778). Although Kant did not, like some of his predecessors, inspire the American and French revolutions of the eighteenth century, which gave birth to the modern constitution, he played a pivotal role in explaining these events philosophically after the fact (Reiss 1991, 3–4). Kant is of course best known as a founding figure of the Enlightenment through his three Critiques, which have tended to overshadow his politico-legal writings (3). The latter texts, which flow from the Critiques, have however received greater attention in recent years, as can, for example, be seen in the influential writings of John Rawls and Jürgen Habermas.[1] With respect to constitutionalism, and as appears in more detail later, Kant championed the notions of human freedom and of self–government as well as the limitation and separation of state powers. Kant furthermore proposed a constitutional-type arrangement on the international and cosmopolitan levels for the sake of securing peace.

Jacques *Derrida* is known for his *deconstruction* of the Western philosophical tradition. He is regarded by many as one of the most important philosophers of the twentieth century. Kant plays a central role in Derrida's readings, whom he both follows and challenges. As we will see in what follows, this often happens through an analysis of Heidegger's engagement with Kant. With respect to constitutionalism, Derrida's 1990 essay "Force of Law: The 'Mystical Foundations of Authority'" is probably the best known (Derrida 2002a, 230–98).² In the first of the essay's two parts, Derrida draws a distinction between law and justice, and defines the latter in excessive terms as a gift without exchange and as entailing a madness beyond reason. Whereas for Kant, as we will see, justice can be attained by the state if it adheres to certain principles, this is not possible in Derrida's thinking on justice. In the second part of the essay, a close reading of Walter Benjamin's essay "Critique of Violence" takes place, with Derrida pointing to the moment of the founding of a constitution as well as its subsequent enforcement, as occasioning an abyssal, self-destructive, a-legal "moment," where no existing law is in place to regulate what takes place. Kant likely would not have denied this, but he did not explicitly attach any consequence to this "moment," apart from prescribing that the new constitutional order so established should be respected irrespective of the a-legal manner in which it came about (Kant 1996b, 6:318–23). The second part of "Force of Law" thus ties in closely with the first part and opens the way to a radically different approach to modern constitutionalism, which is explored further in *Deconstructive Constitutionalism*.

Derrida's texts on politico-legal issues indicate that the structure of decision-making in "Force of Law" is not restricted to the judiciary, but necessarily extends also to the other state branches (Derrida 1997c, 2005c). "Force of Law" is not further analyzed here, but it serves as an important source of reference for the analysis that is to be undertaken. The focus in *Deconstructive Constitutionalism* is on texts of Derrida that touch either directly or indirectly on what is at the heart of Kant's ethical, political and legal thinking. Justice nevertheless remains at the forefront here, as appears from the first chapter on Derrida's engagement with Kant's moral law. In addition to this engagement with the moral law, *Deconstructive Constitutionalism* explores the way in which Derrida reads other central Kantian notions such as freedom, reason, and the pursuit of peace within the context of modern constitutionalism. The aim is to investigate how the foundations of modern constitutionalism, as spelled out in Kant's thinking, can be differently conceived to address some of the challenges of the twenty-first century. We now explore these elements of the title and their significance in more detail.

Kant and Modern Constitutionalism

Writing between the First and the Second World Wars, Carl Schmitt identified the aim of the modern constitution as the protection of the sphere of freedom of the individual, which is in principle unlimited, and which precedes the establishment of the state:

> The modern, civil, rule-of-law constitution is, in respect of its historical development and its basic structure, which still dominates today, in the first place a liberal (*freiheitliche*) constitution, particularly in the interests of civil freedom (*bürgerlichen Freiheit*). Its meaning and purpose, its *telos*, is not in the first place the power and splendor of the state, not glory (*gloire*) according to the classification of Montesquieu . . . , but liberty (*liberté*), protection of the citizen from the abuse of state power. It is, as Kant said, established "in the first place according to the principles of the freedom (*Prinzipien* der *Freiheit*) of the members of a society as human beings." (Schmitt 2008, 170, trans. modified)

Schmitt then quotes from "Toward Perpetual Peace," where Kant refers to the principles of the civil condition, that is, the freedom and the equality of everyone before the law, as well as the independence of citizens. He further notes the importance of Kant's formulations in this respect, seeing that "they contain the clearest, most definitive expression of the principal ideas of the civil Enlightenment, which until now have not been replaced by any new, ideal foundation" (170, trans. modified). According to Schmitt, the modern constitution seeks to protect freedom from state abuse in two primary ways: by entrenching fundamental rights and by way of the separation of powers. State power is in other words distributed among the various branches and is in principle limited and calculable in terms of a previously enacted law. The traditional state forms, that is, monarchy, aristocracy, and democracy, are all retained, but modified for the sake of the protection of freedom (235).

There can be little doubting the accuracy of Schmitt's assessment at the time. Kant (1996b, 6:237) regarded freedom as the only innate right, and the classical liberal constitution was indeed focused primarily on protecting the freedom (and property) of the individual against the state.[3] The classical liberal constitution lost its dominance after World War II, yet the constitutionalism that arose in its wake is still fully aligned with Kant's thinking.[4] Kant's influence on constitutionalism today is most frequently described with reference to human dignity.[5] This shift in emphasis from freedom toward human dignity corresponds with the shift in emphasis in constitutional discourse after World War II from the "formal" to the "material" elements of the constitutional state (*Rechtsstaat*).[6] It is however important to note that the notion of human dignity, which has become so central to modern constitutional thinking, is very closely related to freedom in Kant's thinking and that the material elements of the constitutional state did not replace the formal elements, but were added to the latter.[7] Freedom in Kant, in other words, is inherently linked to practical reason and the moral law, and therefore it is perhaps not strange that after the atrocities of World War II, Kant's thinking on human dignity would come to play a central role in constitutionalism. After 1945, a number of international and transnational legal instruments as well as national constitutions gave explicit recognition to human dignity, with Kant generally being credited as one of the main sources for this inclusion.[8] Kant's own understanding of dignity furthermore has been important in interpreting the relevant human dignity provisions within these documents, both in the courts and in scholarly reflection.[9] This development is nonetheless somewhat peculiar, as Kant developed the notion of human dignity within a discussion of the moral law and never argued for, or seems to have envisaged, the constitutionalization of this notion.[10]

The German Basic Law was one of the first constitutions to recognize human dignity, not simply as a right, but as a foundational value of the whole constitutional order (Botha 2009, 178–82). Article 1 of the Basic Law, echoing the preamble of the United Nations Charter and the Universal Declaration of Human Rights, posits the respect and protection of human dignity at the basis of all human rights. It furthermore links human dignity to "peace and justice in the world," in a similar way that Kant does with freedom.[11] The German Basic law has become paradigmatic in the design of constitutions since World War II (Ackermann 2012, 1, 13). This happened, for example, in South Africa, also because of the similarities between the policy and practices of apartheid and the atrocities in Nazi Germany. The German Basic Law served as a model for the South African constitution in a number of respects, for example, in the establishment of a Constitutional Court, the institutionalization of a quasi-federal system, and the foundational value of human dignity.[12] Human dignity indeed became a central value and principle within the post-apartheid constitutional dispensation.[13] In the early years of the post-apartheid era, the South African Constitutional Court both explicitly and implicitly relied on Kant in expounding the notion of human dignity as well as its interconnection with freedom.[14] To be noted, with respect to the discussion in chapters 2, 4, and 5, is that human dignity is, similar to the position in Germany, regarded as central to the objective normative value system established through the Constitution, and thus also to legal reasoning.[15] This objective normative value system "acts as a guiding principle and stimulus" for the legislature, the executive, and the judiciary, and all law and action need to comply therewith (Ackermann 2012, 49, 97). In view of the discussion in chapter 5, it is furthermore interesting to note that the South African Constitutional Court has declared the death penalty unconstitutional, inter alia on the basis of human dignity. This is ironic, of course, as Kant was a strong, principled defender of the death penalty, precisely on the basis of human dignity. The Constitutional Court has furthermore, in relation to the propriety of imprisonment, viewed human dignity as conceived by Kant to be a central consideration.[16] The notions of criminal guilt and punishment as such have not, however, as yet been placed in question on constitutional grounds. The obviously exclusionary nature of the Kantian notion of human dignity, that is, the exclusion of everything non-human from the protection and respect it accords, was furthermore not regarded as a problem in the early years of the post-apartheid state.[17]

Insofar as the international legal order is concerned, it is generally acknowledged that it today reflects Kant's eighteenth-century vision of a voluntary association of states, in the form of the United Nations, as well as of a cosmopolitan order through the recognition of universal human rights.[18] The transnational and international legal orders are furthermore today increasingly thought of in terms of constitutional orders, and thus as different levels of multilevel constitutionalism.[19] A discussion of Kant's essay on "Perpetual Peace" (chapter 6) therefore is not out of place in *Deconstructive Constitutionalism*, also because this text and other texts of Kant continue to play an important role in contemporary thinking on the development of such a global constitutional order.[20]

Context, Challenges, and Alliances

Despite the references earlier to the German and South African constitutions, *Deconstructive Constitutionalism* does not focus on any specific country's constitution. *Deconstructive Constitutionalism* was nonetheless written within the context of a specific constitutional order, and it may be useful to briefly convey that background, as it inevitably informs the arguments presented here. The writing of *Deconstructive Constitutionalism* started during a three-month stint in Berlin, Germany, but was written for the most part in and around Cape Town, South Africa. As noted earlier, South Africa underwent a constitutional transformation in the 1990s and today is governed by a supreme constitution, which entrenches fundamental rights, the rule of law, separation of powers, and democracy. This constitutional transformation is often described in Kantian terms as a movement away from a culture of authority to a culture of justification, that is, requiring that every exercise of state power must be justifiable (Mureinik 1994, 32). The Constitution is furthermore frequently referred to as being "transformative" or as "post-liberal" in nature (Klare 1998, 150–51). Despite the democratic transition almost thirty years ago, the country today is still marked by acute poverty, food insecurity, stark inequality, and high unemployment. There furthermore is evidence of endemic corruption and a dysfunctional public service on all three levels of government. South Africa moreover has one of the highest crime rates in the world. Anticipating the analysis in chapter 4 of this volume, violence against animals is increasing at a rapid pace, as is the case almost everywhere else in the world. This country, on the southernmost tip of Africa, is of course not immune from other global currents such as climate change, which in 2017–18 contributed to taps in the second-largest city (Cape Town) almost running dry. South Africa moreover has been severely affected by the COVID-19 pandemic, which was responded to by the declaration of a state of national disaster with sometimes draconian regulations, and which has further exacerbated the poverty, unemployment, and inequality mentioned earlier. Because of its relative economic strength on the African continent, South Africa attracts large numbers of migrants, which in turn has led to violent and deadly xenophobic incidents on a large scale.[21] Recent technological developments likewise pose fundamental challenges to democracy today, also in South Africa. This is due, inter alia, to the possibility of the manipulation of elections through propaganda, an increase in the spread of conspiracy theories and disinformation, as well technology's enabling of extremism and increasing polarization (including racial polarization) within society. Further challenges to democracy in South Africa and elsewhere include the demise of traditional and independent news media, voter apathy and loss of trust in public institutions, censorship, as well as power imbalances, specifically between big tech companies and state powers with respect to technology. The impact of other developments on the international level is also felt in South Africa. These include globalization, which is evoking vehement responses, such as religious fundamentalism and authoritarian populism, the latter which appears to combine itself with a peculiar form of capitalism (Scheuerman 2019, 1175–78). In addition, authoritarianism in rising global powers such as Russia and China, as well as authoritarian populism in "democratic" countries, is placing the international legal order under severe strain.[22]

Returning to the theme of constitutionalism within the South African context, the lack of progress in addressing inequality, specifically systemic racial inequality, as well as historical injustice, especially the failure to address the issue of land restoration to the original inhabitants, has recently led to calls for the amendment or even the abolition of the constitution, which is regarded as still being rooted in colonialism.[23] The Enlightenment, German, and Kantian "presence" within the South African constitution, as outlined earlier, would seem to provide further evidence of its Western, colonial heritage.[24] Indeed, it can hardly be denied that the South African constitution, and the same most likely can be said of most, if not all modern constitutions, is the product of a long history of Western metaphysical thinking.

The "radical" critique expressed by certain South African scholars against the "colonial" constitution, that is, a constitution based on Western, and thus metaphysical, thinking, and the search for an alternative jurisprudence, in a strange way resonates with the analysis undertaken here. Similar to these "radical" critics, *Deconstructive Constitutionalism* is concerned with the mostly unnoticed and unstable foundations, the injustices, failures, complicities, and exclusions of not only the South African constitution, but of modern constitutions in general.[25] It follows Derrida, who has argued that the "origin" of the modern constitution does not only lie in Western metaphysical thinking, but in a certain beyond to metaphysics (Derrida 2014a, 9–30; Goosen 2010, 255–59). It is arguably from this "beyond" that a challenge to existing constitutional arrangements, principles, and values needs to be launched. *Deconstructive Constitutionalism* agrees that "interpretation" as traditionally conceived may not be adequate to bring about justice, and that a certain kind of "abolition" of the modern constitution may be needed. It is, however, contra these critics, somewhat skeptical of the possibility of establishing a truly post-colonial constitution, which would succeed in completely freeing itself from the metaphysics of presence. This is because simply opposing and overturning Western metaphysical thinking as it finds expression in modern constitutionalism risks simply replicating the system (Derrida 1981, 41–42). Such a strategy, more specifically, risks retaining the founding belief in the value of "presence," here of a collective subject with the power to enact a postcolonial constitution for itself (Maris and Jacobs 2011, 322–24; chapter 3 of this volume). Moreover, as Derrida (1981, 12; 1998b, 39; 2001a, 86, 88) has pointed out, neither metaphysics nor colonialism can be completely escaped from. Deconstructive constitutionalism arguably presents the only chance for such an "escape," even though this "escape" cannot be experienced in time and space.[26]

The analysis undertaken here furthermore resonates with the North American variants of critical legal scholarship, or what is now sometimes called "critical realism," and finds itself in alliance with the efforts of these movements to bring about egalitarian and democratic social change. *Deconstructive Constitutionalism* thus aligns itself in broad terms with the political stance taken by those belonging to these movements.[27] Albertyn and Davis (2010, 202) capture this stance succinctly as follows with respect to the South African constitution: "In our view, the best interpretation of the Constitution and its transformative impulse is an egalitarian one. This requires, inter alia, achievement of socio-economic equality and individual well-being through the dismantling of structures of exclusion and oppression and the development of a caring and inclusive society." *Deconstructive Constitutionalism* further agrees with the view of these critical legal scholars that adjudication inevitably involves lawmaking and that law cannot be rigorously distinguished from politics. Yet it takes a distance from these critics concerning the way in which such lawmaking should be conceived, how "politics" should be understood, and the central role that subjectivity continues to play in much critical legal writing.[28] *Deconstructive Constitutionalism* finds itself philosophically closer to the UK variants of critical legal thinking that rely primarily on continental philosophical and psychoanalytical thinking in reflecting on law, though slight differences remain.[29] These differences are due mostly to variations in interpretation of the same texts and reliance on other thinkers.

"Method" and Limitations

The challenges faced by South Africa and the South African constitution of course are not unique. Similar challenges, with variations on the themes outlined previously, exist in many countries today, as well as transnationally and internationally. The challenges facing modern constitutionalism include injustices that often go unnoticed, yet that Kant seemed to find more or less unproblematic, such as the exclusionary practices of democratic constitutionalism, material inequality, criminal punishment, the human-animal relation, and war in its many forms.

It should by now be clear that the aim of the reading undertaken here is not to simply restate and confirm the foundations of constitutionalism established by Kant, but a radical reconceptualization thereof. *Deconstructive Constitutionalism* thus differs from other sympathetic readings of Kant, such as a "pure" reading à la Geismann or an "updated" reading à la Habermas and Rawls. *Deconstructive Constitutionalism* adopts a different approach, because it is not certain that these and other, similar readings of Kant go far enough in exposing the realities of the current age and in the search for justice in the current age. *Deconstructive Constitutionalism* thus proceeds through a close reading of Kant, primarily by way of Derrida, a reading that explores not only the unity of Kant's thinking, but specifically the tensions within Kant's texts, and that seeks to go beyond Kant's conscious intentions. This is arguably the only way in which Kant can remain relevant in relation to the questions that need to be addressed by constitutionalism today. The analysis undertaken here is informed by a particular reading of Derrida's texts, as elaborated on and explored in earlier publications.[30] This reading differs in various respects from many of the perhaps more well-known readings of Derrida within the field of law.[31] *Deconstructive Constitutionalism* does not lay claim to being the only correct reading of Derrida in the constitutional context, though it does modestly lay claim to a contextual and coherent understanding of Derrida's texts. This understanding takes account of Derrida's "project" as well as his reliance on other important thinkers, such as Heidegger and Freud. For Derrida, as pointed out elsewhere, metaphysics is never at one with itself, and exceeds itself.[32] The same is true of Kant's texts. As shown in the discussion that follows, Heidegger's reading of Kant is very influential in Derrida's own reading, specifically with respect to reason and freedom (chapters 2 and 3). These Kantian notions are read by Heidegger as reflections on the Being of beings, thereby bringing about a radical shift in the meaning of Kant's texts. The groundlessness of Being in Heidegger's texts furthermore resonates with Freud's equally abyssal reflections on the death drive in "Beyond the Pleasure Principle" (2001, 18:3–64), which likewise plays an important role in Derrida's reading of Kant. This drive involves a radical dislocation or interruption of the self and thereby also of Kantian notions such as freedom, responsibility, autonomy, reason, the subject, and the decision (Derrida 1990, 4).

The reading of Kant via Derrida engaged in here does not seek in the first place to address or provide solutions to the previously mentioned national and transnational issues. The issues and context of every country and region are furthermore different, and the seeking for solutions needs to take account of that context. Such solutions will furthermore always entail restrictions of the "unconditional," which as we saw is at stake in Derrida's texts and is his main concern. The aims of *Deconstructive Constitutionalism* are therefore more modest. It is concerned first of all with a conceptual analysis of the Kantian foundations of the modern constitution, namely the moral law, reason, freedom, democracy, and peace. In line with Derrida's thinking, the analysis undertaken here challenges some of the traditional and intuitive understandings of these concepts, which we tend to take for granted. These concepts furthermore are explored with reference to, inter alia, the human-animal relation, as well as criminal law and punishment, that is, with reference to some of the marginalized issues of inclusion/exclusion within the context of constitutionalism. The reconceptualization at stake here nevertheless has potentially important implications for a wide range of constitutional and societal questions, including those alluded to earlier. The conceptual analysis can in other words assist in framing a "theoretical starting point," or by providing a "normative framework" through which answers to these questions can be sought. This "normative framework" ties in closely with Kant's thinking, which as indicated, has been highly influential in modern constitutionalism (Ackermann 2012, 54, 60). Yet it seeks to bring about fundamental changes to the Kantian normative framework so as to enable modern constitutionalism to meet some of the challenges of the twenty-first century. Because of its main focus and aims, *Deconstructive Constitutionalism* restricts itself to providing the broad outlines of the possible implications of such a reading of Kant. The discussion that follows starts with a brief overview of Kant's thinking—adopting a fairly standard reading for this purpose—insofar as it is relevant for the rest of the analysis.

From Kant's Moral Law to Perpetual Peace

In the *Critique of Pure Reason*, Kant seeks to establish whether or not all phenomena can be said to be subject to the laws of causation. If that were to be the case, there of course would be no room left for freedom or morality. Kant shows through what he refers to as the "transcendental method" that our relation to the world is based on certain necessary conditions, or ways in which we view the world, including by way of our a priori intuition of space and time and by way of the a priori categories of understanding (such as causality). We do not therefore have direct access to the world, but only by way of our perception of it, or the way in which it appears to us. This happens, in short, through the interaction between reason and the senses (Maris and Jacobs *Law* 2011, 177–78). Reason thus cannot on its own provide theoretical knowledge of the world—this easily leads to illusionary ideas (Reath 1997, vii)—and neither can empirical observation. Although reason structures observation, the content or material of such observation is provided by sensory experience (Maris and Jacobs 2011, 171). Scientific observation, as we saw, is restricted to the phenomenal world, and therefore cannot provide knowledge of the nonobservable or noumenal world, examples of which are God, the soul, freedom, and morality (Maris and Jacobs 2011, 178; Reath 1997, xi). These matters cannot be observed by the senses, and their existence therefore cannot be proved or disproved, at least not by theoretical reason. By establishing the existence of synthetic a priori reason, Kant nevertheless shows that pure reason provides us with knowledge about the world independent of experience (Korsgaard 1997, ix–xi). This opens the door for reason to give insight into the noumenal world. In the *Critique of Pure Reason*, the focus is on that which theoretical reason tells us of the world as it is, or rather, as it appears to us, whereas in the *Groundwork* and the *Critique of Practical Reason*, the focus is on practical reason, which provides us with knowledge about the way things ought to be (Korsgaard 1997, x–xi). Practical reason can in other words provide us with the necessary grounds to draw conclusions about the noumenal world (Reath 1997, xi–xii).

As outlined by Kant in the *Groundwork* and in the *Critique of Practical Reason*, our conscience suggests that there is a domain beyond the phenomenal world, that is, some *noumenal* or intelligible world that is not subject to natural causation. Although the existence of this "world" cannot be proved through scientific observation, and therefore we cannot have empirical knowledge of it, it can and must be assumed for practical or moral purposes. Looking specifically at the human being, our conscience imposes unconditional obligations on us irrespective of the benefits to us or the consequences for us of performing such obligations (Maris and Jacobs 2011, 179). Human beings thus appear, at least to a certain extent, to be free from the causal determinations of nature. One can also say that, as beings belonging to the intelligible or noumenal world, the conduct of human beings is not completely determined by the sensible world of which they are nevertheless likewise members. They can act on the basis of duty rather than simply on the basis of their inclinations, from which they can distance themselves by subjecting these inclinations to a moral judgment (180–81). The moral "world" at stake here allows for self-legislation, that is, the ability by way of reason to adopt maxims for one's actions, which can be applied universally. To act in an ethical manner, one should ask oneself namely whether the maxim for one's actions in a specific case is such that it could become a general rule, that is, a rule that applies to everyone under similar circumstances. In another formulation of what Kant terms the "categorical imperative," which, as we saw earlier, was influential in the role that human dignity has come to play in modern constitutionalism, each person should be treated as an end in him- or herself and not as a mere means.[33] This is the terrain of virtue or ethics and is aimed at regulating the *internal* freedom of human beings. No one can, however, be forced to act ethically (184).

In view of the aforesaid, human beings thus belong to two domains: first, to the domain of natural causality with respect to their inclinations, and, second, to the domain of reason, morality, and freedom, which distinguishes them from non-human animals (Kant 1997b, 4:453–55; Korsgaard 1997, xxix). It is especially the second, noumenal domain to which human beings belong that determines Kant's conception of law, although he takes due account of the first domain. Prior to the civil condition (*bürgerlichen Zustand*), human beings find themselves in a state of nature and thus in a potential state of irresolvable conflict with others. This is because in the state of nature everyone acts as his or her own judge with respect to the scope and limitation of rights, and there is no higher power, which can provide clarity through positive laws or resolve conflicts by adjudication.[34] What then is the relation between the laws established in the civil condition and the moral law? In the *Metaphysics of Morals*, the doctrines or theories of law and of virtue are treated separately, but as two elements of a general morality. By virtue of this morality, practical reason places certain demands on law, in the first place, the establishment of a civil condition, which regulates the scope and protection of everyone's external freedom, thereby making possible their peaceful coexistence. This happens through a constitution, the idea of which Kant describes as "an absolute command [*absolutes Gebot*] that practical reason . . . gives to every people" and which is "*sacred* and irresistible [heilig *und unwiderstehlich*]" (Kant 1996b, 6:372). As we saw earlier, the constitution in question should be republican in nature, providing for a separation between the three spheres of power, recognizing the lawful freedom of all human beings, equality of everyone before the law, and the independence of citizens (Kant 1996a, 8:290–97 ["On the Common Saying," 1996b, 6:313–18 (para. 45–49)).[35] Although, according to Kant (1979, 159, 165; 1996a: 8:297), pure reason does not necessarily prescribe a democratic constitution, the laws enacted should be such that every citizen could have rationally agreed thereto. A similar structure thus applies here as regards moral self-legislation: the laws enacted by the state should be universalizable (Kersting 1992, 344, 355; 2007, 26). This requirement at the same time makes possible a distinction between legislation that is just and unjust, which in Kant's thinking takes place primarily by way of the principles of equality and freedom (Kersting 1992, 355–56; 2007, 26, 275–77). A law that, for example, imposes an obligation only on a certain part of the population cannot be said to comply with the requirement of universalizability (Kersting 1992, 355). The same would apply to paternalistic legislation that seeks to improve the morality of the population, thereby violating their freedom (356). Citizens may indeed criticize such injustices, but they may not revolt against them so as to seek the violent overthrow of the constitution (Kant 1996a, 8:299; 1996b, 6:319–22). This would lead to the annihilation of the lawful condition established by such constitution, even if only for an interim period (Kant 1996b, 6:355). Whereas Kant's moral law is perfectionist in nature, as noted, this only applies in the internal sphere, that is, with respect to inner freedom. The state's actions should be restricted to the external relations between individuals and refrain from regulating their internal thoughts and pursuits, even indirectly (Geismann 1996, 9–10).[36] The state should, in other words, as we saw earlier, not attempt to make its citizens morally good, but simply protect their freedom through laws. This necessarily means that it can enforce the law and impose punishment after a finding that someone has broken the law. As Kant (1996b, 6:362) puts it in the *Metaphysics of Morals*, "the mere idea of a civil constitution among human beings carries with it the concept of punitive justice belonging to the supreme authority." Such punishment may include the imposition of the death penalty under certain circumstances, for example, in the event of murder or a revolt against the state (6:320 and 6:334). The citizens of a state are thus assumed to possess the freedom to choose and to take responsibility for their actions (Maris and Jacobs 2011, 172–73).

Kant further realized that establishing a peaceful order within the state under a republican constitution is an important but insufficient step to ensure human autonomy. Sovereign states, similar to human beings prior to entering the civil condition, find themselves in a state of nature without anyone independent to judge who is in the right (Kant 1996b, 6:349 (para. 60); 1996a, 8:355 ["Perpetual Peace"]). War and the constant threat of war with other states thus constantly threaten the civil condition brought about by the national legal system, and thereby human autonomy. Practical reason also demands peace on the international level (Kant 1996b, 6:354) that should be brought about by forming a voluntary and continually expanding federation of sovereign republican states, which in terms of an agreement reached between them do not wage war against each other and protect each other from external attack (Kant 1996a, 8:356; 1996b, 6:344, 6:350, 6:354). To attain eternal peace, a further step however seems to be required by reason, that is, the establishment of a world republic with powers of coercion similar to those that exist on a national level.[37] Kant approaches the latter with some caution, inter alia because a world state poses the threat of despotism on the global level, which could lead to the abolition of the civil condition attained at the national level. The attraction of external sovereignty on the part of states poses a further obstacle. He therefore appears to settle, at least for the interim, for a voluntary federation of states that retain their sovereignty. To attain perpetual peace, Kant finally makes suggestions for what he terms "cosmopolitan law," for an era where state sovereignty will remain in place. In this respect, he proposes a right of foreign visitors to be treated with hospitality in the states they visit, and at the same time a prohibition against the inhospitable conduct of many colonial and imperial states to conquer foreign territory and oppress the inhabitants (1996a, 8:359; 1996b, 6:353).

Outline of Chapters

From the previous discussion, it is clear that Kant's "Theory of Law"[38] stands in a close relation with the moral law, as well as with his conceptions of freedom and reason. In the preface to the *Critique of Practical Reason* (5:4), Kant notes in this regard that the reality of the concept of freedom "is proved by an apodictic law of practical reason," which "constitutes the *keystone* of the whole structure of a system of pure reason, even of speculative reason," and further that the idea of the reality of freedom "reveals itself through the moral law." These three foundational and closely interlinked elements of Kant's thinking (the moral law, reason, and freedom) are given attention to in chapters 1, 2 and 3. Chapter 3, which engages with freedom, also explores the relation between freedom and democracy. Chapters 3 to 6 more specifically explore the way in which these foundational elements play themselves out in modern constitutionalism, as well as the implications of Derrida's reading of Kant for modern constitutionalism. In chapters 4 and 5, the focus is on non-human animals and criminal law, respectively, and in chapter 6, on global constitutionalism. A somewhat more comprehensive outline of the chapters to follow is provided next.

In chapter 1 of *Deconstructive Constitutionalism*, we look at the way in which Derrida, in a variety of texts, engages directly or indirectly with the Kantian moral law, which as we saw rests on the assumption of the human being's autonomy or freedom vis-à-vis his or her natural inclinations. In the background of this analysis is Derrida's engagement with Freud, the latter having argued that the Kantian moral law is located in, and can be equated with, the superego. Derrida challenges Freud's assignation of the moral law (solely) to the superego and suggests that what appears to Kant as the moral law and to Freud as the demands of the superego already involves a limitation of a much more radical demand on the self: that of absolute sacrifice, and which can be understood with reference to Freud's death drive. Derrida refers to this demand as the law of law, that is, the law that makes of the moral law a law. Derrida thus seeks to show that in Kant's portrayal of the moral law, there is already a split, or indications of some law that precedes the moral law—as its origin. The chapter explores in detail Kant's notion of respect that is owed to the moral law, the notion of duty, and the formulation of the categorical imperative by Kant in terms of an "as if." The implications for the legal system of such a split in the moral law are of course profound and go far beyond the demand for the protection of human dignity that we find in modern constitutionalism.

In chapter 2, at stake is the demand of the principle of reason (*nihil est sine ratione*), which was formulated by Leibniz, and the way in which it finds application in the thinking of Kant. The discussion here takes place by way of the analysis of Heidegger in *Der Satz vom Grund* (*The Principle of Reason*). Heidegger in the latter text listens to the statement of the principle in two ways: first as an expression of the demand that reason must be rendered for everything that exists, and, second, as a statement about the Being of beings, in other words, that Being itself plays the role of ground, but that it is itself groundless. At stake in the second tonality is the "origin" of the principle of reason in modernity, which essentially involves calculation, and which finds expression inter alia in Kant's transcendental method. In Derrida's reading, the inherent relation between reason and force is emphasized, also in the legal field. Derrida's reading takes place also by way of a certain psychoanalysis, and the groundlessness of reason, identified by Heidegger, takes on a "moral" dimension. It does so through the notion of the gift, which, also in Heidegger's thinking, "precedes" and "gives" Being and time. Reason, within Kant's thinking and in the legal field as well, thus finds its origin in the pure or immeasurable gift, which involves no return to the self. This places an infinite responsibility on those entrusted with reason in terms of the modern constitution, to calculate with the incalculable. The demands of the pure gift should in other words be the abyssal starting point before starting to engage in politico-legal calculations.

We saw earlier that freedom is central in Kant's thinking, and that specifically human freedom provides the foundation for his theory of law.

Chapter 3 inquires by way of the reading of Kant's texts by Heidegger, Nancy, and Derrida into the notion of freedom. It looks into Kant's understanding of freedom, specifically in the *Critique of Pure Reason* and the *Critique of Practical Reason*, as well as the relation he posits between freedom and causality. The understanding and location of freedom in these analyses hold important implications for our understanding of democracy today. If "freedom" does not belong to the human subject, but is instead located beyond Being, as the event or gift of Being, it would mean that we have to look beyond the variety of forms taken by democracy today, toward the democracy to come. The latter would no longer be characterized by mastery, sovereignty, and power, but instead by a welcoming of the unforeseeable and incalculable event. Such an understanding of freedom and democracy would in turn have important implications for the exclusions and limits traditionally imposed by democracy, as well as for its location beyond the nation-state.

In chapter 4, an inquiry is undertaken of Kant's thinking on the non-human animal and Derrida's reading thereof. Derrida shows how the subjection, mastery, and domestication of the non-human animal is at the heart of Kant's thinking on morality, as well as of his construction of subjectivity and of the establishment of society. One could indeed say that Kant's whole thinking on morality and law is based on the human-animal distinction. It is after all only human beings who share in two worlds: the sensible and the intelligible, which enable them to give themselves practical laws by their own reason and not be led purely by their senses, as animals are presumed to be. Subjectivity and the civil constitution, according to Kant, are both made possible by a certain power or ability that the human being has in comparison with animals. In his reading of Kant's *Anthropology from a Pragmatic Point of View*, Derrida points to the underlying assumptions of Kant's analysis, as well as certain tensions in Kant's text, which undermine the foundations of the dominant Kantian discourse. It appears that the subjection of the animal in Kant takes place through the "repression" of a certain otherness, abyss, or "animal" within the (human) self. Derrida's analysis of Kant has potentially important implications for the scope of protection afforded by constitutions as well as for democratic participation.

Chapter 5 inquires into the implications for criminal law of Derrida's analysis in the Death Penalty seminars. The seminars include a reading of Kant's *Metaphysics of Morals*, specifically Kant's reflections on legal responsibility, the sovereign right to punish and grant clemency, the purpose and measure of punishment, as well as the possibilities of reform of the criminal justice system. Kant's texts are read in conjunction with the reflections of Freud and Reik on the relation between the unconscious and crime, as well as Nietzsche's reflections on morality, punishment, and cruelty. What comes to the fore in Derrida's analysis is a system of economic exchange operating on an unconscious level, of which criminal law forms an intrinsic part. Derrida's analysis of the "origin" of crime in the seminars poses serious questions to the assumption of freedom underlying modern criminal law. The links that Derrida posits between sovereignty, cruelty, and forgiveness, and between punishment and political theology, as well as his exposure of the incalculability of punishment, likewise challenge the existing theories and forms of punishment. What the seminars call for in the name of the Kantian Enlightenment is a radical break with economic circularity as it operates with respect to crime and punishment.

Chapter 6 discusses Kant's essay on perpetual peace, looking specifically at the preface of the text, Kant's definition of peace, as well as his proposals for the reform of international law and cosmopolitan law in seeking to secure peace. Derrida analyzes Kant's "Toward Perpetual Peace" in a number of his texts, usually in the context of a discussion of the concept of hospitality, but also of the democracy to come. Whereas Kant's concept of hospitality, invoked within the context of a discussion of cosmopolitan law, is a restricted one in a number of ways, Derrida seeks to show that this concept also has an unconditional dimension by exploring the tensions in Kant's text. These tensions are, for example, to be seen in Kant's notion of perpetual peace, which has both a political dimension and a dimension beyond the political, the latter of which Derrida reads as a reference to absolute hospitality. Derrida's reading of Kant has important implications for the principles as well as institutions of international/cosmopolitan law, which require radical reform, in order to come closer to this demand of absolute hospitality and of the democracy to come.

"Kant after Derrida" summarizes the findings of *Deconstructive Constitutionalism* in relation to the reading of Kant undertaken here. It looks at the consequences of Derrida's reading of Kant for the foundations of modern constitutionalism. As we saw, these include justice, reason, freedom, self-government, legal personality, rights, criminal responsibility, and peace. Derrida's reading of Kant does not lead to the confirmation of these foundations or to the establishment of new foundations. It instead brings to the fore the abyssal nature of the Kantian foundations, thereby enabling us to approach the challenges of the twenty-first century in a different, and perhaps more just, way.

Chapter 1

The Moral Law

We saw in the "Introduction" how the Kantian notion of human dignity has, somewhat surprisingly, come to play a central role in modern constitutionalism. Kant's mention of this notion takes place in the analysis of the moral law, which is to be found primarily in the *Groundwork for a Metaphysics of Morals*, the *Critique of Practical Reason*, and *The Metaphysics of Morals*. In the *Groundwork*, the argument is in brief that the human being, as both a phenomenal and a noumenal being, is not simply subject to the laws of nature. Conscience and the guilt associated with it suggest that the human being has the freedom or autonomy to decide whether or not to act morally. Practical reason, and not the inclinations, must therefore provide guidance in moral actions based on this freedom. One should namely ask oneself whether the subjective maxims of one's actions could also serve as a universal law. These contentions are refined in various respects in the *Critique of Practical Reason*, for example, in relation to freedom, as well as the incentives and the postulates of practical reason, whereas in the *Metaphysics of Morals*, Kant sets out first a theory of law based on the need to regulate reciprocal external freedom, followed by a system of legal duties, and, second, a system of duties of virtue or of ethics. Kant's moral law has been the topic of countless commentaries, criticisms, and attempts at reconstruction or transformation. Of these, Freud's attempts to understand Kant's moral law with reference to his own model of the psyche and the readings that have followed in the wake of Freud are arguably the most thought-provoking.

On a standard reading, one could say that Freud (2001, 19:167; 22:61–65) equates the Kantian categorical imperative with the superego.[1] According to Freud (21:126; 22:60–62), the superego, with different measures of strictness in different individuals and even at different points in time in the same individual, takes the place of external parental authority by internalizing such authority. The superego is, because of this relation to the parents, viewed by Freud (19:34–36, 48; 22:64, 66–67, 79) as a successor to the Oedipus complex. The experience of guilt is furthermore a result of the tension between the demands of the (punishing) superego and the actual performances of the ego (19:37, 53; 21:123, 125, 127–28; 22:61). The consequence of Freud's thinking in this regard has been to cast serious doubt on the possibility of the Kantian notions of freedom and self-legislation. It appears that even such self-legislation in accordance with conscience or the moral law is determined by "external" causal factors, that is, by parental figures who influence the constitution of one's superego, and thus "pathological" (Maris and Jacobs 2011, 277).

The radicalization of Kant's moral law in the readings of Lacan and Derrida can be understood as a response to Freud's analysis. Like Freud, they are concerned with finding the origins of morality, but they seek this "origin" elsewhere, with reference to other texts of Freud.[2] Lacan (1989, 1992, 1998) in this respect invokes inter alia the realm of the Real, *jouissance*, the Thing, the Freudian superego, desire, guilt, punishment, and the death drive, as well as figures like Antigone and Sade.[3] Despite the (for the most part) different terminology and style of writing employed by Derrida and Lacan, as well as the different fields in which they operate, there are a number of similarities in their readings of Kant (and of Freud),[4] more specifically with respect to the role and significance of the death drive. To the traditional Kantian scholar it may appear that Derrida (and Lacan) is simply misreading, or even completely misunderstanding, the Kantian system.[5] This is not the case.

The analysis undertaken here closely follows Derrida in his readings of Kant's moral law, also when he takes a detour through other texts, such as Kafka's "Before the Law," Freud's "Totem and Taboo," Nancy's *Psyche*, Patočka's *Heretical Essays*, and Kierkegaard's *Fear and Trembling*, to illustrate what is at stake in his reading of Kant. This gives a different perspective on Derrida's thinking in relation to "ethics" as well as on law, the former of which is as a rule explored primarily with reference to Levinas.[6] The focus in the present chapter is on the nature of the relation (of respect) vis-à-vis the moral law, which includes an analysis of the nature of this law itself, of the untouchability of this law, as well as of the "feeling" that according to Kant gives rise to respect for the moral law. Apart from showing the split nature of the moral law, the analysis seeks to provide a better understanding of the location of the moral law, the nature of the demands that the moral law places on one (of self-sacrifice), and its relation to the Freudian death drive. The nature of this demand is explored further in the following section, which focuses on the notion of duty. At stake in the moral law, as this section shows, is an absolute or excessive duty, beyond the notion of duty as debt. Finally, the chapter explores the formulation of the categorical imperative by Kant in terms of an "as if." Derrida's analysis shows that the moral law does not derive from the imagination, as one might expect, but instead from the "if," the "perhaps," or what can be termed the "fantastic," which is closely related to the Freudian death drive.[7] What comes to the fore here is a law—the law of law—that precedes the Kantian moral law, a law that may not be touched, that does not show itself, and that prescribes a duty beyond duty. At stake here is not a fictional law, but a law that arises from the fantastical.[8] This law goes far beyond the restrictions of human dignity and, it will be contended, lies at the origin of modern constitutionalism. It consequently should always inform the interpretation, amendment, and replacement of the relevant constitutional texts.

The (Non-)Relation of Respect for the Law

According to Kant (1997b, 4:400), the morality of an action lies in its being done "*out of respect for the [moral] law*" (aus Achtung fürs Gesetz).[9] The law is moreover the only thing that deserves our respect. Respect for a person, because of his or her observance of the moral law, "is actually only respect for the law (of righteousness, etc.,) that that person exemplifies" (4:402n).[10] Of all Derrida's texts on this issue, *On Touching Jean-Luc Nancy* is perhaps the most elaborate in this respect and is worth quoting at some length. Here Derrida (2005a, 66–67) notes that for Kant it is—

> first of all [about] respect for the law, respect for which is precisely the cause of respect, that is to say, in the first place, to respect the law rather than the person. This only gives an example of it. Respect commands us to keep our distance, to touch and tamper neither with the law, which is respectable, nor—therefore—with the untouchable. The untouchable is thus kept at a distance by the gaze,[11] or *regard*, in French (meaning

respect in its Latin provenance), or in any case at an attentive distance, in order to watch out carefully, to guard (as in *achten, Achtung*, in German)[12] against touching, affecting, corrupting.

The notion of respect for the moral law in Kant's thinking is referred to in a number of Derrida's texts in passing, while in a few of his published texts it can be said to play a significant role in the analysis. An (as yet) unpublished seminar also exists where Derrida is said to engage in more detail with chapter 3 (of Part I, Book One) of the *Critique of Practical Reason* ("On the incentives of pure practical reason" 5:72–89), and where respect is the main theme.[13] We can gain a few clues concerning the content of the seminar on respect from other texts of Derrida.[14] His comments in these published texts nevertheless remain enigmatic, and a close reading thereof would be necessary to understand the implications of his analysis. In brief, it appears that for Derrida, the notion of respect for the law concerns a certain "untouchability" of the law, and thus has to do with its peculiar "nature" or "structure" as well as with what this law requires of one.

As regards its structure or nature, Derrida reads the moral law as presented by Kant as split within itself. According to Derrida (2018, 35), Kant seems at first sight to portray the moral law as having no history, no derivation, no genesis, no origin. Yet such an account, at least with respect to (not having a) history, would today be regarded as doubtful, especially after Marx's "On the Jewish Question" (1843) and Nietzsche's *On the Genealogy of Morals*.[15] In "Faith and Knowledge," Derrida (1998a, para. 15) points in this regard, a bit like Nietzsche, to the indissociable link between the Kantian moral law and the Christian religion, as spelled out by Kant in *Religion within the Limits of Reason Alone*. If the Kantian moral law is then indeed historically determined, this raises the question of its "origin" or condition of possibility, a question that, in Derrida's reading, "tempted" Freud, leading him (that is, Freud) to repression (as well as to the question of what lies behind repression), to an organic link between repression and standing upright, and later to the story of the primal horde (Derrida 2018, 37–40, 44–46).[16] Derrida consequently reads Kant's moral texts as speaking not only of the moral law in its historical appearance, but also of the law itself, or what he refers to as the law of law, that which makes of the moral law a law.[17]

The Law of Law

In *Before the Law*, Derrida (2018, 33) notes that he was persecuted (*harceler*) by Kafka's "Before the Law" in the previously mentioned seminar, precisely while he was engaging with the Kantian moral law. Derrida's reading of Kafka thus appears to involve at the same time a radicalization of Kant's moral law. This is perhaps the text that most explicitly speaks of and explicates the relation without relation (of respect) one has vis-à-vis the (moral) law, as well as the "nature" of the (moral) law itself. It thus calls for our attention here. As he does in *On Touching*, Derrida here notes that "respect is due only to the moral law, which is the only cause of it[18] even though that moral law never presents itself," and that no direct access to the law is possible; that one is never immediately before the law; and that this can involve an infinite detour (2005a, 66–67; 2018, 34, 43). Derrida furthermore speaks of the law of law as what is not to be touched; as a secret, a secret of nothing that can be presented or represented,[19] but nonetheless needs to be guarded carefully;[20] as having no essence; as obscene; as what is not there, but which there is (*il y a*);[21] as a non-truth; as calling in silence, even before moral conscience, and requiring a response; as neuter, and with reference to Maurice Blanchot, as being neither a man nor a woman, but having the form of a feminine silhouette; as fantastical; as that which we (can) have no knowledge of;[22] and as neither a multiplicity nor a universal generality, but an idiom, which Derrida refers to as the great insight of Kant, that is, it has a single gate destined for a singular being, without being able to reach it (2018, 43, 46–47, 53–58, 61–62).

An Interrupted Relation

In Kafka's "Before the Law," the door of the law before which the man from the country appears cannot be entered. He comes in a sense to a standstill before the law, which Derrida likens to the Kantian notion of respect (for the law) as "nothing but the *effect* of the law" (2018, 43).[23] A guardian defers such entry, and he warns against further and even more powerful guardians behind him (49–50). The guardians can be understood as respecting the law, but also as causing the law to be respected (47). The guardians are the representatives of the law, who at the same time interrupt and delay the relation with the law (51). The relation of respect for the law appears to be dependent on this interruption (51–52). Derrida consequently describes the prohibition of the law, including the power of the guardians in enforcing this prohibition, as involving a *différance*, an unending *différance*, that is, a delay, a postponement, a deferral, a differential relation between forces, rather than an imperative constraint (53).[24] The Kantian notion of freedom, that is, the freedom to act independent of empirical conditions, to act in terms of the law that one makes for oneself, which is revealed

24 | Deconstructive Constitutionalism

through the moral law and serves as the latter's condition,[25] is here both retained and canceled out: the man from the country has the freedom to act in self-determination, yet he must ultimately give himself an order: not to *obey* the law, but to *not enter* the law (51–53). He is both a subject of the law and an outlaw (52–53; chapter 3 of this volume).

In Derrida's reading of Kant via Kafka, it is ultimately the pre-origin of *différance*, that is, the law of law, which cannot and must not be approached, presented, represented, or penetrated (2018, 53). Derrida's employment of "penetration [*pénétrer*]" here, which is what he notes the man from the country wishes to do in relation to the law, points to a link between the law of law and a certain pleasure or desire (60–61). This also seems to be alluded to by the depiction of the guardian with a big sharp nose, a beard, and a fur coat, the sight of which causes the man to decide to wait until he gets permission to enter (41). In his analysis, Derrida links this scene with Freud's account of the origin of morality: as a movement away from the impure, a certain elevation,[26] of standing upright, thereby distancing the human being from what smells unpleasant, from what cannot be touched, that is, from the anal and genital sexual zones (38–39). Derrida of course does not with his analysis seek to simply overturn Kant's analysis, by linking morality to the empirical inclinations or, in Freudian fashion, linking it to the superego. The exploration of touch in the next section seeks to determine the location of the moral law, as well as the relation we ought to have with it.

A Law of Tact

The untouchability of the (moral) law, as we saw earlier, also comes to the fore in *On Touching—Jean-Luc Nancy*, with Derrida (2005a, 66) linking it to the Kantian notion of respect for the law.[27] The law is here explored from another end, that is, through an exploration of the concept of touch, which itself operates according to a law: the same law of law at stake in Kant's moral law. Derrida speaks in *On Touching* of a prohibition of touching the thing itself and, more specifically, of a law of tact, of tact as the origin of law, which prescribes that one must (know how to) touch without touching that which does not allow itself to be touched. This prohibition of touching, Derrida (66) contends, precedes all cultural and religious (as well as neurotic) prohibitions in relation to touching.[28] The latter issue is raised a few pages earlier, when Derrida (47) refers to Aristotle's analysis of touch. He notes there that for Aristotle (*Peri psuchēs, On the Soul, De anima*), this is the most important of the senses: an animal can do without seeing, hearing, and tasting, but if it loses the sense of touch, it will die. Likewise, but conversely, according to Aristotle, death will follow if the animal is affected by an excessive sensitivity to touch. For Derrida, this gives rise to the following question:

> Couldn't one say that this measure, this moderation of touch, remains at the service of life to the sole extent, precisely, that some kind of reserve holds it on the brink of exaggeration? A certain tact, a "thou shalt not touch too much," "thou shalt not let yourself be touched too much," or even "thou shalt not touch yourself too much," would thus be inscribed a priori, like a first commandment, the law of originary prohibition, in the destiny of tactile experience. Ritual prohibitions would then come to be determined, afterward, and only on the background of an untouchability as initial as it is vital, on the background of this "thou shalt not touch, not too much," which wouldn't have awaited any religion, ritual cult, or neurosis of touch. In the beginning, there is abstinence. And without delay, unforgivingly, touching commits perjury. (2005a, 47)

At stake here is what can be referred to as the condition of possibility of the sense of touch, a sense that has been privileged in the Western philosophical tradition (including Kant's *Anthropology from a Pragmatic Point of View*)[29] because touch seems to testify to a certain directness, an immediacy, a presence of self to self, thus to a haptocentric tradition, or to what Derrida elsewhere refers to as the metaphysics of presence (2005a, 41). This reading of Aristotle is explored by Derrida together with Nancy's glosses[30] on Freud's penultimate note of August 22, 1938: "Psyche is extended, knows nothing of it" (*Psyche ist ausgedehnt, weiß nichts davon*).[31] This note, as well as its analysis by Nancy and Derrida, is important for our analysis of Kant, because it points to the "location" of the (moral) law as well as the way in which one should relate to it. In Derrida's reading of the note, Freud is not saying that the soul is outside, expelled into space, but that space itself is a projection: "the spatiality of space, its exteriority would only be an outside projection of an internal and properly speaking psychical extension. In short, the outside would only be a projection" (43). Is Nancy saying the same thing when he suggests that Psyche is extended and thus outside?; or, as Derrida puts it, is he thinking "on the contrary, of an exteriority resisting any projection even if it makes possible some projection effects?" (43). It seems that an affirmative response can be given to both of these possible readings.

Nancy retells in less than a page the mythical tale of Eros/Cupid and Psyche, the latter usually translated as life (force), the principle of life, breath, animation, the soul, the mind, the spirit, but here she is a person, a woman (Nancy 1993a, 393). Psyche is asleep (a deep, deathlike sleep) under the shade of a walnut tree, and is "contemplated" by Eros, both flustered and mischievous. She knows nothing of this. Then Psyche is dead, in a coffin, about to be inhumed, with some of those around her hiding their faces and others staring at her body, and again, she knows nothing of this.[32] Those around her, however, know this, with an "exact and cruel knowledge." Derrida (2005a, 15–16) points to inter alia the following in this tale: Psyche lacks sense, sense of herself, which is what becomes intolerable for those who watch her. Although she has a body, this is an intangible body that remains untouchable for others, and Psyche also does not touch anything, not even herself (16–17). An incarnation of Psyche is thus at stake here, or what can, with reference to the scene of mourning that plays itself out here, be referred to as an "incorporation" (17).[33] Coming to Eros, Derrida notes that it is both Psyche's pose (in sleeping) and her lack of knowledge and self-touching that seems to seduce him, that is, that conditions desire (51, 282). Influential in Derrida's reading of Nancy seems to be Freud's final note, written on the same day as the penultimate note: "Mystik die dunkle Seibstwahrnehmung des Reiches ausserhalb des Ichs, des Es" (2001, 23:300). At least two translations are possible, as Derrida notes: "Mystical is the obscure self-perception of the realm outside of the ego, *that is, the id*," or alternatively ". . . outside of the ego, *outside of the id*" (12, emphasis added). At stake in Aristotle's comment about excess (a constant "theme" in *On Touching*), as well as in Nancy's "Psyche," thus appears to be (part of) the soul (beyond the ego and the id) that is unknowable and untouchable, and which appears to correspond with what Derrida elsewhere refers to as the crypt (Derrida 1986). As we saw earlier, this "soul" calls for a certain law of tact—not the (lack of) tact of the man from the country in "Before the Law," who as we saw persists in wishing to enter the door of the law, to make the law present, but the tact of Eros: his desire having been provoked (by Psyche), he nevertheless touches (Psyche, the untouchable) without touching (her).

In view of our main concerns in this chapter, one could no doubt continue here with an analysis of *On Touching*, as Derrida also engages in this text with Nancy as a thinker of absolute generosity; with the relation between touching/the caress and (Levinas's) ethics of the face; as well as with the notion of being bound to a secret, which is how Derrida (2005a, 65) refers to Psyche's absence of knowledge. One could also compare Derrida's (hetero-affective) analysis in *On Touching* with the reading by Heidegger (1997, 111 [para. 30]) in *Kant and the Problem of Metaphysics*, who contends that the origin of practical reason is to be found in the transcendental imagination, and that the feeling of respect for the law concerns the becoming manifest of the I as an acting self, that is, as a submitting to self as pure reason and an elevating of self to a free creature that determines itself. But let us restrict our gaze to Derrida, Kant, and the moral law and now inquire specifically into Derrida's reading of the relation between "feeling" and "respect" for the (moral) law—where the true nature of practical reason comes to the fore—as well as into the consequences of this relation for the demands of the moral law.

FEELING AS DRIVING FORCE

Kant raises the notion of respect for the law as a "feeling" for the first time in the *Groundwork*. Here he points out that although respect involves a feeling, it is different from feelings that arise because of inclination and fear. He defines respect here as "the direct determination of the will by the law, and the awareness of that determination." We should therefore, he contends, "see respect as the *effect* of the law on a person rather than as what *produces* the law" (1997b, 4:402n). This analysis is expanded on in chapter 3 of the *Critique of Practical Reason* ("On the incentives of pure practical reason [*Von den Triebfedern der reinen praktischen Vernunft*]"). Here Kant (1997a, 5:73) likewise seeks to exclude all sensible impulses and inclinations that are based on (sensible) feeling as incentives to moral action, while in the same breath he speaks of the feeling of respect as an effect of practical reason:

> There is no *antecedent* feeling in the subject that would be attuned to morality: that is impossible, since all feeling is sensible whereas the incentive of the moral disposition must be free from any sensible condition. Instead, sensible feeling, which underlies all our inclinations, is indeed the condition of that feeling we call respect, but the cause determining it lies in pure practical reason; and so this feeling, on account of its origin, cannot be called pathologically effected but must be called *practically effected*. (5:75)[34]

In "Passions," Derrida (1992b, 14) notes that the notion of respect for the law inscribes a "disturbing paradox" into the heart of morality. This is because of the notion of affect, feeling, or sensibility (*Gefühl*) within which morality is inscribed, and which, as we saw in the previous quotation, Kant at the same time seeks to exclude as incentive or motivating force of pure practical reason.[35] In fact, morality prescribes that "everything that would obey this sensible inclination" needs to be sacrificed (Derrida 1992b, 14). The latter notion alludes to Kant's employment of the word *Aufopferung* (sacrifice, self-sacrifice, or self-abandonment) in chapter 3 (1997a, 5:84 and 5:85), which is specifically emphasized by Derrida. He notes that the "object of sacrifice there is always the order of the sensuous motives [*mobile sensible*]" (1992b, 14). According to Kant, as Derrida (14) notes, "the secretly 'pathological' interest" must be " 'humbled' before the moral law."[36] In *The Gift of Death*, Derrida (1995d, 93) similarly notes that access to pure duty[37] necessarily goes along with "a sacrifice of the passions, of the affections, of so-called 'pathological' interests; everything that links my sensibility to the empirical world, to calculation, and to the conditionality of hypothetical imperatives." Derrida is here preparing the ground for taking Kant's comments on sacrifice to their logical extreme, suggesting thereby that the moral law lays down an unconditional command, an absolute duty.[38] Derrida (93) consequently speaks here of the "unconditionality of respect for the law . . . [that] dictates a sacrifice (*Aufopferung*) which is always a sacrifice of self."[39] An example[40] of such a sacrifice is to be found in Abraham—the focus of the discussion in this text analyzing Kierkegaard—who, in getting ready to kill Isaac, "inflicts the most severe suffering upon himself, he gives to himself the death that he is granting his son" (93). A certain violence is clearly at stake here, a violence that according to Kant (as glossed by Derrida) is dictated by "the unconditionality of moral law" and is "exercised in self-restraint (*Selbstzwang*) and against one's own desires, interests, affections, or drives" (Derrida 1995d, 93; Kant 1997a, 5:84). In Derrida's reading, "one is driven to [this violence or] sacrifice by a sort of practical drive, by a form of motivation that is also instinctive, but an instinct that is pure and practical, respect for moral law being its sensible manifestation" (93). Derrida seems to be alluding here to Kant's contention that the moral law itself, alternatively respect for such law, serves as the motivating force (*Triebfeder*, *elater animi*, driving force) for moral action (Kant 1997a, 5:78 and 5:88). Derrida's glosses on Kant make it scarcely possible to avoid thinking here of Freud's description of the operation of the drives or instincts in "Beyond the Pleasure Principle."[41] This is also the case in relation to Kant's use in this passage of the notions of *Selbstzwang* (self-constraint) and *innere Nötigung* (inner necessitation), as well as his employment of the notions of pleasure and unpleasure in relation to respect.[42] With this somewhat mysterious force, drive or instinct, as the motivating force of the Kantian moral law, we seem to return to Kafka's guardians, who guard an untouchable and unknowable law,[43] as well as to Nancy's equally untouchable and unknowable Psyche. This force, that is, the death drive, needs to be guarded against for life to conserve itself.

Duty

In the *Groundwork*, Kant invokes the concept of duty in connection with a good will, the latter being the only thing that, according to him, is good without qualification (1997b, 4:393). A good will is the will of a finite, rational being to act solely out of duty or from duty (*aus Pflicht*), thereby overcoming his or her inclinations.[44] Acting out of duty thus entails more than simply conforming to the requirements of the moral law, for example, a shopkeeper who does not overcharge customers, because of (commercial) self-interest; or, similarly, someone who is compassionately disposed, and thus finds inner joy in helping others (4:397–98). In the case of the shopkeeper, his honesty means that he *indirectly* complies with duty, while the philanthropist complies *directly* with duty by helping others. Such actions are indeed in accordance with the moral law, yet according to Kant, they have no moral worth. To have moral worth, the action must go beyond mere compliance, that is, beyond action in accordance with or in conformity with duty (*gemäß Pflicht*), thereby attaining the status of what Kant refers to as *morality*. Important in this regard is furthermore not the consequences of the action but only the (subjective) maxim on which such action is based (4:400). Kant in the *Groundwork* (4:400) and in the *Critique of Practical Reason* (1997a, 5:81) speaks of such actions solely out of duty, as conduct of subjective respect for the law and objective accord with the law. Important for our analysis here is that Kant, in the *Critique of Practical Reason* (5:82), furthermore speaks of this relation as one of *Schuldigkeit* (translated as "what is owed," also "obligation" or "duty").[45] According to Kant (1997b, 4:407), the distinction between acting out of duty and acting merely in conformity with duty is nevertheless impossible to establish with empirical certainty:

> It is in fact absolutely impossible to identify by experience, with complete certainty, a single case in which the maxim of

an action—an action that accords with duty—was based exclusively on moral reasons and the thought of one's duty. There are cases when the most searching self-examination comes up with nothing but duty as the moral reason that could have been strong enough to move us to this or that good action or to some great sacrifice [*Aufopferung*]. But we cannot conclude from this with certainty that the real determining cause of our will was not some secret impulse of self-love [*geheimer Antrieb der Selbstliebe*], disguising itself as that Idea of duty. So we like to flatter ourselves with the false claim to a nobler motive [*Bewegungsgrunde*] but in fact we can never, even with the most rigorous self-examination, completely uncover the hidden motivations [*die geheimen Triebfedern*]. For when moral worth is the issue, what counts is not the actions which one sees, but their inner principles, which one does not see.

In the *Critique of Practical Reason*, Kant furthermore concerns himself with the origin or root (*Wurzel*) of this duty, referring to the latter as a "sublime and mighty name," as "hold[ing] forth a law that of itself finds entry into the mind [*Gemüte*]," and as "a law before which all inclinations [*Neigungen*] are dumb, even though they secretly work against it [*wenn sie gleich in Geheim ihm entgegen wirken*]" (5:86). Kant is here directly addressing duty, and he further asks, "what origin is there worthy of you [*welches ist der deiner würdige Ursprung*], and where is to be found the root of your noble descent [*die Wurzel deiner edlen Abkunft*] which proudly rejects all kinship with the inclinations [*Neigungen*], descent from which is the indispensable condition of that worth which human beings alone can give themselves?" (5:86). Kant ultimately finds this origin in personality, that is, freedom and independence from the mechanism of nature (5:87).

In Derrida's (2003, 133) reading, duty in Kant's thinking appears to remain inscribed within a circular economy. We can see this, for example, in Kant's earlier-mentioned description of the relation to the moral law as one of *Schuldigkeit* (obligation, duty, what is owed),[46] as well as his positing of such obligation vis-à-vis moral fanaticism (introduced by novelists and sentimental educators), which requires restraint and subjection, and which can presumably be seen (although Kant does not mention this here specifically) in the examples of Abraham and Jesus (1997a, 5:84–86). Kantian duty is in other words very closely linked with or even rooted in the acquittal of a debt or can be said to amount to a duty of restitution (Derrida 1992b, 26 n4). The etimologico-semantic analyses of Benveniste and Malamoud that Derrida (1992b, 27–29 n4) cites in "Passions" similarly indicate the rootedness of duty in debt in certain languages and cultures, as well as the close link that exists there between duty/obligation, debt (German: *Schuld*), and fault (German: *Schuld*). According to Derrida, a certain feeling (*sentiment*), presumably related to the "feeling" that we came across earlier, nevertheless suggests that a duty understood simply as the discharge of a debt, as restitution, as returning what was lent or borrowed, would be a-moral (26 n4). "Pure morality," Derrida contends, "must exceed all calculation, conscious or unconscious, of restitution or reappropriation" (26 n4). It is in other words necessary to "go beyond duty, or at least beyond *duty as debt:* duty owes nothing, it must owe nothing, it ought at any rate to owe nothing" (26 n4, Derrida 2001d, 66).

The preceding discussion, read with Kant's definition of duty as "the necessity of an act done out of respect for the law" (1997b, 4:400), suggests that a reading of Kant in line with a conception of duty as beyond debt may indeed be possible. What Kant says concerning the roots of duty,[47] secret driving forces, as well as the solemn majesty and severity of the moral law point in a similar direction (1997a, 5:77). As Derrida points out, we find further allusions to such a duty beyond debt in Nietzsche's *Genealogy of Morals*,[48] Heidegger's *Being and Time*,[49] and Freud's "Totem and Taboo" (1992b, 27 n4).[50] Derrida consequently speaks of back-and-forth movements (*aller et retours*) taking place between all these texts, including Kant's reflections on duty in the *Groundwork* and in the *Critique*, as well as the relation posited between debt and culpability in the *Metaphysics of Morals* (27 n4). Nietzsche, Heidegger, and Freud all in a certain way concern themselves with an arche-ethics or a law beyond the moral law, which seeks to account for morality.[51] Something similar seems to be alluded to in the text of Malamoud, as cited by Derrida, when he, for example, speaks of man in an originary state of indebtedness (29 n4).[52]

Derrida explores such a different conception of duty in a number of texts, speaking in this regard of a duty to act beyond all debt, economy, and obligation as well as without rule or norm.[53] He also refers to this as a counter-duty, an over-duty, an absolute duty, and a deontology beyond deontology (1992b, 8; 1993a, 16; 1995d, 66, 67; 2014a, 24). The concept of duty understood thus would go beyond the Kantian notions of acting "in accordance with duty" (*Pflichtmässig*) and "out of (pure) duty" (*aus (reiner) Pflicht*).[54] This does not of course mean the rejection of the whole Kantian analysis of duty as debt. One can indeed raise the question, as Derrida

(1992b, 26 n4) does, of whether there is such a duty beyond debt. If there is (that is, the question of the perhaps, to be discussed later in the current chapter), and as Kant also indicates, duty as debt would continue to haunt this other duty, making a good conscience impossible (26 n4).

The relation between the duty beyond duty and duty as debt is, as noted, explored in detail by Derrida in the *Gift of Death* with reference to Patočka's *Heretical Essays on the Philosophy of History* and Kierkegaard's analysis in *Fear and Trembling* of the sacrifice of Abraham. These two analyses conjoin insofar as Patočka investigates the origins and essence of Christian and philosophical responsibility in the surpassing or subjection of the demonic secret or the orgiastic sacred, and Kierkegaard inquires into the domestication by Christianity of an absolute duty that is, for example, imposed by God on Abraham (alluding thereby to the passion of Jesus (Derrida 1995d, 81). At stake in both these texts, in Derrida's reading, is the question of giving death, thus of a certain relation to death, sacrifice, the gift, and the secret (10, 29–30). Kierkegaard in *Fear and Trembling* is in conversation with Kant, whose texts as we saw earlier likewise speak of sacrifice, of a certain majesty and severity of the moral law and of secret inclinations (92–93).[55] In seeming opposition to Kant, Kierkegaard contends that simply acting out of duty entails a dereliction of one's absolute duty, the latter requiring a gift or sacrifice that functions beyond debt and duty, beyond duty as a form of debt (63). At stake in such absolute duty can also be said to be a call, such as the call to Abraham, which needs to be kept a secret. This absolute duty involves a heteronomy, a "trembling" in secret of the identity of the self, in contrast with a Kantian autonomy where one acts in terms of a law that one makes for oneself (91–92).[56] This secret is not related to some hidden truth, but to a frightful mystery, which makes one tremble (53).[57] With respect to whence it comes or its repetition, it is not something we can have knowledge of (54–67). This absolute or infinite duty is linked to an originary responsibility, guilt, and indebtedness before any particular fault or determined debt (31, 52).[58] Abraham, in complying with this absolute duty, has to betray duty, ethics, and responsibility as conceived by Kant (59–67).[59] With reference to Husserl's notion of appresentation,[60] Derrida extends this relation without relation of Abraham to God, to every other: *tout autre est tout autre* (every other is wholly other) (78). Yet the question of whether this absolute duty (toward every other) has indeed been complied with, whether the action concerned has indeed managed to step outside the circle of a sacrificial economy, will, as we saw earlier, necessarily have to remain open.[61] This is not, in contrast with what the earlier quotation from the *Groundwork* suggests, because of some empirical or phenomenal limit, but, as Derrida puts it, because

> its possibility is linked *structurally* to the possibility of the "out of pure duty." . . . Impurity is principally inherent in the purity of duty, that is, its iterability.[62] Flouting all possible oppositions: there would be the secret [*là serait le secret*]. The secret of passion, the passion of the secret. To this secret that nothing could confine, as Kant would wish, within the order of "pathological" sensibility, no sacrifice will ever disclose its precise meaning, because there is none. (1992b, 33 n12)

The "As If"

In *Before the Law*, Derrida specifically points to the second formulation of the categorical imperative by Kant (1997b, 4:421) in the *Groundwork of the Metaphysic of Morals*: "act as if the maxim of your action were to become by your will a universal law of nature."[63] Derrida (2018, 34) notes that with the "as if," Kant introduces "narrativity and fiction virtually into the very heart of his thought on law, at the very moment when law begins to speak and to question the moral subject." Derrida is of course not interested here in characterizing the moral law as fictional or as literature, but in that which lies at the origin of the moral law. This he finds in Kafka's "Before the Law" as well as in Freud's reflections in the Letters to Fliess and in "Totem and Taboo." These texts allude to what Derrida, as we saw earlier, refers to as the fantastical[64] or the law of law, which lies beyond the imagination, and which is therefore unimaginable and unpresentable.

Derrida's analysis of the figure of the double in *Dissemination* can assist in understanding what is at stake here. Derrida (2004a, 201) in the latter text points out that in the metaphysical tradition, the double has been understood as the copy of something original, as the imitation of the truth. In Plato's *Philebus* as well as in Mallarmé's *Mimique*, Derrida however finds allusions to a different, non-present understanding of the operation of the double. While the *Philebus* lays the basis for the metaphysical approach to the relation between truth and copy—the relation of the mime to the mimed being always that of a past present, the imitated coming before the imitation (203)—it also raises the question (within a broader discussion of the relation between pleasure and memory) of whether it is perhaps possible that the imitation can precede the imitated, that it can in other words relate to an imitated that still has to come. This question should according to Derrida be read in conjunction with the distinction Plato draws in the *Sophist* between two forms of the mimetic: "[1] the making of likenesses (the *eikastic*) or faithful reproduction, and [2] the making of semblances (the fantastic), which simulates the *eikastic*, pretending to simulate faithfully and deceiving the eye with a simulacrum (a phantasm)" (287 n14).[65] In Derrida's analysis in *Before the Law*, a subtle transformation thus takes place of the Kantian "as if" (which can be understood as mere simulacrum) into the "(as) if" or the "perhaps" of the event, of the impossible, which Derrida (2002d, 210–13, 233–35) explores further in "The University without Condition."[66]

A Law of Welcome

We saw in our analysis that Derrida, in his transformation and radicalization of Kant's moral law, nevertheless remains close to Kant. In *Limited Inc.*, Derrida (1988, 152–53), for example, notes that his employment in different contexts of the notion of "unconditionality" happens "not by accident to recall the character of the categorical imperative in its Kantian form."[67] Something similar can be said about the absence of knowledge that exists concerning the (moral) law, its impossibility, and the question of respect for the moral law. Remaining with the latter point, we saw the frequent appearance in Derrida's texts of the Kantian notion of respect for the law and for persons insofar as they give an example of such law. At stake here appears to also be a repetition that alters. We should in other words understand this law and hear this demand or feeling of respect differently from Kant's seeming intention. We saw in our analysis that the law that Kant speaks of can be understood as a law beyond the moral law. The law is namely one of interruption, of the self, of subjectivity, before the appearance of the other (person) and thus before the ethical relation. This law appears in the call to Abraham and in his (trembling) response: "Here I am." "Here I am": the first and only possible response to the call by the other, the originary moment of responsibility such as it exposes me to the singular other, the one who appeals to me. " 'Here I am' is the only self-presentation presumed by every form of responsibility: I am ready to respond, I reply that I am ready to respond" (Derrida 1995d, 72). It is this law, which can also with reference to Levinas be referred to as a law of welcome, of hospitality, where the subject becomes a hostage, guilty, persecuted, that makes a relation (of respect) to the other possible in the first place (De Ville 2011a, 21–28).[68] In "I have a Taste for the Secret," Derrida (2001b, 63) likewise refers to the Kantian relation of respect for the other in terms of "a certain disarming quality," "a moment of absolute weakness and disarmament," and "exposing ourselves to what we cannot appropriate." At stake here can be said to be a certain structure of the self: "The other is in me before me: the ego (even the collective ego) implies alterity as its own condition. There is no 'I' that ethically makes room for the other, but rather an 'I' that is structured by the alterity within it, an "I" that is itself in a state of self-deconstruction, of dislocation" (84). The call to Abraham to sacrifice his son, a call that disrupts subjectivity, is as we saw contrasted by Derrida (2001d, 69) with traditional conceptions of morality, politics, and law, which allow us in good conscience to sacrifice others so as to avoid sacrificing ourselves.[69] Derrida's analysis in *Gift of Death* of the phrase "every other is absolutely other" entails that every other (not restricted to human beings—chapter 4 of this volume) makes a claim on me as God does in relation to Abraham. What is called for is a certain "radicalization" of the Kantian moral law and the notion of sacrifice employed by Kant, a call thus for an absolute duty beyond reason, an absolute sacrifice of the self, that is, of economy: "The sacrifice of economy, that without which there is no responsibility that is free and relative to decision (a decision always takes place beyond calculation), is indeed in this case the sacrifice of the *oikonomia*, namely of the law of the home (*oikos*), of the hearth, of what is one's own or proper, of the private, of the love and affection of one's kin" (Derrida 1995d, 95). Derrida's analysis thus shows the "existence" of a law preceding the moral law, the latter which, as we saw, in turn precedes, and makes possible law and ethics/virtue. This law of law or "justice," as Derrida (2002a, 230–98) would later call it in "Force of Law," imposes a demand on the law or the juridical in Kant of self-sacrifice, of a duty beyond duty, that is, to do the impossible. This demand of (unconditional) justice precedes and makes possible the modern constitution (268–73). In the "Introduction," we saw how Kant's moral law, at first by way of freedom, and since the mid-twentieth century by way of "human dignity," has become the aspirational ideal that informs and guides the interpretation of the modern constitution as well as other founding legal documents.[70] Derrida's reading of Kant shows that a much more radical demand is at stake here, calling for the sacrifice of "We, the People" as self-legislating collective subject. This demand comes to the fore not only at the time of founding, but in each of its iterations. To heed this call, a suspension of the constitution is required in every application thereof. This holds implications for legal reasoning as well as for the way in which we understand freedom and democracy, human rights, criminal law and punishment, as well as peace.[71]

Chapter 2

The Principle of Reason

In the "Introduction" and in chapter 1 we saw the close relation in Kant's thinking between the moral law, freedom, and reason. It was noted that, according to Kant, human beings belong to two domains: first, to the domain of natural causality with respect to their inclinations, and second, to the domain of reason, morality, and freedom. Throughout the philosophical tradition, human beings have been said to be endowed with reason, in contrast with non-human animals. Reason has furthermore been posited in opposition to faith, madness, mysticism, the instincts, and so forth. In the legal field, the question of reason is closely tied to the question of the nature or concept of law, and thus to the different schools of legal thinking. In other words, what is regarded as a reasonable or rational argument can be said to be dependent on the specific school of thinking. The legal positivist and utilitarian thinker Jeremy Bentham's reference to the notion of "natural rights" as "simple nonsense" and of "natural and imprescriptible rights" as "rhetorical nonsense, —nonsense upon stilts" is telling in this regard (1843, 501). Depending on the nature of law, as contended for by the specific school of legal thinking, permissible legal reasoning in the sphere of adjudication may consequently be restricted only to rules, or to in addition allow for considerations of justice, policy, principles, values, politics, or structural relations of power.

One of the most thought-provoking analyses of legal reasoning in recent years has come from the critical legal scholar Pierre Schlag (1998) in *The Enchantment of Reason*, which seeks to analyze the operation of reason in the US legal system. Although written in a different register, Schlag here interestingly anticipates in a variety of respects the discussion that follows of the principle of reason. He, for example, observes a belief in the "rule of reason" in the legal system (24–26), as well as the pervasive role of power, force, and violence in legal reasoning (20–21). He further identifies an "objectivist aesthetic" in law through the operation of reason, which, as he points out, makes possible the stability, identifiability, and visibility of law (100–4, 106). At the same time, Schlag detects a "subjectivist aesthetic" in law, which points to an uncanny, magical power issuing from law, and which he compares to "hearing voices" (104–8). These two aesthetics raise the question as to where the objective character of law and its power come from (110–11), and moreover, point toward a pathology of reason (116–19), reason having self-destructive tendencies (47). Reason is furthermore said to be "grounded in an unthought that it cannot know," to have an "unstable identity," as well as a "constitutive vulnerability" (78–79). Schlag additionally comments on the impossibility of justifying reason by resorting to reason, or as he puts it, "to ground reason in reason" (60–61). There is in other words an infinite regress at stake in reason, which points to its abyssal foundations, yet hidden from sight by the previously mentioned belief in reason (30–33, 61–63). Finally, Schlag notes the effect of the rule of reason on the legal self, that is, a self that is caught within the "play of dominance and submission" of the "force fields of law" (139).[1]

This chapter touches on Kant's understanding of reason and, passing by way of Heidegger, arrives at Derrida's reinterpretation thereof. Kant, in brief, draws a distinction between theoretical reason, which relates to knowledge of nature, and practical reason, which concerns morality. Kant's "Theory of Law" (*Rechtslehre*) is itself derived from the demands of practical reason, and focuses on reconciling the external freedom of each person with another in accordance with a universal law (Kant, 1996b, 6:230–31, 237). Reason therefore also prescribes that a civil condition be established, which will guarantee and enforce such freedom by way of law and force (6:312 [para. 44]; Kant 1996a, 8:297 ["On the Common Saying"]). According to Kant, reason in its different dimensions nevertheless has a common principle, which is simply applied in different fields (1997b, 4:391; Derrida 2019, 24). Reason for Kant is in other words one, as an inseparable unity exists between theoretical reason and practical reason. At the same time, theoretical reason is subordinate to practical reason (Derrida 2005c, 132; 2019, 24). For Kant, reason needs to be rigorously distinguished from mysticism, which poses an inherent threat to it (Derrida 2019, 24). Kant therefore seeks to strictly specify the conditions of possibility of reason, as well as its limits.

The analysis of Kant via Heidegger undertaken in this chapter proceeds specifically by way of Heidegger's *Der Satz vom Grund* (1957), translated as *The Principle of Reason* (1991). In this text, Heidegger gives a detailed analysis of the principle of reason as formulated by Gottfried Wilhelm Leibniz, and in doing so, also engages with Kant's thinking on reason. Heidegger suggests listening to the statement containing the principle of reason (*nihil est sine ratione*) with two tonalities. In the first tonality, it states that beings exist only insofar as reason can justify their existence.[2] In the second tonality, the statement speaks to us not only of beings, but of the Being of beings. In this tonality, the principle of reason points to the relation between Being and ground/reason (*Grund*). Being grounds, but, different from beings, does not have a ground itself. The principle of reason is established in modernity through the sending of Being, which at the same time withdraws. In modernity, beings become calculating objects for the cognition of a subject, as elaborated on by Kant, whose thinking is firmly ensconced within the principle of reason. The Being of beings is in other words understood as objectness and will. Finally, the sending of Being takes place by way of language and thus also by way of human beings, who, similar to Being, in their essence are without ground.

The analysis of Heidegger's *Der Satz vom Grund* is followed by a reading of primarily four texts of Derrida that engage with Heidegger's text as well as with Kant's thinking on reason: "The Principle of Reason: The University in the Eyes of Its Pupils" (1983), as published in Derrida *Eyes of the University* (2004b), *Given Time* (1992a [1991]), *Death Penalty* II (2017 [2000–2001]), and *Rogues* (2005c [2002]). In these texts, Derrida stays close to Heidegger's analysis of the principle of reason, yet takes a distance from it in certain respects, specifically in relation to the gathering of Being, the epochal sending of Being, and the relation of the human being toward death.[3] A shift in focus thus takes place away from Being toward what can be referred to as the abyss, the withdrawal, play, or gift of Being, from which the demand to render reason issues forth. In *Eyes of the University*, Derrida is similarly concerned with the abyssal "origin" of the principle of reason, as well as the demand that issues from this origin, which can be said to precede Kantian practical reason. In *Given Time*, this "origin" is explored in terms of the gift, more precisely the pure gift, which does not involve any subject or return to the self, and is thus characterized by a certain madness, a duty beyond duty. In the second volume of the *Death Penalty Seminars*, Derrida extends Heidegger's analysis of the principle of reason to the legal field, which is characterized by calculation or measure, yet made possible by a gift, another name for death, which is not itself measurable. This gift imposes an infinite responsibility for the death of the other. In *Rogues*, Derrida explores the seemingly inherent threat that reason poses to itself, with reference to the notion of autoimmunity, which opens reason to the future and makes possible the welcoming of the other.

Heidegger on the Principle of Reason

Modern Thinking and the Principle of Reason

The principle of reason,[4] namely that nothing is without reason, ground, or cause (*nihil est sine ratione/Nichts ist ohne Grund*),[5] states something very obvious about human understanding, that is, that human beings always look for the reasons why that which they encounter exists as well as concerning its way of existing. These reasons include proximate reasons, but also more remote reasons, in other words, reasons that require going to the bottom (Heidegger 1991, 3, 10–11, 53). This search for reasons or grounds has always been there and can be detected in the earliest writings of Greek philosophy. The principle of reason was nevertheless formulated for the first time by Leibniz in the seventeenth century. Why did it take so long, that is, 2,300 years since the dawn of Western philosophy, for this principle to be formulated? (3–4). As Heidegger points out, the statement in relation to the principle appears to be simple, but it is actually enigmatic. It can be noted that it contains a double negative: "nothing" and "without," which means that it can also be restated in a positive way: everything that exists has a reason (5). The principle appears to be formulated as a rule: that in general every being has a reason for existing and for being the way it is. Yet rules have exceptions. The principle of reason, by contrast, does not allow for exceptions, as is indicated by the double negation. The principle in effect says: every being necessarily has a reason, thereby raising the question of where this necessity comes from or what its basis is (6). The principle further expresses something unconditional. In doing so, it shows its nature as a fundamental principle, and even as the highest fundamental principle. It is in other words more fundamental than any other fundamental principle, for example, the principles of identity, difference, and contradiction (8).

As noted earlier, the principle of reason provokes us to ask the question as to the reason for or the ground of the principle of reason itself. Does the principle have a ground/reason itself, or is it exempted from this demand, which it poses? Is the principle itself without reason/ground? (11). Does it perhaps have a different kind of reason/ground? If, as one may be tempted to expect, at stake here is the most eminent reason, do we not risk falling into groundlessness by retreating ever further to the reason of reason of reason? (12). If on the other hand the principle of reason were to be without ground, it would be in contradiction with itself. The principle of contradiction namely provides that that which contradicts itself cannot be. Modern science indeed proceeds in this manner, that is, it seeks to rid itself of contradictions. Yet, as we saw earlier, in relation to the principle of reason, the principle of contradiction is a secondary principle (17). Furthermore, Hegel's dialectic showed that what is contradictory is not necessarily not real (18). That the principle of reason may itself be without ground/reason seems inconceivable, but that does not mean that it is unthinkable.

One can also state the question of the ground or reason of the principle somewhat differently, that is, from where does the principle of reason speak? (20–21, 32). Leibniz, who described the principle as fundamental, supreme, mighty, and noble, also referred to the principle as the *principium reddendae rationis*—for every true proposition, a reason can, or rather *must*, be rendered or given back. A truth is in other words a truth only if a reason can be given for it. Truth, one could also say, is a true proposition or a correct judgment (118). The reason for the "must" lies in the normativity of the strict formulation of the principle, thereby issuing a demand. This is where its power lies, what gives the principle its strength (24, 26–29). Phrased thus, one can also say that the principle requires that cognition (*Vorstellen*) must give back (*zurückgeben/reddere*) to cognition the reason for what is encountered, that is, to the I, the discerning I (22). For Leibniz, the principle of reason is a principle for sentences and statements, primarily concerning philosophical and scientific knowledge (22). The mightiness of the principle lies in the fact that it "pervades, guides, and supports all cognition that expresses itself in sentences or propositions" (22). The principle of reason is nevertheless not restricted to cognition or knowledge. It extends to everything that exists in some manner, in other words, to all the objects of cognition (22–23, 27). It is valid for every object, everything that "is." Its power lies in the fact that it is the principle for everything that "is" (23). Heidegger (119) summarizes as follows the essence of modern thinking as captured by Leibniz:

> After Descartes, followed by Leibniz and all of modern thinking, humans are experienced as an I that relates to the world such that it renders this world to itself in the form of connections

42 | Deconstructive Constitutionalism

> correctly established between its representations—that means judgments—and thus sets itself over against this world as to an object. Judgments and statements are correct, that means true, only if the reason for the connection of subject and predicate is rendered, given back to the representing I. A reason is this sort of reason only if it is a ratio, that means, an account that is given about something that is in front of a person as the judging I, and is given to this I.

Leibniz managed to hear the decisive claim of the principle and put it into wording, a principle that had for centuries existed, but not been captured before (23). The principle of reason lies at the foundation of modern science, which, as noted earlier, moves by way of the principle of reason in seeking a contradiction-free unity of judgments (30, 123). The same could be said of law, which, in the words of Schlag (1998, 24), functions like a "grid of intelligibility that enables legal propositions and legal artifacts (rules, standards, principles, policies, values) to be linked to each other in a pleasing and intelligible network of actual and potential connections." Heidegger specifically mentions the modern university in this context, which is grounded in the principle of reason (24, 28). Modern technology likewise gives expression to the principle of reason, with everything becoming calculable (121). Modern technology pushes toward the greatest possible perfection, that is, the complete calculability of objects. The closely related conceptualization of language as an instrument of information in the modern era in turn makes possible thinking machines and large-scale calculation (29, 124). Information, Heidegger contends, informs but at the same time forms. Information enables humanity to establish its dominance over the whole earth and beyond.

The Principle of Reason as a Saying of Being

We return now to the question posed earlier, that is, from where does the principle speak, or, phrased differently, who or what makes the demand to render reason? (Heidegger 1991, 39). Does the demand come from human beings or from reason itself? We would only know whether the demand comes from reason if we knew the essence of reason. Yet the principle of reason tells us nothing directly about the essence of reason (39). The principle of reason (nothing is without reason) is not a statement in the first place about reason, but about beings insofar as there are beings (44). As noted earlier, the question that necessarily arises is whether the principle itself has a ground or, phrased differently, is there a reason/ground (*Grund*) that is dissociated from every "why" and "because," and still is a reason/ground (*Grund*)? (43). At this point, Heidegger (45) suggests that we listen to the statement concerning the principle of reason with a different tonality. If we emphasize the words "is" (*ist*, a conjugation of "to be" [*sein*]) and "reason/ ground" (*Grund*) in the statement, we hear what was unheard before. It then reads that "nothing," that is, no being whatsoever, exists or "is" without ground/reason (*Grund*) (49). Heard in this way, the principle of reason speaks to us not only about beings, but also about the existence or Being of beings. It indicates that there is a close relationship between the Being of beings and ground/reason. It says namely that "*to Being there belongs something like ground/reason. Being is akin to grounds, it is ground-like* [Zum Sein gehört dergleichen wie Grund. Das Sein is grundartig, grundhaft]" (49). Being is not here said to have a ground, but to "*reign in itself as grounding* [Sein west in sich als gründendes]" (49). The principle of reason can in other words be read as a saying of or concerning Being (*sagen vom Sein*), though in a concealed manner.

Heidegger thus suggests that we should hear what remains silent in the principle of reason. This hearing does not concern only the ear, but also the essence of the human being, that is, the attuning of the human being to what determines his or her essence. In this determining (*Be-stimmung*) the human being is touched and called forth by a voice (*Stimme*), which "resounds all the more purely the more it silently reverberates through what speaks" (50). The change in tonality allows us to hear the accord between Being and reason/ground (*Grund*) in the formulation of the principle "nothing *is* without *reason*." To Being there thus belongs something like ground/ reason (*Grund*). As noted, this does not mean that Being has a reason or that Being is grounded. Only beings have a ground/reason; only beings are grounded. "Being is as Being grounding" (*Sein ist als Sein gründend*). With the new tonality, the principle of reason is revealed as a principle of Being (*Satz vom Sein*) (51). In shifting toward the question of Being (*Seinsfrage*), the search for the essence of reason/ground, which was raised earlier, is not abandoned. The discussion of ground/reason only moves into the relevant realm (*zuständigen Bereich*) through this focus on Being. Being and ground/ reason (*Grund*), as we saw, belong together (51). From this belonging together with Being as Being, ground/reason receives its essence, or, stated differently: Being as Being reigns (*waltet*) from the essence of ground/reason (51). Being and ground/reason are the same (*das Selbe*) but not the equivalent (*das Gleiche*). There is thus a difference between Being and ground/reason (*Grund*). Being is in essence ground/reason. For this reason, Being does not have a ground and is thus the abyss (*der Ab-Grund*). Insofar as it grounds, Being nevertheless allows beings to be beings (125). It is important to note that Being does not fall within the realm (*Machtbereich*) of the principle of reason; only beings do (51). Furthermore, we cannot strictly speaking say that Being "is," as we have in fact repeatedly stated until now. This is so because the word "is" can actually be used only with respect to beings. The "is" itself, or Being, "is" not (51). It is not present in the same sense as, for example, a wall. We could instead say "Being and ground/reason: the same"; or "Being: the abyss." These "sentences" or "phrases" (*Sätze*) are no longer propositions (*Sätze*) in the sense of affirming or denying (the truth of) something (51). Hearing the principle of reason as a principle of Being does not happen by way of a theory or through sorcery, but by building a path that brings us close to where we need to be (52). This change in tonality requires a leap in thinking as thinking is brought into another realm. The earlier discussion of the principle of reason according to the first, ordinary tonality helps us to prepare for the leap (53). It brings us, so to speak, to and through a field, from where we can undertake the leap. As we saw earlier, *Satz* also bears this meaning of a leap (*Sprung*). It is in this sense that the principle of reason is a leap (*Satz*) into the essence of Being (*das Wesen des Seins*), into Being as Being (*das Sein als Sein*), into Being as ground/reason (*als Grund*) (53).

The Withdrawal of Being in its Sending

We can say that the sovereignty of reason is established by the principle of reason, which, as noted, is described by Leibniz as the supreme fundamental principle (Heidegger 1991, 55). In accordance with the *principium reddendae rationis sufficientis*, all cognition now has to respond to the demand that sufficient reasons be rendered for every being (55, 71). Because of the sovereignty of reason so established, the possibility of the principle of reason being recognized as allowing for a leap into Being did not come into view for a long time. The establishment of the sovereignty of reason happens by way of the withdrawing of Being, which occurs at the same time as its proffering or sending in beings (61). In modernity, Being as Being withdraws even more, yet what withdraws at the same time shines forth through beings and the way in which they appear. As we saw, in modernity beings appear as objects, or heard with the second tonality, Being comes to shine in the objectness of objects, which in turn has an effect on the subjectivity of subjects. This relation between subject and object in other words determines the way in which the Being of beings is determined, that is, solely in terms of the objectness of the object. This peculiar appearing of Being in modernity can be described as a new epoch of withdrawal, where Being adapts itself to the objectness of objects, yet in its essence as Being, withdraws (55). At this point, we can return to the question posed at the start of this analysis as to the reason for the lateness of the arrival of the principle of reason. We can say that the incubation period of the principle of reason ends with Leibniz, yet the incubation of the principle of reason/ground as a principle of Being remains for a longer time (55–56). As we will see in the further discussion, with the extreme withdrawal of Being in objectivity, the essence of Being (as ground/reason) yet paradoxically comes to the fore (56). This seems to align with human nature: we only notice something when we no longer have it.

We now return again to the question from where the demand comes to render reason, which has in a sense already been answered, albeit implicitly (59). This is in other words a question about the site of the principle, yet the site is not a place in space. To reach the site, it is again a question of the path. We saw earlier that a leap is required here, as no gradual transition from one tonality to the next is possible. Yet it is important to note that that from which one makes the leap is not abandoned in the leap, albeit that it is viewed differently after the leap. The principle of reason by way of this path becomes a saying of Being, speaking of Being as such (61). The notion of the sending (*Geschick*) of Being can only be understood once we have made the leap. We can now understand this sending, which is at the same time the history of Being, as encompassing the entire history of Western thinking (61). The "sending" (*Geschick*) at stake here does not simply mean destiny or fate, whether good or bad, but also preparing and ordering (61). The sending of Being involves us being spoken to (*zuspricht*) as well as the preparing of a temporal play-space in which beings can appear by way of lighting and clearing (*lichtet*) (62). The history of Being is not to be confused with a (Hegelian) history of what happened in the past, which is characterized by a process. The sending of history instead means that the essence of history is viewed from the perspective of the sending and withdrawal of Being. Although Being differs through its sending, something remains the same, which can nonetheless not be represented by a general concept and does not have a definite characteristic or feature that can be extracted (62). Being furthermore does not lie over against us like beings do. Being, as we saw, hides itself, withdraws itself (63). Incubation is simply another word for the self-withdrawal of Being into concealment, which remains the source of every revealing. The end of philosophy arrives when Being withdraws completely in the absolute self-knowledge of absolute spirit (65). We can in other words speak of epochs of incubation. The end of the incubation period of Being as such paradoxically goes along with the sovereignty and rule of the mighty/fundamental principle of reason (65–66). As we saw, Being here withdraws more and more decisively, revealing itself as objectness (and as will) in this withdrawing (65). Kant's philosophy takes the decisive step in fleshing out Being as objectness and will (65–66).

Before we discuss Heidegger's reading of Kant, a few more comments about the leap at stake in hearing the principle of reason with the second tonality are required. Heard in the first tonality, the principle of reason is a saying about beings. Heard in the second tonality, we hear that reason/ground and Being are the same. We now start to think Being as Being, and no longer by way of a kind of being. The leap that is required here lays claim to our being/our essence (68). It is only in the sending of Being that we become sent-like Beings (*geschicklich*), and therefore compelled to find what is fitting/sent (*das Schickliche*) and at the same time enmeshed in missing (*verfehlen*) what is fitting/sent (*das Schickliche*) (68). We seldom experience this sending of Being, which lays claim to us, which needs us. As noted earlier, the nature of Being is furthermore such that it withdraws in the sending (68). It is important to note that the self-revealing of Being is not a characteristic of Being, but what Being "is" in its essence—it belongs to Being as a property (69). Being can be said to reign (*walten*) as withdrawal in the history of thinking. Leibniz formulated the principle of reason in such a way that it awakens and gathers Western thinking in a new way. The claim of the principle of reason as highest fundamental principle (*Grundsatz*) comes to the fore here, as well as the concealing/sheltering/salvaging power (*bergende Machte*) of this claim. With reference to Leibniz, Heidegger notes that the greater the work of a thinker, the greater is the unthought (*Ungedachte*) in his work. One can say this about the principle of reason in Leibniz's work through which modern thinking first found its depth (71).

Kant and the Principle of Reason

Heidegger's discussion of Kant takes place primarily in Lectures 9 and 10. We focus here on three main features of this reading: (1) the notions of critique and of reason; (2) the phrase "a priori conditions of possibility" and its relation to the principle of reason; and (3) the transcendental method and its relation to the sending of Being. Heidegger first points to the notion of critique (*Kritik*) that appears in the titles of all three of Kant's main texts. Critique is not to be understood as criticism here, that is, as an examination of or as placing bounds (*Schranken*) on reason. Critique is instead to be understood here in the Greek sense of a limit, specifically the limits (*Grenzen*) of reason. A limit in this sense is not that where something stops, but that from which and in which something commences, emerges as what it is. The Kantian notion of critique resonates with the Greek *krinein*, that is, to distinguish in the sense of "a 'separating out,' in which something important comes into relief" (72). This appears inter alia from the fact that his three *Critiques* focus on what he refers to as "a priori conditions of possibility" (72). Reason, more specifically pure reason, that is, reason that is not determined by sensibility (71, 76), and that includes theoretical as well as practical reason, is furthermore the main theme of all three these texts, and central to the thinking of Kant in general. Reason is to be understood here as the faculty of judgment according to a priori principles or as the "faculty of principles, that is, of grounding principles (*Grundsätze*), of the giving of grounds (*Grundgebung*)" (71–72), thus resonating with Leibniz's principle of reason.

The phrase "a priori conditions of possibility" is the leitmotiv that comes to the fore in all of Kant's work (72). The term "a priori" (from the earlier) is the later echo of what Aristotle called *proteron te phusei*, in other words, that which, with respect to self-revealing, is earlier, insofar as it precedes what is more manifest. For Kant, the conditions of possibility are a priori in this sense. "Possibility" here means enabling or making-possible (*Ermöglichung*). What do the a priori conditions of making-possible relate to? They relate to what the *proteron te phusei* relate to for Aristotle, that is, to what in relation to us and for us is the most manifest vis-à-vis *phusis*, Being. In other words, the a priori conditions of possibility relate to beings (*das Seiende*). Under the title "a priori conditions of possibility," Kant reflects on the making-possible of that from where beings are determined for us as such and as a whole. From where does this happen? The two regions of beings where we as humans, as *animal rationale*, are placed, that is, first, our belonging to the realm of nature and, second, our belonging to the realm of reason, freedom, and will (72, 76). Behind the formula "a priori conditions of possibility" hides the rendering of sufficient reasons, the *ratio sufficiens*, which as *ratio*, is pure reason (73). According to Kant, only by way of recourse to reason can something be determined as to what it is and how it is a being for the rational creature, that is, for human beings. For Kant, as we saw, reason (*Vernunft*) means and is *ratio*, in other words, the faculty of fundamental/grounding principles (*Vermögen der Grundsätze*), that is, of grounds (*des Grundes*) (76). Reason (*Vernunft*) is thus the ground that grounds (*der gründende Grund*). Only when it is reasonable (*vernünftig*) is ground (*Grund*) pure reason. When Kant, in accordance with the leitmotiv of his thinking, contemplates the a priori conditions of possibility of nature and of freedom, this thinking amounts to the presentation of sufficient grounds for that which can appear to human beings as beings and what cannot, as well as for the way in which what appears can appear and the way in which they cannot (76).

Finally, how does this connection between the critique of pure reason and the principle of sufficient reason assist us in understanding the sending of Being in the modern epoch? How does Being in other words send itself in Kant's thinking, and how does Being withdraw? According to Heidegger, Kant was the first thinker since the ancient Greeks to posit the Being of beings as a question to be answered. Kant does so by reflecting on the path that traces beings with respect to their Being, that is, on method (76). This of course happens in a way that differs radically from what happened in ancient Greek thinking. The path of Kant is characterized by *ratio—ratio* as reason (*Vernunft*) and as ground (*Grund*).[6] In line with the thinking of the modern age, Kant's thinking moves in the realm of reason (*Vernunft*). Reason as the faculty of foundational principles here functions as the faculty of representing something as something. Descartes expressed this as "I think/*ego cogito*." Kant goes further: "I place something as something in front of myself." The focus of the three critiques—of theoretical, practical, and technical reason—is thus on the I-ness of the I, the subjectivity of the subject: "It is in relation to the I as subject that beings, placed before the I in representation, have the character of an object for a subject" (77). We can also say that "beings are beings as object for a consciousness" (77). The ground, which gives or hands over (*zureicht*) to an object its possibility as object, describes that which we call the objectivity of the object. Objectivity is the Kantian understood Being of objects that can be experienced. The objectivity of objects is clearly the ownmost (*das Eigenste*) of objects. At the same time, the objectivity of an object does not cling to it like some or other quality. It rather lends itself to (*eignet*) the object, and it does not do so after the fact, but before it appears as object, so that it can appear as such (77). The critical enclosing of the objectivity of objects thus surpasses/transcends the object. This surpassing of the object amounts to a surpassing into the realm of the founding fundamental principles (*gründende Grundsätze*), into the subjectivity of reason (*Vernunft*). The transcendence beyond the object toward objectivity is the entry into reason (*Vernunft*), which only herewith comes to the fore in its ground-setting essence. This transcendence of the object and entry into subjectivity is referred to in Latin as *transcendere*. For this reason, Kant calls his critical procedure, which inquires into the a priori conditions for the possibility of objects, the "transcendental method" (77). The transcendental method speaks of the Being of beings in accordance with the principle of reason.

The Sending of Being and the Human Being

Before we conclude this discussion, it is necessary to briefly explore (1) the relation between the sending of Being and human beings; and (2) the link that Heidegger posits between the play of Being, or Being as the abyss on the one hand, and death on the other. As for (1), Heidegger (1991, 94) describes the sending of Being as the conjuncture (*Gegeneinanderüber*) of Being and human beings. The sending of Being is more precisely both a demand (*Zuspruch*) and a claim (*Anspruch*) of the saying (*Spruch*), from which all human speaking speaks. This ties in with Heidegger's well-known statement that language speaks (2000, 188) and that language is the house of Being (1993, 237). Here he adds that language speaks historically (1991, 96). In the sending of Being, Being furnishes the Free (*das Freie*) of the temporal play-space (*Zeit-Spiel-Raumes*), and in this way frees human beings into the Free (*ins Freie*) of the possibilities of essence sent to them in each instance (*jeweils schicklichen Wesensmöglichkeiten*) (94; chapter 3 of this volume). The historical speaking of language is thus sent (*beschickt*) and determined (*gefügt*) by a particular sending of Being. Human beings speak only insofar as they answer to language in accordance with the sending (*geschicklich die Sprache entspricht*). Human beings are in other words addressed differently at different times by the sending of Being. In this manner, Kant, by virtue of his translation of *ratio* into reason (*Vernunft*) and by inquiring into the conditions of possibility for the appearance of objects (grounds/*Grund*), responds to the claim of the principle of sufficient reason and brings this response to language (97–98). Leibniz's principle of sufficient reason, which, as we saw, is lodged in the representing "I," the subject conscious of him- or herself, provides the point of departure for this sending of Being in modernity (101). In this era, the principle ultimately becomes the unconditional and universal claim to render mathematical-technical calculable grounds, in other words, total rationalization (103).

The second link that remains to be explored likewise ties in with the earlier-mentioned conjuncture between (the sending of) Being and human essence (94). We saw earlier that Heidegger speaks of Being as the abyss (*Sein: der Ab-Grund*) or as groundless (*grund-los*) (110). For Heidegger, this is not because Being grounds itself, but because every grounding by Being in its epochal sending where, as we saw, Being is inevitably turned into a being remains disproportionate (*ungemäß*) to Being as ground (*Sein als Grund*) (110). Thinking now becomes abyssal as we no longer contemplate Being in terms of a ground, that is, in terms of beings. The leap into the second tonality of the principle of reason nevertheless enables us to contemplate Being as Being. It allows us to contemplate that which brings thought into play with that on which Being as Being rests (*ruht*). The "play" (*Spiel*) at stake here needs to be thought in its essence, that is, with respect to what it plays and who plays it. This mysterious and most elevated play cannot be thought as something that "is," and thus in terms of the dialectic of freedom and necessity. Being as abyss needs to be thought in terms of the play to which we are brought as mortals (*Sterbliche*), insofar as we live in proximity to death. Death, Heidegger notes, is the "as yet unthought measure (*Maßgabe*) of the immeasurable (*Unermeßlichen*), in other words, the ultimate (*höchste*) play in which humans are engaged on earth, a play in which they are at stake" (112). Why this play? What is its ground in other words? The play, like Being itself (126), is without ground/reason and thus without why. It plays because it plays (113). Being as grounding has no ground, plays as the abyss (*Ab-Grund*) plays the play that, as sending, passes on Being and ground/reason (*Grund*) to us (113).

Derrida

THE UNIVERSITY AND THE PRINCIPLE OF REASON

In "The Principle of Reason: The University in the Eyes of Its Pupils," a text dating from 1983, Derrida (2004b, 129–55) reflects on the principle of reason with reference to the university, more specifically Cornell University. Cornell University was established in 1865 in an area where there were greater possibilities of expansion, and which also provided a view of the village, the hills, and the lake. These views, it was thought, made the campus fit for reflective contemplation of life and death. The scenery is furthermore marked by gorges, which are spanned by bridges. Derrida notes here the controversy concerning protective barriers that were installed in 1977 on the bridges to prevent suicides from happening on campus, but also affected the view from the bridges. The institutional scenography as described here alludes to some relationship between reason and life-death, as we also saw in Heidegger (1991, 133–34). The essence, purpose, mission, or raison d'être of the university, its justification for existence as required by the principle of reason/ground, is precisely reason, or the idea of reason, as Kant indicated in *The Conflict of the Faculties* (1979, 129–30, 134–35).[7] As Derrida (135) points out, no university has ever been established against reason.

Leibniz's principle of reason, as Derrida (136) notes, speaks of an obligation or demand for it to be rendered, as we also saw in Heidegger earlier. The "rendering" or "giving back" in the *principium reddendae rationis* seems to suggest that reason "gives rise to exchange, borrowing, debt, donation, restitution [*donne lieu à échange, circulation, emprunt, dette, donation, restitution*]" (136). If this is indeed the case, questions would arise as to who is responsible for that debt or duty and to whom (136). Heidegger's analysis, as we saw earlier, suggests that this is partly the case, depending on the tonality with which the principle of reason is heard. Derrida appears to agree, noting that *ratio* in the phrase *reddere rationem* is not to be understood (only) as a faculty or power of human beings, as it is usually understood in the metaphysical tradition, specifically by Kant. *Ratio* as employed here is furthermore not to be understood as a thing encountered among beings or objects in the world to be rendered or given back. Reason here stands in a close relationship with the "one must" and the "one must render" in the statement of the principle of reason. At stake here is our relationship to a principle, which points to "a demand, debt, duty, request, order, obligation, law, imperative [*l'exigence, la dette, le devoir, la requête, l'ordre, l'obligation, la loi, l'impératif*]" (136). If reason can be rendered (*rendi potest*), it must also be.

This "must" of reason cannot without precaution be equated with a moral imperative in the Kantian sense of practical reason. The latter instead presupposes and calls on the "must" of the principle of reason. The "must" of reason is therefore to be distinguished from practical reason, ethics, and theoretical reason. At stake here is clearly a certain kind of responsibility, a call that we need to respond to. Heidegger refers in this regard to an *Anspruch*, which Derrida (136) translates as "requirement, claim, claim/demand, demand, command, or summons [*exigence, prétention, revendication, demande, commande, convocation*]." Derrida here seeks to draw a distinction between responding *to* the principle of reason and answering *for* the principle of reason (*répondre au principe de raison et répondre du principe de raison*).[8] "Responding to" points to the first tonality that we came across in the reading of Heidegger. To "answer for" the principle of reason refers to the second tonality; in other words, it means not simply obeying the principle, but raising questions about the origin or ground of the principle itself. This brings us back to the gorge, in the case of Cornell University, the void, the abyss, that is, the impossibility of the principle of reason/ground to ground itself. As we saw in Heidegger, the principle of reason establishes its empire, but it does so by keeping hidden from itself the abyssal question of Being, and thus of its own foundation (Derrida 2004b, 139). This is particularly true of the modern university, which can be said to be built both on the principle of reason and on what remains hidden within the principle (140). The dissimulation of the origin in fact makes the development of the modern university possible. Yet this all happens over an abyss. It happens on a ground that is itself without ground (140). This raises important questions about the (future) task of the university, and of thinking in general. Can it simply respond *to* the principle of reason, as it tends to do, without also answering *for* the principle, as both Heidegger and Derrida seek to do by raising questions about its origin?

In *The Principle of Reason*, as we saw earlier, Heidegger (1991, 124) captures the essence of what he calls the modern (atomic) era, where the rational mixes with the technical, in the concept of information (Derrida 2004b, 145–46). This concept of information or of technical instrumentalization also determines the modern university (147). In his analysis, Derrida shows that both basic and end-orientated research are and can potentially be used today for military-technological purposes across all fields and that even philosophy and literary theory are not immune to such utilization (140–44). All forms of research become "information," which, as Heidegger pointed out, not only informs but forms as well. It ensures calculability and safeguarding, positioning human beings in a way that enables their mastery on earth and beyond (145–46). Within the university, this technical instrumentalization gives rise to the focus on the provision of professional education by the university (151). Derrida then calls for a community of thinking that (1) accepts the permeability of the border between basic and end-orientated research; (2) operates in terms of reason *and* is prepared to inquire into the origins of the demand for reason; and (3) is prepared to investigate the consequences of such an inquiry (148–50). At stake here is a new responsibility, which does not entail simply opposing end-orientated research, the principle of reason, new technologies, or professional education (146, 147, 153). With reference to Cornell University, this responsibility would mean not only contemplating the heights, the bridges, and the barriers to the abyss, but also the abyss itself (150). The abyss here of course refers to the impossibility of the principle of reason/ground to ground itself, and thus having to keep itself suspended above the void. Thinking in other words needs to engage with the principle of reason as well as with what lies beyond this principle, both with the *arche* and with an-archy (153). Derrida finally points to the strange position of the university vis-à-vis society: on the one hand, the university is projected to the outside, emancipated, and on the other, jealously guarded, controlled (153–54). This double movement gives the opportunity for a certain freedom of play, an empty place for chance, for the event that would tear up time, thereby bringing us close to the abyss (154–55).[9]

The Gift and the Principle of Reason

Derrida's *Given Time: I. Counterfeit Money* was published in 1992 (in French in 1991) but has its roots in a series of lectures dating from 1977 to 1979. Here Derrida (1992a) analyzes inter alia Marcel Mauss's *The Gift*, which explores the structure of the giving of gifts in archaic societies, showing that such gifts are characterized by circular economic exchange and economic self-interest. Derrida points out that the gift as described here cancels itself out as gift. Returning implicitly to the analysis in "The Principle of Reason: The University in the Eyes of its Pupils," Derrida notes that a gift would be such only if there are no traces of calculation, reciprocation, debt, or gratitude, whether in consciousness or in the unconscious of the giver or the receiver. This indeed seems impossible, as the intention to give appears to automatically give rise to a process of self-approval and thus circular return. Derrida nevertheless finds indications of such a notion of the pure or perfect gift in Heidegger's *Time and Being* (1962) where he speaks of the *es gibt*, that is, the gift of Being and of time. At stake here is an event (*Ereignis*) or interplay (*Zuspiel*), which as Derrida (1992a, 20) points out, entails a giving "without giving anything and without anyone giving anything—nothing but Being and time (which are nothing)." This gift-event thus in a certain way precedes Being and time. It is not possible to give an account or to render reason of the pure gift in accordance with the principle of reason, and Derrida (35) accordingly refers to the gift as involving a certain madness, an *a-logos*. The gift entails a desire to give the impossible, it never takes place in the present, and "is" therefore non-localizable, *a-topos* (35). The gift "is" furthermore excessive and measureless, and is a stranger to Kantian practical reason as well as theoretical reason (91). Derrida (156) outlines the relation between the principle of reason and the gift as follows:

> The gift would be that which does not obey the principle of reason: it is, it ought to be, it owes itself to be without reason, without wherefore, and without foundation. The gift, if there is any, does not even belong to practical reason. It should remain a stranger to morality, to the will, perhaps to freedom, at least to that freedom that is associated with the will of a subject. It should remain a stranger to the law or to the "il faut" (you must, you have to) of this practical reason. It *should* surpass *duty* itself: duty beyond duty [*Il* devrait *passer le* devoir *même: devoir au-delà du devoir*].

Derrida's *Given Time* thus proceeds somewhat further than "The Principle of Reason: The University in the Eyes of Its Pupils" in giving a certain "content" to the abyss, play, and the event that lies at the origin of the principle of reason. The event now takes on a certain "ethical" dimension, involving an excessive responsibility, which is linked here with a certain psychoanalysis. Derrida (16–17) namely speaks of the pure gift as involving a radical or an absolute forgetting, which he distinguishes from repression in the unconscious.[10]

THE DEATH PENALTY AND THE PRINCIPLE OF REASON

The relation between the principle of reason and law, specifically criminal law, is explored in the second volume of Derrida's *Death Penalty Seminars* (2000–2001), in the sixth session, where Derrida (2017) refers to and discusses Heidegger's *The Principle of Reason*. Derrida notes here the fact that Heidegger, in reflecting on the principle of reason, does not refer to the death penalty or to criminal law (145). One can nevertheless draw certain conclusions about law and the death penalty from what Heidegger says about, for example, calculation. As we saw earlier, Heidegger in his address on the principle of reason points to the relation between the principle of reason as formulated by Leibniz, and calculation, that is, the condition of existence of having to be "securely established as a calculating object for cognition" (Derrida 2017, 145; Heidegger 1991, 120). It is also interesting to note Heidegger's comment that the word *ratio* in the formulation of the principle of reason has an age-old link not only with accounting, but also with "justifying, of confirming something as being in the right, of correctly figuring something out and securing something through such a reckoning [*rechtfertigen, etwas als zu Recht bestehend, als richtig errechnen und durch solche Rechnung sichern*]" (Heidegger 1991, 120). Heidegger here invokes the language of law (*Recht, richtig, rechtfertigen*), which, as Derrida (146) notes, points to an inherent link between calculation and law. Heidegger (120–24) further elaborates on the way in which the human being, by way of the principle of reason, increasingly becomes a reckoning creature, which, as we saw earlier, finds expression in modern technology, where rational calculation rules. Toward the end of the address, Heidegger (129) points to the determination of the human being as rational animal and wonders whether this determination can be said to exhaust "the essence of humanity [*das Wesen des Menschen*]." The word *ratio*, as he points out, was originally a word used in Roman commercial language (*der römischen Kaufmannssprache*), as can for example be seen in the texts of Cicero (129). For Derrida (147), this points to the fact that legal reasoning, in Heidegger's assessment, essentially is mercantile reasoning; that legal calculation in other words essentially amounts to market calculation. In the criminal law field, this essence of law—as commercial law—can, for example, be seen in the centrality of the *talio* principle (147–48; chapter 5 of this volume).

Further reflecting on the absence of a discussion of punishment and the death penalty in Heidegger's reflections on the principle of reason, Derrida notes that for Heidegger the death penalty would be a secondary issue, that is, coming after Dasein's being-toward-death. The death penalty would furthermore be an inauthentic and improper way of dying, involving some machine or tool, which nevertheless can only happen to the human being (Derrida 2017, 149). The death penalty would thus be proper to the human being only, as the animal in Heidegger's thinking does not die, but merely perishes (149). One can again draw certain conclusions about Heidegger's assessment of law and punishment from some of his remarks, for example, his remark in passing that Leibniz was the inventor of life insurance and that this is essentially what reason is, that is, about seeking insurance or security, about safeguarding life (Heidegger 1991, 124). As Derrida (150–51) points out, law can be said to be one of these life insurance measures, whether in the form of the inalienable right to life, thereby banning the death penalty, or in providing for the death penalty, thereby seeking to ensure through deterrence the security of the social body.[11] Although he would thus attach a negative connotation to the death penalty because of the inauthentic relation to death as well as the objective legal calculation that it entails, Heidegger would not necessarily condemn the death penalty (Derrida 2017, 149).

In concluding this discussion, Derrida turns to lecture 13 of Heidegger's *The Principle of Reason*, which we briefly discussed earlier. Derrida (152–53) here notes the many possible interpretations of the title *Der Satz vom Grund*, specifically of *Satz*, which, as noted, points to a leap, but also to a venturing, positing or wagering (*gesetzt/Setzung/Setzen*). Derrida (153) refers here to the second tonality with which Heidegger (111) seeks to hear the principle of reason, where Being is thought as abyss, as groundless, as without reason. Heidegger (111) also notes that Being is now, by way of the leap, thought as that which gives measure (*das Maß-Gebende*), though in itself is immeasurable (*Unermeßlich*) (Derrida 2017, 154).[12] Notable here is the appearance of the gift, of measure and the immeasurable. We saw earlier that Heidegger also refers to this leap into the realm of Being as a play (*Spiel*) where the essence of the human being is placed at risk or in play (Derrida 2017, 154–55). In this abyssal ground or play, human beings become who they are (155). The essence of the human being is in other words to be thought in the first place "on the basis of this being wagered, posited, set in play, in the measureless gift of the measure, in the gift of the measure of the immense" (155).[13] Such a contemplation of the human being must precede the contemplation of the essence of the human being as *animal rationale*, of the human being as end in him- or herself, as having dignity, as one finds, for example, in Kantian discourse (155). The legal rationality at stake in the Kantian discourse on the death penalty can in view of Heidegger's analysis thus be said to "obscure this play, to evade and hide from oneself the abyss of the incalculable at the bottom of the calculable" (155). What links together for Heidegger the play, the immeasurable, the abyss, as we saw earlier, is death in whose proximity we mortals dwell. Death is, in other words, another name for the

> as yet unthought gift of the measure of the unmeasurable, of the immense, that is, of the most elevated Play in which humans are engaged on their earthly path, and in which, once again, they are *gesetzt*, posited, played, risked, wagered [*gagé*], at stake [*engagé*]. Death is a gift (death gives or is given), it is an as-yet unthought gift, but the gift of a measure of what cannot be measured. . . . The measure is death. The first or the last measure, and giving the measure, it is not measurable; thus it gives the measure of the unfathomable from the unfathomable. And

this holds true for the thinking of the gift without ground and without exchange, without calculation, as well as for the thinking of the grounding without ground, of *Grund* as *Abgrund* or of the Measure and the Calculation of the noncalculable unfathomable. (Derrida 2017, 155–56)

Derrida (157) concludes the session by noting that the Heideggerian discourse allows one to both support and oppose the death penalty. Derrida's position is, however, different. For him it is about taking responsibility and negotiating between the immeasurable gift, on the one hand, and the measurable or calculable drive to safeguard and secure, on the other (158). For Heidegger, the reflection on death is ultimately about making human beings die their own death properly, about saving or immunizing humanity, whereas for Derrida (242) it is about dying *for* the other. The latter is not to be understood in a literal sense (Derrida 1995d, 43–45), but as imposing an infinite responsibility for the death of the other. In the sixth session, Derrida, for example, points in this respect to a broader understanding of the death penalty, as not only including a judicial sentence, but also including ways of letting die. One needs to think, for example, of the impact of poverty and of certain kinds of work on life expectancy, and thus as a kind of structural death penalty imposed on some. We also tend to value certain lives more than others, as can be seen in media reports on earthquakes, terrorism, or war in poorer countries, which allows us to absolve ourselves from responsibility (Derrida 2017, 143). The position is even worse when it comes to non-human animals, seeing that the dominant view today is still that killing these animals does not constitute murder (Derrida 1995d, 69).[14] Many deaths due to hunger and disease are furthermore caused by the pursuit of self-interest by states and multinational companies (85–86). The infinite responsibility at stake here would involve viewing every death as premature and therefore as murder, for which I am responsible (Derrida 2002a, 385). One can speak here of an originary guilt with respect to the death of the other, or an a priori debt of the living as survivor, and therefore a need to seek forgiveness for one's own being-there (Derrida 2002a, 383–84; 1995d, 52).

Reason to Come

In both *the Beast and the Sovereign I* and part I of *Rogues*, Derrida interrogates La Fontaine's fable *The Wolf and the Lamb* (1668), which declares that the reason of the strongest is always the best. Derrida (2005c, xi, 92–93) relates the fable to the Kantian insight that law is always (potentially) accompanied by force or coercion, and therefore needs to be distinguished from justice (Kant 1996b, 6:312 [para. 44]). La Fontaine is in other words describing a state of affairs, that is, the reason of the strongest tends to prevail, although such reasoning is not necessarily just. The political examples that Derrida (2005c, 13–14; 2009a, 11–13) gives are of democratic sovereign states as well as the United States, which in the international law context often acts like the wolf in the fable (2005c, xiii, 103–4; 2009a, 208–9), as well as the five permanent members of the Security Council, which of course includes the United States (2005c, 100). Yet the fable also can be read in a Freudian sense as a reference to the forces at war in the psyche (Derrida 2009a, 183), which includes a certain "weak force," a force without power, which "opens up unconditionally to what or who *comes* and comes to affect it" (Derrida 2005c, xiv). In a related sense, the fable can be said to hint at the analysis of Heidegger discussed earlier and in *Introduction to Metaphysics*, where he raises the question of how *logos*, which as we saw is at first a word for Being, becomes logic and reason, and in this form dominates and rules over Western philosophy (Derrida 2009a, 317–20).[15]

In part II of *Rogues*, Derrida (2005c, 122, 123, 127) links the notion or phrase of "saving the honor of reason" with Husserl's *The Crisis of European Science and Transcendental Phenomenology*, Heidegger's *Der Satz vom Grund*, as well as with Kant's analysis of reason, and again brings to the fore the connection made earlier with the relationship between life and death. In referring to Heidegger's text, Derrida (122) notes that a detailed analysis would show that "everything here gets played out between the calculable and the incalculable, there where the *Grund* opens up into the *Abgrund*, where giving reasons [*rendre-raison*] and giving an account [*rendre-compte*]— *logon didonai* or *principium reddendae rationis*—are threatened by or drawn into the abyss." This tension between the calculable and the incalculable is linked by Derrida (121–22) with Husserl's invocation of a heroism of reason, which Derrida likens to a "saving" of reason from running aground, that is, the threat of its own illness, loss, crisis or demise, which appears to be inherent to the structure of reason. The same is true of the antinomies of reason, which, according to Kant (1998a, A474–76/B502–4), likewise threaten the architectonic or system of reason (Derrida 2005c, 120, 128; 2019, 33). Derrida (2005c, 123) refers to this threat that reason poses to itself, a threat arising from within reason, as autoimmunity, a notion that gives expression to the self-destructive or death drive of an organism neutralizing its own defenses against external intrusions. This autoimmune structure of reason, even though it threatens reason from within, at the same time allows it to be open to the future, to the event, to what or who comes (152). It allows for the welcoming of the other[16] and, as we saw earlier, prescribes an excessive duty—beyond the Kantian notion of acting out of pure duty—toward, and the taking of responsibility for, the other, through an interruption of subjectivity, ipseity, sovereignty, economy, and the inevitable calculation of law (148–53). Similar to Derrida's analysis of hospitality, the gift, forgiveness, and justice, a decision involving reason, or what he here refers to as a "reasonable" decision, requires a negotiation between the incalculable and calculation (149–51, 159). Derrida (2005c, 133–34) finds support for such an understanding of reason inter alia in the Kantian understanding of dignity in the Groundwork (1997b, 4:435) as incalculable, and of the "interest" of practical reason as unconditional (*unbedingt*) in nature, in the *Critique of Practical Reason* (1997a, 5:120–22, read with 5:29–30 and 5:106), thereby making possible the subordination of theoretical reason (whose interest is only conditional) to practical reason.[17]

Legal Reasoning and the Welcome to the Other

The analyses of Heidegger and Derrida undertaken here show the problematic nature of reason as it operates today by virtue of the demand of the principle of reason. Apart from its calculating nature, reason is furthermore, especially in the analysis of Derrida, inherently linked to power and force, that is, with the reason of the strongest. Furthermore, the principle of reason requires that reason be rendered or given back, showing thereby its inherent link with economic exchange or circularity. The same observations can be made about legal reasoning, as we saw in Schlag's analysis. Should this leave us skeptical about law and legal reasoning, making us conclude that it simply amounts to politics in disguise?[18] Heidegger, and even more so Derrida, open the door to a different approach to reason. They show that we are indeed all inevitably caught within this demand. Nevertheless, through their analyses of the "origin" of the principle of reason, we arrive at a new understanding of reason, which is relevant also for the legal field. They allow us to reach beyond reason and, especially in Derrida's reading, bring us to a hyperethical or hyperpolitical understanding of reason. Whereas reason has traditionally been viewed as not needful of a ground or as grounded in itself, Derrida, following Heidegger, problematizes this assumption and, following Freud, locates this lack or "origin" of ground in the unconscious. This opens up the possibility of identifying "something," which is not a thing, that is, the pure gift, which lies beyond reason, and with reference to Kant, specifically beyond practical reason (Derrida 1992a, 156). Heidegger and Derrida thus point toward a split in the Kantian notion of the unity of reason, an opening in reason, toward what can be called "reason to come." This split in reason imposes an infinite responsibility on those entrusted with legal reasoning, to calculate with the incalculable. Reason so conceived could, for example, have a significant impact on the way in which modern constitutionalism on all levels addresses the claims of traditionally marginalized and excluded groups in society, such as those living in abject poverty; illegal migrants and refugees; the LGBTQIA+ community; women; minority religious, language, or cultural groups; sex workers; the criminally accused; and non-human animals (chapters 3, 4, and 5 of this volume). In each instance a negotiation would be required between the demands of the pure gift or of absolute hospitality, which can be said to underlie every modern constitution (De Ville 2017, 102–38), on the one hand, and the demands of calculation, on the other. The demands of the pure gift would in each instance be the abyssal and autoimmune starting point before engaging in politico-legal calculations. Such calculation would of course, where relevant, take account of affordability, legal precedent, as well as considerations such as (state) capacity and the separation of powers, that is, who would have the final say as to the measures to be taken and the timeline within which they should be taken.[19] A negotiation in other words needs to take place between the impossible and the possible, seeking to come as close as possible to the impossible. In transitioning from the impossible to the possible, invention in the strong sense is required, and certain forms of traditional legal reasoning may be unsuitable for the task.[20] The demand imposed by reason thus goes far beyond the duty imposed by Kantian practical reason. At stake here, as we saw, is an interruption of sovereignty, of subjectivity and of law, a duty beyond duty, an infinite responsibility toward the death of the other.

Chapter 3

Freedom and Democracy

We saw in earlier chapters that, according to Kant, the human being is the only being that is endowed with freedom with respect to the inclinations. This freedom, established in the *Critique of Pure Reason*, gives rise in the *Groundwork for a Metaphysics of Morals* and in the *Critique of Practical Reason* to a (moral) duty to respect human dignity. Yet, as noted, Kant (1996b, 6:230–31, 237–38, 311) did not foresee that the latter notion would become constitutionalized. Constitutionalism in his thinking is instead founded in freedom. The aim of a constitutional order is for Kant in the first place to secure peace between the members of society by protecting and reconciling their claims to external freedom. Although, as we saw, human dignity has come to dominate constitutionalism in many parts of the world after World War II (Introduction of this volume), this has not detracted from the importance of freedom.[1]

Freedom in Kant's thinking is in principle unlimited and poses a potential threat to the human being him- or herself as well as to others. In the *Lectures on Ethics*, in discussing the duties toward the self, Kant (1997c, 27:344) refers to freedom as constituting the inner worth of the world, yet unrestrained freedom is "the most terrible thing there could ever be." Freedom that "is not restricted by objective rules" would result in "much savage disorder. For it is uncertain whether man will not use his powers to destroy himself, and others, and the whole of nature" (27:344). In the *Lectures and Drafts on Political Philosophy*, Kant similarly remarks that "nothing worse could be thought than that each would be free without law. For each would do with the other what he wants and so no one would be free. The wildest animal is not as frightening as a lawless human being" (27:1320).

Objective rules are therefore required to restrain human freedom, both in relation to ourselves and in relation to others, that is, in its internal and external dimensions (27:347).[2] We are in the present chapter concerned only with external freedom, the protection of which, according to Kant, can be secured best under a republican constitution.[3] Here lawless freedom is forsaken for the sake of freedom under a law one makes for oneself. Freedom is thus inherently linked to self-government (1996b, 6:315–16). In the state of nature, as we saw in the "Introduction," every person can interpret the limits of his or her own freedom, and in the case of conflict with others, there is no third party who can determine these limits and judge who is in the right. Practical reason therefore prescribes that freedom should be lawful and limited under a republican constitution. This gives rise to law (*Recht*), that is, "the limitation of the particular freedom of each by the conditions under which universal freedom can exist" (27:1334). In the *Lectures on Anthropology*, Kant (2012, 25:1424) summarizes the position thus with respect to external freedom:

> The civil constitution includes: 1. Freedom. This includes: 2. the law, or the restriction of the freedom of an individual in order not to disturb the freedom of another; besides this, there must also 3. be an authority that applies the laws. Freedom without laws and force is the freedom of the savages and nomads. With this [kind of] freedom, I am always in danger of losing my freedom. Freedom with law and force creates equality among human beings.

The republican constitution, prescribed by practical reason, is thus characterized by the recognition of lawful freedom, formal equality, and the independence of citizens, as well as by the separation of powers and representative government (Kant 1996b, 6:313–18 [para. 45–49], 1996a, 8:290–97 ["On the Common Saying"]). This form of constitution is reconcilable with the different kinds of state, that is, autocracy, aristocracy, and democracy, which are nonetheless modified and tempered by such constitution.[4] The demand by practical reason that external freedom must be protected also has implications beyond the state. This demand means that war needs to be prohibited and peace be pursued, not only between individuals in the state of nature, but also between free, sovereign states (Kant 1996b, 6:354). The protection of freedom therefore requires not only a republican state, which provides for the greatest possible protection of the external freedom of the individual (Kant 2007, 8:22 ["Idea for a Universal History"], 1998a,

A316/B373), but also a continually expanding federation between sovereign states, and cosmopolitan law, which regulates the conditions of hospitality to be afforded to strangers (Kant 1996b, 6:311 [para. 43]; 1996a, 8:357–60 ["Perpetual Peace"]). Ultimately a world republic under a cosmopolitan constitution seems to be envisaged by Kant to ensure eternal peace (chapter 6).

As noted earlier, freedom remains one of the founding values of the modern constitution, even though it at times appears to be overshadowed by human dignity. In the "Introduction," it was further noted that in Kant's thinking, freedom and human dignity are very closely related.[5] We see something similar in this chapter in the exploration of the relation between the moral law and freedom in Kant's thinking. The main aim of this chapter is to understand Derrida's "reading" of Kant with respect to freedom and the way in which Derrida links freedom to democracy and to sovereignty, specifically in *Rogues*.[6] To arrive at such an understanding, one has to take a detour through the texts of Heidegger and Nancy, as Derrida does not in any of his published texts engage directly, or at least not in detail, with a reading of Kant with respect to freedom. This approach, which includes a close reading of specific texts, that is, of Heidegger's *The Essence of Human Freedom* and Derrida's *Rogues*, with Derrida's reading of Freud in the background, arguably allows for a better understanding not only of freedom in Derrida's thinking vis-à-vis Kant, but also of its peculiar relation to the democracy to come, and allows us to consider some of its implications for modern constitutionalism.

Our inquiry into freedom therefore starts with an analysis of Heidegger's reading of Kant's *Critique of Pure Reason*, the *Groundwork for a Metaphysics of Morals*, and the *Critique of Practical Reason*. In *The Essence of Human Freedom*, Heidegger (2005, 15) focuses specifically on Kant because, as he puts it, "Kant brings the problem of freedom for the first time explicitly into a radical connection with the problems of metaphysics." In other words, the way in which Kant approaches freedom allows for a philosophical inquiry, which involves not simply going-after-the-whole, but at the same time a going-to-the-roots (23–27). Stated differently, it allows one to ask not simply what beings are, but what they are as such, or what beings are as beings, and therefore also what Being is, or what the essence is of Being (28–29). At stake here is not an objective scientific inquiry, but an inquiry that inquires into the one who inquires, into the roots of his or her existence (25, 208). Heidegger's main concern in *The Essence of Human Freedom* is thus with what Kant, in contemplating human freedom, is by implication saying about that which exists, that is, about the Being of beings. How does Kant, in other words, understand Being, and how does this assist us in contemplating the essence of freedom? We see that Heidegger (16) is critical of the "narrowing" that takes place in Kant's engagement with freedom. A central theme in this respect is causality, specifically its relation to freedom in Kant's texts. Kant inquires into Being in terms of beings, and consequently views freedom as a form of causality. He thereby fails to appreciate the essence of Being as well as the relation between freedom and Being. In Heidegger's reading, transcendental (cosmological) freedom and practical (moral) freedom in Kant are clearly linked, with the latter being dependent on the former (18). Heidegger's reading in other words shows, inter alia, that transcendental freedom, that is, freedom as self-causation, as compared with the causation of nature, lies at the foundation of the Kantian system and, thus, of guilt, morality, and rights.[7] If freedom is, however, understood as preceding Being (and time), as proposed by Heidegger, this would have important implications for human freedom. Freedom is then no longer something possessed by human beings, but something that possesses them instead. Although the main focus in the first part of this chapter is on Heidegger's reading of Kant in *The Essence of Human Freedom*, attention also is given to Heidegger's analysis of Schelling's *Treatise on the Essence of Human Freedom*, as well as Heidegger's engagement with freedom in later texts.

In the second part of the chapter, we proceed to Derrida's interpretation of freedom, primarily in *Rogues*, as well as in an interview focusing on freedom, which was published in *For What Tomorrow*. Derrida in these texts at the same time explores the concept and structure of democracy, both as conceived traditionally and as can be conceived in collaboration with a rethinking of freedom. As noted, Derrida does not in *Rogues* directly confront the analyses of freedom by Kant or even of Heidegger. He instead proceeds by returning to the Greek origins of these notions, as well as via Nancy, whose analysis of freedom is itself strongly influenced by Heidegger. Nancy seeks to rethink the Western tradition of freedom in a radical sense, yet—and here the difference between Derrida and Nancy emerges—he wants to retain the word "freedom." We see in our analysis that Derrida, somewhat similar to Heidegger in his later thinking, seeks to take a certain distance from the word freedom, as it seems "to be loaded with metaphysical presuppositions that confer on the subject or on consciousness—that is, on an egological subject—a sovereign independence in relation to drives, calculation, economy, the machine" (Derrida and Roudinesco 2004, 48). Derrida instead detects a certain freedom in the "excess of play in the machine" (48). Derrida follows Heidegger in positioning freedom beyond Being, yet he views freedom more radically, that is, in terms of an incalculable event, "an *arrivance* that would surprise me absolutely and to whom and for whom, to which or for which I could not, and may no longer, *not respond*—in a way that is as responsible as possible: what happens, what arrives and comes down upon me, that to which I am exposed, beyond all mastery" (52). At stake here is what can also be referred to as a pure or unconditional hospitality, or as the democracy to come, which welcomes what or who comes without the imposition of any limitations (59–61).

Heidegger

As indicated, the main focus of Heidegger's reading of Kant's analysis of freedom is its relation to Being. This discussion takes place primarily in Part Two of *The Essence of Human Freedom*. Part One revisits some of the key elements in Heidegger's thinking, including the need for the reawakening of the question of Being in Western philosophy, which has throughout its existence implicitly understood Being as constant presence; the primordial relation between Being and time; the privilege to be accorded to Dasein in the understanding of Being; and the significance of finitude or death in Dasein's encounter of Being, that is, Dasein's being-toward-death (2005, 13–97). The discussion that follows engages first with Heidegger's analysis of transcendental freedom, as discussed in Kant's *Critique of Pure Reason*, and then with practical freedom, as it finds expression in Kant's *Groundwork* as well as his *Critique of Practical Reason*.[8]

TRANSCENDENTAL FREEDOM

In the discussion of transcendental freedom in this section, we proceed by seeking answers to the following questions that arise in Heidegger's reading of Kant:

- What are the main aims of the *Critique of Pure Reason*?
- How does Heidegger proceed, or which questions does he seek answers to?
- What are the limits of the Kantian analysis?
- What perspective does Kant nevertheless open for us?

According to Kant, all experience of nature is subject to the law of causality (Heidegger 2005, 20). Everything that occurs must in other words be the result of something else, which itself must have been caused by something else. In nature, one could say, nothing is the cause of itself (20). By contrast, absolute spontaneity, or what Kant refers to as "freedom of causality," has no previous cause. This is not however something we experience, that is, it is not observed in nature (21). One of the questions to which an answer is sought in the *Critique of Pure Reason* is whether there is still a place for freedom despite the overwhelming evidence of the experience of causation (164). Kant believes that this question is to be answered in the affirmative, and he thus seeks to show that not everything in nature is subject to natural processes, necessity, or the law of causation, that is, a prior state leading to another according to a (natural) law. He ultimately wants to show that there are beings within the world who, although subject to the laws of nature, act freely themselves.

Heidegger (101) is specifically interested in how Kant treats the relation between freedom and causality. In other words, is freedom merely a kind of causality, or is it to be understood in a more radical sense? This question lies behind Heidegger's reading of the "Analogies of Experience" as well as the "Antinomy of Pure Reason" in Kant's *Critique of Pure Reason*. The importance of the "Analogies of Experience" lies in the fact that the "rules that are always pre-represented in every human experience," and which contain the rules of the necessary temporal determination of everything present, are ultimately "ontological principles concerning the being-present of that which is present" (112, 121). In his discussion of Kant's "Antinomy of Pure Reason," Heidegger is first interested in the location of the idea of freedom in Kant's thinking. For Kant, freedom is a metaphysical issue, yet he does not lodge the problem of freedom in the soul or in God, but in the world, that is, "the totality of present beings as accessible to finite human knowledge" (144). Second, despite his critique that Kant also in this section treats freedom in terms of natural causality, he finds the Kantian argument attractive insofar as it seeks to resolve the antinomy (freedom must exist *versus* there is only natural causality) by way of the distinction between the noumenon and the phenomenon. We thus only have access to beings insofar as they are given to us in appearance, that is, given to us in space and time (157–58). The attraction of this argument for Heidegger lies in the fact that it acknowledges the finitude of knowledge, which is in turn necessarily linked to human finitude (162).[9] The distinction between noumenon and phenomenon furthermore makes clear that it is not a question of either nature or freedom, but of both at the same time. It opens the possibility of an intra-temporal being, apart from having intra-temporal causes, also having other causes "which themselves and in their causation are extra-temporal" (165). According to Kant, this problem cannot be resolved at a general ontological level, but only in relation to a specific being, that is, the human being "*as ethically acting person*" (165). The human being's freedom would thus be only one instance of cosmological freedom (181).[10] As we see later, freedom is furthermore noticeable specifically in the will (171). This is because of a particular kind of self-knowledge that characterizes the human being, which takes place by way of what Kant terms "pure apperception" (172). The latter refers to "actions and inner determinations which [the human being] cannot regard as impressions of the senses" (173). Because of the way in which Kant treats the relation between causality and freedom, Heidegger however concludes that causality in Kant "remains the fundamental ontological characteristic" (167).

There are thus, in Heidegger's reading, certain clear limits to the Kantian analysis. Causation is understood by Kant in terms of temporal succession: a cause-effect relation that involves priority and outcome or, one could say, "the succession of that which is in time" (107–8). Kant's thinking with respect to causality is ultimately determined by the metaphysics of presence, specifically in the way in which he thinks permanence or duration, which is said to be central in all experience. At stake in causality is thus some permanent thing that merely changes states, in such a way that one state follows from a prior state, that is, everything arises from something that is already present (125). There is, according to Kant, something permanent in every appearance: the object itself is permanent (117). This is also the case with time, which cannot be perceived in itself, but within which everything present is placed and their specific locations determined (120). Time expresses this permanence (118). Indeed, for Kant no experience of objects in time (succession and/or simultaneity) would be possible unless experience is grounded in something permanent and abiding (118). Permanence ultimately serves as condition of possibility for causality (122). Alteration—a sequence of different states of the same object after one another—is perceivable only if, "beforehand, something permanent is experienced. For it is only upon the basis of, and in relation to, something permanent, that a transition from one state to another can be perceived; otherwise there would be nothing but total displacement of one thing by another" (122). The centrality of permanence can also be seen in Kant's analysis of freedom, where such permanence is located in the acting person (122–23). The idea of permanence is namely tied not only to the experience of beings, but also to man's own experience of himself—of his "ownmost *self-being, self-hood and self-constancy* [*des eigenen* Selbstseins und seiner Selbigkeit, Beständigkeit, Selbst-ständigkeit]" (123). Human finitude does not therefore play a sufficiently important role in the Analogies. It should according to Heidegger have been fundamental in Kant's analysis, seeing that the Analogies furnish "rules which hold up, for every possible experience" (116, read with 118, 121, and 128). Being is consequently not understood in its essence by Kant, but in terms of beings, and more specifically, as constant presence (134). Even though Kant furthermore describes freedom and natural causality as mutually incompatible concepts, he nonetheless refers to both as causalities (132–33). Natural causality furthermore remains dominant, and freedom is determined in terms of the former, that is, as being present (133). Heidegger (133) expresses his objection in this respect as follows: "But freedom is the fundamental condition of the possibility of the acting person, in the sense of ethical action. Thus the existence of man, precisely through the characterization of freedom as causality (albeit as one kind thereof) is *conceived basically as being-present*. This turns freedom into its complete opposite [*eben doch* grundsätzlich als Vorhandensein aufgefaßt *und damit völlig ins Gegenteil verkehrt*]." The human being's way of being cannot "be primarily defined as being-present [*Vorhandensein*]" (134). Kant should instead have treated the causality of freedom primordially and in its own terms and not, as he tends to do, from the perspective of natural causality (134). Heidegger (136–39) shows that also when Kant engages with action, specifically the action of a free being who brings about an event, this is viewed in terms of cause and effect, that is, natural causality.[11] Here too, Kant thus views freedom in terms of natural causality. He in other words "fails to pose the question concerning the particular way of being of beings which are free" and thus to "unfold the metaphysical problem of freedom in a primordial manner" (134). By viewing freedom in terms of causality, Kant does not succeed in inquiring into the essence of the human being or the Being of Dasein (206, 207). As we see later, this has inevitable consequences for how one views freedom as well as democracy.

Finally, despite the limitations of the Kantian analysis, for example, the fact that he remains within the metaphysical tradition by viewing freedom in terms of causality, he does so in a more radical manner than anyone before him (205). Kant further regards the concept of freedom as primary and ultimate in philosophy (134). He opens up the possibility of viewing (transcendental) freedom as first cause, which sets in motion natural causality as well as the possibility of beings in the world also acting by virtue of freedom (150–51). Kant further acknowledges a certain incomprehension with respect to freedom: how such freedom becomes possible is as impossible to explain as it is to explain the possibility of natural causality (151).[12] Kant (1998a, A451/B479) finds support for this thesis (of freedom as first cause) in the philosophers of antiquity, who similarly posited a "first mover for the explanation of motions in the world, that is, a freely acting cause, which begins this series of states first and from itself," Aristotle's unmoved mover being an example. By showing that freedom is not simply a characteristic of the human being, but his or her essence, Kant moreover reveals something about the Being of Dasein. At stake here is in other words a characterization of Being, or rather, as we will see, something that precedes Being and time (Heidegger 2005, 94).

PRACTICAL FREEDOM

Although there is a continuity between the *Critique of Pure Reason* and Kant's texts on practical reason, he does not analyze practical freedom as a kind of causality, but as a specific characteristic of the human being as a rational being (Heidegger 2005, 182), or, as we saw, as the essence of the human being. As in the case of transcendental freedom, the existence of practical freedom cannot be proved, although, as we saw, its possibility was confirmed through Kant's inquiry into transcendental freedom (185). The reality of freedom can nonetheless be experienced, not in the same way as natural causation, but through practical, will-governed action or the practical laws of pure reason (187–88). Earlier, in the discussion of transcendental freedom, Heidegger (150) remarked that the (free) will is a very specific kind of being, that is, not one that we encounter in the mere representation of a present being. Instead, it must be given to us (*sondern das uns gegeben werden muß*). At stake here is the good will that Kant in the *Groundwork* speaks of, which is not concerned with its own effects or ends (191). Heidegger (192) refers to it as a case of willing one's own essence, pure willing, or the law of the pure will. It is thus not about realizing certain values, but "the actual willing to take responsibility . . . the decision to exist within this responsibility" (193).[13] As finite beings inevitably are affected by other motives, this law appears to us as a command, an "ought" (193). This "ought" is not conditional, that is, it is not dependent on attaining certain results, but unconditional (*bedingungslos*), a categorical imperative, as Kant refers to it (193). Heidegger points out that according to Kant we become conscious of the moral law when we construct maxims for the will, and that the categorical imperative impresses itself on us. Heidegger at this point takes a distance from Kant, contending that the categorical imperative, and the notion of a maxim that could serve as universal legislation, is a product of the Enlightenment and the Prussian state at the time, being a "specific sociologically determined philosophico-ethico ideology" (196–97). He however notes that Kant nowhere posits the categorical imperative as a fact (*Faktum*), different from the moral law, which is a "fact" in a specified sense (198). Heidegger thus retains the Kantian idea expressed in the *Critique of Practical Reason* (1997a, 5:29) that we become immediately conscious of the (fact of the) moral law when we formulate maxims of the will for ourselves. This is not about making an effort to will. Actual willing entails the willing of nothing but the "ought" of one's there-being (*will nichts anderes als das Sollen seines Da-seins*).

Heidegger (198) proceeds to refer to the "place" of this willing as a kind of placeless place or a certain real or reality:

> This reality of the "ought" stands very close to us [*steht ganz bei uns*]; it is the reality of our will in an essential, double sense: 1. it is the reality which gives its reality only in and through our will [*Es ist die Wirklichkeit, die ihr Wirkliches nur gibt in und durch unseren Willen*]. 2. It is then and only then the reality which truly characterizes our will as will. The factuality of this fact does not stand opposed to us, but is unique to ourselves, indeed in such a way that we are already claimed for the possibility of this reality, indeed not in this or that, but we are *claimed with the commitment of our being* [*sondern* in Anspruch genommen *sind wir mit dem* Einsatz unseres Wesens].

Even when we do not decide, or when we shirk deciding, or hold forth false motives for our actions, we have actually decided, that is, to turn away from the "ought" (199). In this turning away from the "ought" lies the strongest experience of the "ought" as fact.

Returning to the categorical imperative, Heidegger points out that the basic law of pure reason cannot be equated with the formulation of the categorical imperative that we find in Kant. Following the moral law is thus to be distinguished from the Kantian formula. The latter is one of many possible philosophical interpretations thereof, and Kant himself adopted various interpretations (291). One of the formulations of the categorical imperative in the *Groundwork* reads as follows: "Act in such a way that you treat humanity, whether in your own person or in any other person, always at the same time as an end, never merely as a means" (Kant 1997b, 4:429). At stake here in Heidegger's reading is the personality that constitutes for Kant the essence of the human being as a person, that is, that in the human being that makes possible accountability and responsibility (188).[14] The categorical imperative as formulated here thus says that in one's actions one should always be "essential in one's essence [*wesentlich in deinem Wesen*]" (200–1). At stake is a certain self-responsibility (*Selbstverantwortlichkeit*), not in an egotistical way and in relation to the accidental I, but a responsibility to bind oneself to oneself (*sich an sich selbst . . . binden*), which Heidegger later refers to as "an originary self-binding [*ursprüngliches Sichbinden*]," binding as letting oneself be bound (*Bindung als für sich verbindlich sein lassen*) (201, 207). The understanding of the moral law is thus not about getting to know a formula, a value, or a rule. It is instead about learning to understand the character of the peculiar reality of that which becomes and is a reality in action and as action (201). Despite the fact that Kant did not develop this insight any further, one can indeed say that Kant had a fundamental experience of the peculiarity of the willing real as fact (*Eigenart des willentlichen Wirklichen als Tatsache*), and by virtue of this experience determined the problematic of practical reason within the limits that he regarded as possible and necessary (201).

The proof of the practical reality of freedom consists in and can solely consist in understanding "that this *freedom only exists as the real will of the pure ought* [*daß diese* Freiheit nur ist als wirkliches Wollen des rein Gesollten]" (202). This means that the essence of practical freedom is itself legislation, pure will, autonomy. Practical freedom thereby reveals itself as the condition of possibility of the factuality of pure practical reason. Practical freedom as autonomy is, as we saw, self-responsibility, which is the essence of the personality of the human person, the real essence, the humanity of the human person (202–3). Pure will, pure practical reason, legislation of the basic law of actual action, responsibility, personality, and freedom thus are all the same. They are the same not in the sense of an undetermined, flowing unity, but the same in the sense of in themselves necessarily belonging together. Thereby pure practical reason and freedom acquire their own conditional relationship. Practical reason and its (moral) law are "the condition . . . under which we be become aware for the first time of freedom [as autonomy]," that is, the moral law is "the ground of possibility of the knowledge of freedom (*ratio cognoscendi*)" (Kant 1997a, 5:4n; Heidegger 2005, 203). Conversely, "freedom is the ground of possibility of the being of the law and its practical reason, the *ratio essendi* of the moral law" (Kant 1997a, 5:4n; Heidegger 2005, 203). Heidegger (203) concludes the section by quoting from the *Critique of Practical Reason* where at stake is the interrelationship between freedom and the moral law, or what Kant refers to as the "unconditional practical law" (*unbedingtes praktisches Gesetz*), indicating, in Heidegger's reading, that they are identical.

Freedom, Causality, and Being

We saw earlier that for Heidegger the aim of his reading of Kant is to arrive at the essence of human freedom. Although Kant, especially with respect to practical freedom, goes very far in this regard, he does not ultimately inquire into the essence of the human being, and thus fails to view freedom adequately as a problem of Being (Heidegger 2005, 206). Kant's analysis of practical reason, we can also say, remains lodged within the transcendental freedom of the *Critique of Pure Reason*, which, as we saw, remains a form of causality. The human being, although "free," thus ultimately remains stuck within a fate-like structure of causality (Heidegger 2018, 79–80). To contemplate freedom in its essence, not only the location, region, or field thereof is thus of importance, but also its position within this field (Heidegger 2005, 93). The answer as to location seems obvious—in the human being—yet the human being's nature is enigmatic, and at stake is not simply a particular characteristic or property of the human being, but his or her essence, which precedes any such determination. We can only gain insight into the essence of freedom if we redirect our gaze, that is, if we seek freedom "as the ground of the possibility of Dasein, *as something* prior even to being and time [*Das Wesen der Freiheit kommt erst dann eigentlich in den Blick, wenn wir sie als Grund der Möglichkeit des Daseins suchen, als dasjenige, was noch vor Sein und Zeit liegt*]" (94). This means that causality, movement, and Being would all be grounded in freedom. Freedom is therefore "*not some particular thing* among and alongside other things, but is *superordinate and governing in relation to the whole* [vorgeordnet und durchherrschend gerade das Ganze im Ganzen]" (94). When we seek out freedom as the ground of possibility of Dasein (*Grund der Möglichkeit des Daseins*), this has the further implication that

> freedom must itself, in its essence, be more primordial than the human being [*in ihrem Wesen ursprünglicher als der Mensch*]. The human being is only an *administrator* [Verwalter] of freedom, that is, he [or she] can only let-be the freedom of the free in the way it falls upon him [or her] [*der die Freiheit von Freien in der*

ihm zugefallenen Weise Freiheit sein lassen kann], so that through the human being, the whole contingency [*ganze Zufälligkeit*] of freedom becomes visible.

Human freedom now no longer means freedom as a property [*Eigenschaft*] of the human being, but the *human being as a possibility of freedom* [der Mensch als eine Möglichkeit der Freiheit]. Human freedom is the freedom that breaks through in the human being and takes him [or her] upon itself, thereby making the human being possible [*sofern sie im Menschen durchbricht und ihn auf sich nimmt, ihn dadurch ermöglicht*]. (94)[15]

Heidegger thus wants us to understand freedom as "the ground of the possibility of existence, the root of Being and of time [*Grund der Möglichkeit des Daseins . . . , die Wurzel von Sein und Zeit*]." This means that the human being, grounded in freedom, whose essence is to be found in freedom, is the site and occasion (*Stätte und Gelegenheit*), as well as the being through which the Being of beings and the understanding of Being comes to the fore (95). Heidegger here describes the human being as monstrous (*ungeheuerlich*) and at the same time the most finite (*Endlichste*). In this finitude appears the extant gathering of the conflict (*die existente Zusammenkunft des Widerstreitenden*) within the sphere of beings and thus the occasion and possibility of the breaking apart (*Auseinanderbrechens*) and breaking up (*Aufbrechens*) of beings in their diversity (95). Freedom is thus to be understood as the condition of possibility for the disclosure of the Being of beings, of the understanding of Being (207).[16]

What appears from these passages, and what is of particular importance in our reading of Derrida, is a thinking of freedom as a certain abyss from which Being arises, and which at the same time poses a radical challenge to the human being by placing an excessive demand on him or her.[17] In the essay "On the Essence of Ground," Heidegger (1998, 127) similarly notes that freedom is not itself a ground, but the origin of ground in general (*Ursprung von Grund überhaupt*), the freedom for ground (*Freiheit zum Grunde*). "In grounding," Heidegger further notes, "freedom *gives* and *takes* ground [*Gründend* gibt *Freiheit und* nimmt *sie Grund*]" (127). Later in the same text he refers to freedom as "the unity of excess and withdrawal [*der Einheit von Überschwung und Entzug*]" and as "the abyss of ground in Dasein [*der Ab-grund des Daseins*]" (132, 134).

The notion of *das Freie*, translated as "the Free," the "domain of freedom," the "free space," "the Open," or the "open realm" is already alluded to in *The Essence of Human Freedom* (2005, 134) and in *Schelling's Treatise* (1985, 4), but it becomes more prominent in later texts, especially in *Contributions to Philosophy*. This terminology does not appear to be a departure from the earlier reflections on freedom, but a continuation, as Heidegger likewise links this notion to (the truth of) Being, inter alia its concealing, revealing, and sending.[18] There is furthermore clearly a resonance between the notions of freedom and the Free on the one hand, and what Heidegger (2002, 1–24) refers to in some of his texts as the sending of, the gift of, or the *Ereignis* (event)[19] of Being, on the other. In *The Event*, Heidegger (2013, 123) for example comments that "the event can be experienced only 'in' Da-seyn, which is itself the essential occurrence of the event [*Das Ereignis ist nur zu erfahren »im« Da-seyn, das selbst ist die Wesung des Ereignisses*]." The relation between Being and event in Heidegger nevertheless remains complex. For example, he speaks on the one hand of Beyng, which "essentially occurs/unfolds as event [*Das Seyn west als das Ereignis*]," which suggests that they are essentially the same (2012b, 25).[20] On the other hand, he speaks of the two modes of event, that is, of expropriation and of consignment/appropriation (*der Ver-eignung und der Übereignung*), which is suggestive of a split or division, even if it occurs in Being itself (2013, 129). The event understood thus, that is, as "preceding" and thereby "giving" Being, would not be causally determined; it would not be "something" that is experienced in time and as a present-being. It would instead point to the "location" of a certain battle between forces (the eventuating of Being and its withdrawal, which Derrida refers to as *différance*),[21] and which, as we saw, calls for a self-binding to take place in the human being who, as Heidegger (2013, 140–43) notes in *The Event*, is "dispropriated of the last possibility of his or her essence [*ist der letzten Möglichkeit seines Wesens enteignet*]" in the withdrawal/abandonment of beings by Being.

Derrida

Heidegger's thought-provoking reinterpretation and relocation of freedom has the potential of reshaping modern constitutionalism. This can specifically be said with respect to the understanding of freedom as the essence of Being, as abyss or as event, as prior to and as root of Being and time. In relation to human beings, freedom is, as we saw, understood as being more primordial, as not a property of human beings, but the latter being possibilities of freedom, belonging to and grounded in freedom, mere "administrators" of freedom. Freedom and the moral law are furthermore indistinguishable. This law, located in a placeless place that Heidegger refers to as the "real," claims the human being in his or her essence, calls on him or her to take responsibility in what can be referred to as an originary self-binding, and places an unconditional demand on him or her. Derrida's analysis of freedom in *Rogues* and *For What Tomorrow* is, as we will see, very close to that of Heidegger. He appears to agree with Heidegger about the need to "dis-locate" freedom, not only for the reasons identified by Heidegger, but also because Derrida (2005c, 38) doubts that freedom and morality as defined by Kant, as well as Heidegger's conception of Being and of the Free, manage to escape from the economy of the same. He thus goes beyond Heidegger's analysis through a further radicalization. In view of the inherent relation between freedom and democracy, recognized since Plato (Derrida 2005c, 22–23), the inquiry into Derrida's analysis of freedom enables us to rethink democracy as well, specifically the relationship between democracy and sovereignty.[22]

FREEDOM AS EXPOSURE BEYOND MASTERY

We saw earlier that Heidegger reconceives freedom in close association with Being, that is, as event in his later texts, and Derrida follows suit, but through a further radicalization. In chapter 4 of *Rogues* (Mastery and Measure/*Maîtrise et métrique*), Derrida focuses on Nancy's *The Experience of Freedom*, yet different from Nancy, and as noted earlier, he wants to maintain a certain distance from the word "freedom" because of the associations traditionally coupled to this word, that is, the power, faculty, ability to act, the force to do as one pleases. Following Nancy, Derrida (2005c, 40–44, 54) argues that if the word freedom is to be maintained, it should not be simply understood in terms of mastery or measure, as the autonomy of a subject in control of him- or herself, or, even more broadly, in the traditional philosophical sense, as related to power, force, possibility, ability, and sovereignty.[23] Freedom is instead to be understood, in Nancy's words, in a pre-subjective or pre-cratic sense, in terms of an ipseity being "constituted by and as sharing," or as "spacing" (Derrida 2005c, 45–46). It is to be understood as without power, as an exposure beyond mastery, sovereignty, and autonomy, as absolute generosity, the gift beyond Being; as a welcoming of the unforeseeable or incalculable event, of who or what may come or arrive, that is, as a compromising of the self, an opening of the self to its own destruction (Derrida 2005a, 21–23, 282; 2005c, 45, 47, 52; Derrida and Roudinesco 2004, 45, 49–50, 52).[24]

Derrida prepares the ground for his analysis of freedom, as well as for the analysis of democracy to follow, in chapter 1 of *Rogues*, where he analyzes ipseity, sovereignty, and freedom with reference to the wheel, as involving movement, repetition, a return to itself around a fixed or relatively immobile axis. We focus here specifically on the analysis by Derrida of Aristotle's prime mover, the figure par excellence of ipseity, sovereignty, and freedom, which appears to operate in a similar fashion as democracy, as described, for example, by De Tocqueville.[25] As we saw earlier, Kant invokes Aristotle's prime or unmoved mover in the context of a discussion of the relation between causality and freedom in the *Critique of Pure Reason*. Kant (1998a, A451/B479) there notes that "all the philosophers of antiquity saw themselves as obliged to assume a first mover for the explanation of motions in the world, that is, a freely acting cause, which began this series of states first and from itself." The first mover here in other words appears as the figure of ipseity, freedom, and sovereignty. When Derrida in *Rogues* invokes the figure of the unmoved mover, he points, different from Kant, to the complexity of the movement at stake here, which entails not only a movement of the self toward itself, but at the same time a turn against the self. Derrida here reads and comments on the relevant passages in Aristotle's *Metaphysics* Book XII. The actuality of this pure energy does not itself move and is not moved by anything, yet sets everything in motion in a circular motion of return to the self. This first motion is in Aristotle's analysis induced or inspired by a drive or desire (*un désir*) (Derrida 2005c, 15). God, or the pure actuality of the first mover, is at the same time erogenous and thinkable. Aristotle describes God in this respect as desirable, the first desirable, as well as the first intelligible, as thinking itself, thought thinking thought (15). This "principle," on which the heavens and nature depend, is furthermore referred to by Aristotle as a "life," comparable to "the best which we enjoy, and enjoy but for a short time" (Aristotle 1984, 2:1072b–15). This life, which is lived in a constant, continuous, and unending fashion, is for us impossible (*adunaton*) (Derrida 2005c, 15). The *energeia* of this pure activity is moreover characterized by Aristotle as "pleasure" (*jouissance/hēdone*), or, as Derrida (15) puts it, "the circle of a taking pleasure in oneself." The energy of God is thus at the same time "desired, desirable (*erōmenon, to proton orekton*), and partaking in pleasure [*à la fois désirée, desirable . . . et jouissant*]. A taking pleasure in the self [*Jouissance de soi*], a circular and specular autoaffection that is analogous to or in accordance with the thinking of thought (*noēsis noēseōs*)" (15). A passing remark at this point about the relation between (conscious and unconscious) desire and pleasure on the one hand and the political on the other, in particular the democratic, shows what is at stake here. Such desire and pleasure, Derrida (15) points out, give rise to "calculation and the incalculable [*du calcul et de l'incalculable*]." By noting here the relation between desire and pleasure, the calculable and the incalculable, Derrida incorporates his own detailed analysis of Freud's "Beyond the Pleasure Principle" in *The Post Card* into the analysis of freedom and democracy. There, as here, it was a question of pleasure, being inherently without bounds or limits, that is, without measure, limiting itself, binding itself, to obtain mastery of itself as pleasure (Derrida 1987a, 398–400).[26] Pleasure (*jouissance*) is in other words what makes possible the movement toward the self at stake in ipseity and sovereignty,[27] yet not simply like a wheel turning around its own axle, but rather like a free wheel. The free wheel (*la roue libre*), that is, the title of chapter 1 of *Rogues*, does not involve a repetition of the same, but an incessant haunting, threatening, and persecution of the self, by the search for an unbound pleasure.[28] At stake here is, as was the case in Heidegger's rethinking of freedom, the relation to death, yet not as a being-toward death, but a Freudian drive toward death.

Derrida (2005c, 15–16) continues the analysis of Aristotle's *Metaphysics* in *Rogues* by showing the close relation between sovereignty and the movement of the circle. The *energeia* of the prime mover, itself unmovable, eternal (but not infinite), indivisible, and separate from sensible things, thus puts in motion an imperishable substance that is characterized by eternal movement, circular return, and finitude. Before concluding this analysis, Derrida (15–16) quotes Aristotle to the effect that "the prime mover, which is immovable, is one both in formula and in number; and therefore so also is that which is eternally and continuously in motion." He then notes that in the final paragraph of Book 12, Aristotle quotes Homer's the *Iliad* (book II), thereby invoking Homer's (sovereign) authority on the need for a single ruler. In the relevant passage, Athena, daughter of Zeus, is present, as well as Odysseus, who is compared with Zeus. When Odysseus speaks, he expresses such preference for one ruler instead of mob rule, rule by many, or what Derrida (16) refers to as "the dispersion of the plural." As Derrida points out, kings derive their authority from Zeus, who is in turn the son of Cronos, and the latter of Ouranos. Through a ruse and with the help of his mother, Zeus had tricked and defeated his father (time), as did Cronos. Freud's Oedipus complex and his related story of the primal horde, with the sons killing the father, loom large here (Derrida 2005c, 16–17).[29] Ancient and modern political theology can both be said to reflect this structure of sovereignty, which Derrida (17) characterizes as phallo-paterno-filio-fraterno-ipsocentric.

This structure can however be imposed only through the suppression of a certain pre-origin, that is, of absolute desire, of pleasure (*jouissance*).

FREEDOM AND DEMOCRACY

For Nancy, as Derrida (2005c, 44) notes, freedom is to be understood in terms of a *who* being free. This *who* is no longer a subject in charge of its will and decisions. The *who* "exists free," without necessarily "being free" (44). Freedom is furthermore not limited to human beings, but "is extended to everything that appears in the open. . . . to the event of everything in the world" (54).[30] Similar to Heidegger, Nancy speaks of freedom in terms of a "(transcendental) force" (54). This conception of freedom has the potential of displacing the power or sovereignty (-cracy) located in democracy itself. In *Rogues*, Derrida (14–15) in similar vein compares democracy, conceived as the ipseity of the One, a return to the same, with democracy conceived of in terms of "heterogeneity, the heteronomic and the dissymmetric, disseminal multiplicity, the anonymous 'anyone,' the 'no matter who,' the indeterminate 'each one,'" that is, the free wheel. If the human being is no longer to be understood as the privileged place for the unfolding of freedom (as Heidegger [2005, 95] still seemed to think), this also raises questions about the scope of democracy, that is, the limits that are traditionally imposed on it and by it. Should it end at the limits of the nation-state, be restricted to only human beings, or even to only the living? (Derrida 2005c, 53–54).

These questions are raised in view of the analysis of Plato's *Republic* in chapter 2 of *Rogues* where two conceptions of freedom as well as two corresponding conceptions of democracy are at stake, that is, the good of democratic liberty or freedom and the bad of democratic license (*la liberté démocratique et . . . la license démocratique*). In the *Republic*, Plato discusses democracy as a regime, and, as Derrida notes, the democratic man (*l'homme democratique*) is brought forward for judgment, that is, his way of being, acting, and speaking. Certain young men (referred to as the *akolastoi*) are said to be characterized by indiscipline, licentiousness, intemperance, delinquency, and wasteful expenditure, and what is more, no one acts against or disciplines or corrects these rogues by way of the law; there is a complete loss of authority (Derrida 2005c, 22). The oligarchs have an economic interest in maintaining this debauched life: to eventually acquire their estates, they lend money against the property of these men to enrich themselves even further through speculation. The *akolastoi* are in debt, do not work, and are plotting a revolution against the oligarchs and the other citizens (21–22). Plato associates the democratic man with freedom (*eleutheria*), which in turn is linked to license (*exousia*), that is, whim, free will, freedom of choice, leisure to follow one's desires, the faculty to do as one pleases (22).[31] As Derrida points out, Plato reports this as a commonly held view about democracy, that is, this is what we are told about it: that democracy entails being free (*eleuthoroi*), a place where freedom (*eleutheria*) reigns, and freedom of speech, as well as the license to do as one likes (*exousia*). The inherent link between freedom (in its two forms) and democracy is thus posited here: freedom and democracy as self-rule, as the faculty or power (*kratos*) to do or decide as one likes, but also as self-destruction, that is, a general abdication, a complete loss of authority, lawlessness, a conception from which Plato wants to take a certain distance (21, 22).[32] Aristotle likewise speaks of freedom (*eleutheria*) as a condition that is generally attributed to democracy, and that includes living as one likes, tied to the claim not to be governed by anyone, or, failing that, to govern and be governed in turn (23–24). The link between freedom and democracy posited here is important for Derrida, as well as the link between a certain understanding of freedom (as license) and the self-destructive nature of democracy. Freedom in Plato and Aristotle is however still linked too closely to a faculty or power. Derrida ultimately wants to go beyond these seemingly opposing conceptions of freedom and of democracy, thereby providing a different kind of "ground" for a likewise very different understanding of democracy, that is, as "to come" (25).[33] In anticipation of the development in chapter 4 of this different conception of freedom, which is no longer associated with mastery, power, faculty, or force, Derrida in chapter 2 again invokes the free wheel, with respect to both freedom and democracy.[34] At stake here is "the semantic vacancy or indetermination at the very center of the concept of democracy that makes its history turn" (24). This indetermination or freedom of play (*une liberté de jeu*) is already to be found in Plato when, in the *Republic*, he does not speak about democracy as a specific type of constitutional form, but as an all-inclusive "form," as a beautiful multicolored patchwork, which seduces and provokes, like a *roué* (26).[35] This patchwork, thinking also of its modern forms, and including regimes that present themselves as such, would include inter alia monarchic democracy, plutocratic democracy, tyrannical democracy, parliamentary democracy, popular democracy, direct or indirect democracy, liberal democracy, Christian democracy, social democracy, and military or authoritarian democracy (26–27). One can thus say, as Derrida (32) will point out later, that there is in Greek no proper, stable, and univocal meaning of the democratic. It appears to rather be characterized by mutability, plasticity and indeterminacy, being a concept without concept.³⁶

Plato's characterization of democracy provides the opportunity for rethinking the two component elements of democracy—*demos* and *kratos*—and to separate them: to think a *demos* without *kratos* (or at least without a force belonging to the people), the latter (*kratos*) being a remainder of the onto-theological dimension of sovereignty despite its secularization. It is therefore necessary to rethink the structure of democracy in line with the stricture of *différance* (Derrida 1987a, 350–51).³⁷ With reference to Algeria, France, Germany, and the United States, and proceeding in a manner similar to Freud in "Beyond the Pleasure Principle" in analyzing the strange repetition compulsion, Derrida shows the autoimmune or suicidal structure of democracy, that is, its tendency to destroy itself. There is in other words a certain weakness located within democracy. This can, for example, be seen in the "by or taking turns" of democracy, its regular elections, which open up the possibility that an undemocratic party (for example, the Islamic Salvation Front, the National Front, the National Socialist German Workers' Party) can gain power and thereafter abolish democracy. The 1991–1992 elections in Algeria, for example, show how sovereignty can be relied on to avert this risk, that is, to protect democracy from its autoimmune nature (in line with Carl Schmitt's thinking), but not without in the process itself destroying democracy. This weakness (the perversion of the democratic by sovereignty) and the contrast between sovereignty and democracy can also be seen in the United States, where the latter can be said to have opened itself through its democratic hospitality (as well as the supply of weapons to "freedom fighters" in protecting/advancing its own sovereignty) to the 9/11 attacks, and the (sovereign) suspension of democratic rights and freedoms in (protective) response. These phenomena—of democracy destroying itself—are in other words made possible by the structure of democracy, its essence, that is, by the taking of turns, by allowing criticism of itself up to the point of its own abolition, its own hospitality, the placing of itself at risk. Democracy in its pure form, that is, without power, and thus extending a welcome to all, even to the enemies of democracy, nonetheless remains deferred. For democracy to have a future, it has to be thought in terms of this openness, this weakness within its own structure.

Kant, Freedom, and Democracy

Kant's engagement with freedom, as we saw, starts with *The Critique of Pure Reason*. Here it is for Kant about showing that human beings rise above natural causality and that, different from animals, they therefore enjoy a certain freedom from their natural inclinations. In the *Groundwork*, the *Critique of Practical Reason*, and other texts on morality, freedom again comes to the fore as well as the need for its restraint (chapter 1 of this volume). Human beings not only have the ability, in comparison with animals, to rise above their natural inclinations: they live under the obligation to deny or sacrifice these inclinations, in obeying the moral law (chapters 1 and 4). Freedom in Kant is thus to be understood in two senses: as transcendental (cosmic) freedom, and as practical (moral) freedom, the latter being dependent on the former. Freedom yet again comes to the fore in the *Metaphysics of Morals* and other texts on law, where the question arises inter alia how freedom should be conceived of within a republican state. For Kant (1996b, 6:239), ethics or virtue (the terrain of internal freedom), as well as the whole politico-legal system (the terrain of external freedom) is based on and made possible by (transcendental) freedom.

If freedom as conceived by Kant is rethought in line with the readings of Heidegger, Nancy, and especially Derrida, what would be the implications for modern constitutionalism? We saw previously that Kant, in Heidegger's reading, indeed treats (transcendental) freedom in an ontological sense, and thus as an issue that concerns Being. Kant nevertheless remains within the metaphysical tradition, and thus contemplates Being in terms of beings, without inquiring into the essence of Being itself. Kant therefore views Being as constant presence, which in turn determines the way in which he understands freedom, that is, as a form of causality, and as a property of human beings. By inquiring into the essence of Being, it becomes clear that freedom is not grounded in causality, but causality in freedom. This is because freedom has an essential relation with Being, preceding both Being and time. Human beings, in Heidegger's analysis, can therefore no longer be said to possess freedom, but to instead be administrators of freedom, the latter being more primordial than they are. Freedom, in this sense, is synonymous with the moral law, which Heidegger understands as an unconditional, pure ought, and that calls on human beings to will their own being or essence, to bind themselves to themselves. Derrida follows Nancy in further radicalizing Heidegger's reading. If freedom is indeed prior to Being, that is, the event or gift of Being, then one can hardly speak of "freedom" any longer. Ipseity, the mastery of the self, the return to oneself in freedom, does not simply amount to a circular economy, but is the result of the binding of absolute pleasure, pleasure being inherently without bounds or limits, exceeding any economy. At stake here is thus no longer the being or essence of human beings, as one finds in Heidegger's reading of Kant, but their lack of essence, absolute a-stricture, unbinding. This also applies to the people (*demos*) in a democracy, who can likewise no longer be viewed as a (collective) subject characterized by mastery or sovereignty, but instead by the welcoming of the unforeseeable or incalculable event. This has important implications for the notion of constituent power, which can similarly no longer be viewed as the freedom or sovereignty to enact simply any constitution that the people want, in view of its history and the prevailing economic, social, and political conditions (De Ville 2017, 74–89). The welcoming injunction of the democracy to come prevents the ineradicable drive to sovereignty (Derrida 2002d, 258), that is, the presumed yet hidden foundation of modern constitutionalism, from simply returning to itself in a calculating fashion. This injunction precedes, conditions, and undermines all restrictions and exclusions imposed by modern constitutionalism, that is, of the "unlike," the "dissimilar,"[38] thereby challenging the legitimacy of the phallo-paterno-filio-fraterno-ipsocentric democratic tradition in its core.

It should, in conclusion, be clear that this chapter does not seek the abolition of freedom and democracy in view of Derrida's analysis. It does, however, call for the revisiting of the notion of freedom, understood as autonomy and as the foundation of modern constitutionalism. If freedom is to be understood as prior to Being, that is, as the welcoming of the unforeseeable or incalculable event, or as the gift of Being, a radical reconception of modern constitutionalism is called for. This applies not only to the rights derived from freedom (chapter 4 of this volume), but also to the notion of democracy in its alliance with sovereignty. The limits of freedom and democracy should in other words be placed in question in each instance where the modern constitution is in need of interpretation and application, as well as amendment and reenactment. A negotiation is thus required in each instance between the unconditional welcome as abyssal foundation of the modern constitution, and the limiting provisions of this constitution. The latter, we now know, does not simply involve a return to the sovereign self of a people, but instead an incessant haunting, threatening, and persecution of the self, an openness to its own destruction. "Freedom" is possible as impossible only by escaping from a circular economy, by way of the unconditional gift.

Chapter 4

Animal, Subject, Constitution

In the "Introduction," we saw how Kant's notion of human dignity has become central in modern constitutionalism since World War II. It was noted there that human dignity is viewed in many constitutions and international legal documents as a foundational value, and thus as part of an objective normative value order that needs to be pursued by all state branches or relevant organizational structures. This has undoubtedly been a significant development, and there is still a long way to go before the dignity of every human being in the world will be acknowledged and protected. This remains an important goal to pursue by constitutionalism on all levels. Yet the exclusionary nature of "human dignity" as a foundational value for constitutionalism cannot be denied. Whereas in the twentieth century this inherent injustice went by largely unnoticed, it is becoming clear that it cannot continue for much longer. The interlinked foundational values of the modern constitution, such as human dignity, freedom, equality, and democracy, consequently require urgent reconsideration. This chapter continues this process.[1]

Within the Cartesian tradition, "the animal" is generally viewed as a mere automaton or machine, which cannot reason, think, speak, or respond to questions.[2] Kant is one of the philosophers, together with Descartes himself, Levinas, and Heidegger, as well as the psychoanalyst Lacan, whose texts Derrida (2008) analyzes in *The Animal That Therefore I Am* as remaining within this tradition. In contemplating the differences between "the human" and "the animal," it is generally assumed by the theorists at stake here that there is a single, indivisible line or limit separating the two. As Derrida (2008, 89–91) points out, in these analyses, no distinction is furthermore drawn between the different species of animals, and no account is taken of animal sexuality (except in Lacan to some extent), of modesty, or of nakedness between animals and humans. Another common feature is that "the animal" is presumed not to have access to language, but only to a fixed code, and therefore is not able to respond, but merely to react. These theorists moreover do not give serious attention to the violence imposed on animals by human beings, and in fact reaffirm the necessity of animal sacrifice. Finally, very little, if any, account is taken of ethological and primatological studies by these theorists in their discussion of animals.

The focus in the particular section of *The Animal That Therefore I Am* dealing with Kant is on Kant's version in *Anthropology from a Pragmatic Point of View* (2006) of Descartes's *cogito* or "I think" as well as Kant's comparison between animal and human society.[3] We will see in the analysis of this section in *The Animal That Therefore I Am* that Derrida follows the same strategy that he follows elsewhere in engaging with reflections in the philosophical tradition on the animal question.[4] In the first place, Derrida problematizes the lack that is traditionally posited concerning the animal, that is, the characteristic, ability, or power, such as language, response, reason, a relation to death, culture that is attributed only to the human being, and that the animal in general is said to fall short of. In doing so, he points to evidence that many non-human animals in fact share with human beings the characteristics that non-human animals are said to lack. Second, he raises questions about whether human beings can in fact be said to have the specific characteristic or ability that is attributed to them exclusively, for example, autonomy, responsibility, morality, or having access to death as such. By raising these questions, Derrida points to a certain commonality between the human animal and other animals. The aim of Derrida's analysis in *The Animal That Therefore I Am* is not to argue that there is some continuity between the human being and non-human animals, that is, no differences, but to challenge the single and indivisible line or limit that is said to separate "the human" and "the animal" (29–31). One should in other words not speak of a simple opposition between "the human" and "the animal," but about differences between human beings and certain animal species, in view of that which defines life, that is, as we will see, a certain lack of power, of inability.

We start our analysis with a broad outline of Kant's position as regards non-human animals, focusing specifically on the moral law, the virtues, the exposition of public law, as well as his texts on anthropology. Derrida's analysis in *The Animal That Therefore I Am* of certain passages in Kant's *Anthropology from a Pragmatic Point of View* is the main focus of this chapter, showing how the subjection, mastery, and domestication of the non-human animal is at the heart of Kant's construction of subjectivity and of civil society, as well as his thinking on morality. As we will see, subjectivity and a civil constitution are, according to Kant, both made possible by a certain power or ability, which the human being has in comparison with non-human animals. According to Kant in *Anthropology from a Pragmatic Point of View*, this is the power to say "I" as well as the ability to enter the "civil condition." This discussion is followed by a brief analysis of the moral implications of such subjection, an analysis that shows that despite their so-called "civil condition" and their "good moral will," Kantian human beings remain at heart beasts because of their endless war against non-human animals. The possible implications of this analysis for the scope of the constitutional protection of claims to justice, as well as for the concepts of democracy, representation, and the modern constitution, are briefly pointed to in the final section.

Kant, the Animal, and the Human

As we saw in earlier chapters, according to Kant, human beings share in two worlds: the sensible and the intelligible. Their share in the intelligible world enables them to give themselves practical laws by their own reason and not be led purely by their inclinations, as animals are presumed to be (Kant 1997b, 4:428). The existence of a rational being has an absolute value in itself. Rational beings can never be regarded merely as a means. They are called "persons" (*Personen*) and are worthy of respect (Kant 1997a, 5:76; 1997b, 4:428).[5] Beings without reason and without consciousness of their own existence, on the other hand, have no value in themselves (Kant 2016, 27:1319). They only have relative value, as a means, and are therefore "things" (Kant 1997b, 4:428).[6] Although animals have a will, this is not their own will, but the will of nature (Kant, 2016, 27:1320). In the *Groundwork*, Kant (1997b, 4:428) captures the essence of what was stated earlier in the second formulation of the categorical imperative: "Now I say that the human being and in general every rational being exists as an end in itself, not merely as a means to be used by this or that will at its discretion; instead he must in all his actions, whether directed to himself or also to other rational beings, always be regarded at the same time as an end." In the kingdom-of-ends formulation of the categorical imperative, Kant places the emphasis on the human being's capability of morality as the qualifying mark to be regarded as a being with an end in itself. This gives dignity to the human being, and this exalts him or her above that which bears a market price, in other words, that which is replaceable by something equivalent (Kant 1997b, 4:435). In *Anthropology from a Pragmatic Point of View*, as discussed in more detail later, Kant (2006, 127)[7] views the ability of the human being to represent him- or herself as an "I" (*in seiner Vorstellung das Ich haben kann*) as the defining characteristic, which raises him or her above all other living beings with respect to rank and dignity (*Rang und Würde*). This consciousness of the self makes of the human being a "person." Kant (322–25) furthermore notes three distinguishing characteristics that "markedly" distinguish human beings from other living beings: First, their technical predisposition, that is, their ability to manipulate things, which is made possible by their hands, fingers, and fingertips; second, their pragmatic predisposition, that is, to be educated and to become cultured so as to achieve progress as a species; and third, their moral predisposition, that is, by way of reason to live in a society with others under laws that protect freedom.

In describing the duties of virtue in the *Doctrine of Virtues* section of the *Metaphysics of Morals*, Kant (1996b, 6:410, 442) confirms that pure reason only imposes duties on a human being toward him- or herself and toward other human beings. Kant distinguishes here between, on the one hand, duties "with regard to" or "in view of" other beings (*in Ansehung anderer Wesen*) and, on the other hand, duties "to" or "toward" such beings (*gegen diese Wesen*).[8] Supposed duties toward other (non-human) beings are actually only duties *in view of* such beings, and therefore duties to the self. One therefore should not destroy what is beautiful in inanimate nature, or plants, or be cruel to animals, yet this is not because of a duty owed directly to nature, plants, or animals. In the latter case, cruel treatment "dulls [the human being's] shared feeling of their suffering and so weakens and gradually uproots a natural predisposition that is very serviceable to morality in one's relations with other men" (Kant 1996b, 6:443). Kant consequently prescribes that if animals are to be killed, this should be done quickly and without pain; if they are made to work, they should not be strained beyond their capacity; animals should not be experimented on for the sake of mere speculation; and one should show gratitude toward an animal that had been in service for a long period of time (6:443).

With respect to law, and as we saw earlier, Kant, similar to other philosophers of his time, posits a state of nature that precedes the entry into civil society. Unlike in Hobbes, the state of nature prior to the establishment of a sovereign state is not however depicted as one where a war of all against all necessarily rages. The state of nature could also be one of society, though not civil society. Within the state of nature, private rights exist, though without any public laws or judges to protect these rights (Kant 1996a, 8:383 ["Perpetual Peace"]; 1996b, 6:242).[9] As we saw in the "Introduction" and in chapter 3 of this volume, practical reason places an obligation (only) on human beings to leave the state of nature and enter the civil condition, regulated by public law, ideally in the form of a republican constitution. This obligation does not follow as a result of experience, which shows the violent nature of human beings toward each other. It follows instead from pure reason, which points to the insecurity of the state of nature for human beings, peoples, and states (1996b, 6:312). In the state of nature, each person namely has a right to do what seems right and good to him- or herself and not be subject to the opinion of another (6:312). Those who refuse to enter the civil condition can be compelled to do so by force (6:312). As noted in the "Introduction" and as we will see in more detail in chapter 6, Kant similarly regards sovereign states as existing in a state of nature vis-à-vis each other as here there is likewise no general law that applies to it and no court that can give a binding judgment with respect to disputes (Kant 1996b, 6:343–44 and 354: 1996a, 8:353–57 ["Perpetual Peace"]; Schmitt 2006, 147). Kant (1996b, 6:343) views sovereign states in this regard as moral persons with natural freedom, and describes this condition as one of constant war. Sovereign states act here like lawless savages, and the right of the strongest prevails (6:344).[10] Practical reason likewise compels sovereign states to leave the state of nature and enter into a civil condition, although no state can be compelled to do so by force (Kant 1996a, 8:355–56 ["Perpetual Peace"]; 1996b, 6:354). The civil condition here consists of a voluntary federation of sovereign states and eventually a world republic under a cosmopolitan constitution, which will secure peace to human beings across the earth (Kant 1996a, 8:311 ["On the Common Saying"]; 1996b, 6:354; 2007, 8:24–26 ["Idea for a Universal History"]).

Empirical observation of human nature does not contribute to the development of Kant's legal theory, which as noted is based on practical reason alone. It is nevertheless important for our purposes here to take note of Kant's texts on anthropology, which appear to stand in tension with the texts referred to earlier, as they do not simply depict the human being as raised above the animal, but as animal-like in a strange, uncanny way.[11] According to Kant (2012, 25:677–78), empirical observation indicates that the human being is by nature more dangerous than any other animal:

> The human being can greatly beware of all animals, if he already once knows their kind and nature, but not of his own kind, for since this is a cunning creature [*weil dieses ein listiges Geschöpf ist*], he thus cannot detect its snares; he can pretend to be friendly, and yet act malevolently [*doch boshaft handeln*], he knows how to dissemble, and disguise himself [*sich zu verstellen, und zu verheelen*], and always conceive of new means of becoming dangerous for the other [person].[12]

Kant (25:678) further remarks that the human being is not by nature a beast of prey [*Raubthier*] vis-à-vis animals, but is such vis-à-vis other human beings "since he is mistrustful, violent, and hostile [*mißtrauisch, gewaltthätig und feindseelig*] toward his own kind." Somewhat similar to what we will see happens in *Anthropology from a Pragmatic Point of View*, Kant here notes that this is "no longer as manifest in the civil state, since the human being is there held under constraint, but which still does very much sprout up, and a great deal of the animal state still adheres to us" (25:678). Should law and order no longer be maintained in such a state, everyone would fear at night that someone would break in and subject them to violence. And it is not only the mob (*Pöbel*) who would do this, Kant notes, because all human beings are by nature mob-like: "This maliciousness lies in the nature of all human beings [*Diese bösartigkeit liegt allen Menschen in der Natur*]" (25:679). Kant then proceeds to seek a purpose in the way in which nature designed human beings: he finds it in God's will that they spread across the earth, which would not have happened if they simply lived together in peace; that they then seek protection of their property against their neighbor; and thus establish law to do so, and eventually a civil constitution. The latter is in other words the direct result of the human being's evil nature (*die bösartigkeit der menschlichen Natur*) (25:681). If the human being was meek and good-natured, no civil constitution would thus have emerged (25:681).[13]

Derrida Reading Kant

Subjectivity

Derrida starts his reading of Kant with the first page of *Anthropology from a Pragmatic Point of View*, where it is for Kant about the representation of an "I," that is, the power or ability to say "I," which the human being is said to have access to, which enables a continuity over time, and which gives rise to subjectivity. This power to say "I," according to Kant, raises the human being above the animal and gives him or her power over the animal. The relevant passage that is the focus of this part of Derrida's analysis is located in Book I of Kant's *Anthropology from a Pragmatic Point of View* titled "On the cognitive faculty," with the heading "On consciousness of oneself." Section I starts as follows:

> The fact that the human being can have the "I" in his representations raises him infinitely above all other living beings on earth. Because of this he is a *person*, and by virtue of the unity of consciousness through all changes that happen to him, one and the same person—i.e., through rank and dignity an entirely different being from *things*, such as irrational animals, with which one can do as one likes. This holds even when he cannot yet say "I," because he still has it in thoughts, just as all languages must think it when they speak in the first person, even if they do not have a special word to express this concept of "I." For this faculty (namely to think) is *understanding*. (127)

As noted, for Kant, only the human being has access to the representation of an "I," that is, the power or ability to say "I." The "I" here points to the unity of consciousness, which remains the same over time despite modifications (Derrida 2008, 92). At stake in the "I think," one can say in Kantian language, is "the originary unity of the transcendental apperception that accompanies every representation" (92).[14] This power or ability—to experience a continuity over time—as noted gives rise to subjectivity, that is, to the subject of reason, of morality, and of law. Over against the subject, clothed with position (*Rang*) and dignity, stand things, that is, irrational animals, over which the subject has power and authority and can do with as he or she pleases. As Derrida (93) points out, this power over animals is in Kant's thinking not a mere attribute of the human being, but constitutes the human being, makes out his or her essence. In his analysis of the human-animal relation, Kant follows not only the account of Descartes, but, going much further back in time, also the account in *Genesis* on the origin and destination of the human being. The Kantian account of the ability to present oneself as an "I" points in Derrida's terminology to a belief in self-presence, that is, the ability to present oneself to oneself, to be present to oneself (93). This self-presence makes possible the "response" of the human being vis-à-vis the mere "reaction" of the animal and thus also his or her responsibility as a subject in a variety of senses: theoretical, practical, ethical, juridical, and political (93). As is clear from the quotation, Kant is nevertheless careful not to link the ability to say "I" to actual speech: the potential ability is sufficient, for example, in the case of an infant who cannot as yet speak, or a (human) language that does not provide for such a word. As long as the "I" or selfness exists in thinking—and this is the case in all human languages, at least implicitly—the subject with all of his or her powers, dignity, and responsibilities is in existence. The animal by contrast has no autobiographical relation to itself (93). The distinction between being a subject and being subjected thus ultimately lies in the ability or power to think, to understand, which is a faculty that all human beings have access to, but which animals are said to lack. For the sake of clarity, Derrida (94) notes that this Kantian account does not concern the ability to relate to the self, to feel the self, or to move spontaneously, hence of auto-affection or auto-motion. It is generally accepted, even by Descartes, that all living beings have these abilities.[15] It is instead here, as Derrida (94) puts it, about the "power to make reference to the self in deictic or autodeictic terms, the capability at least virtually to turn a finger toward oneself in order to say 'this is I.'" The non-human animal is in other words thought to lack this "auto-deictic or auto-referential self-distancing" (94). The non-human animal is deprived of the "I," and consequently also of the "I think," of reason, understanding, response, and responsibility (94).

In challenging this Kantian account, Derrida relies on the strategy as outlined earlier. First, Derrida acknowledges that many animals appear to lack this pointing to self, ascribed by Kant solely to the human being. Derrida (95), however, notes that there is some evidence that this autodeicticity is a characteristic of the genetic system in general, "where each element of the genetic writing has to identify itself, mark itself according to a certain reflexivity, in order to signify in the genetic chain."[16] This pointing to self finds expression in a more sophisticated and complex way in various animals, for example, in the case of seduction or sexual combat, where a form of narcissism is on display by way of "colors, music, adornments, parades, or erections of all sorts" (95).[17] Those animals are in effect saying: "follow me, who is (following) you" (59–60, 95). Second, Derrida refers to the problematic nature of the self-presence that Kant ascribes to the human being, pointing here to the fact that there can be no pure autonomy of the self, which is always touched by some hetero-affection. Derrida does not engage with this aspect in detail here, as he undertakes the challenge to the so-called "metaphysics of presence" in many of his other texts, by way of both phenomenology and psychoanalysis, for example, through an analysis of Husserl's account of signs, Heidegger's analysis of Being and of Dasein, Levinas's account of the ethical relation, and Freud's account of the unconscious and the death drive (De Ville 2011a, 13–37). This "otherness" or abyss within the self is nonetheless alluded to throughout *The Animal That Therefore I Am*, for example, by way of Derrida's description of the abyssal and secret gaze of the animal (2008, 12); his depiction of the scene of Creation, a time before time, where God exposes himself to the event, that is, to what is going to happen between the human being and the animal (15–18); his analysis of the Chimera, which he links to the evil genius in Descartes—a kind of perverse beast (39–40, 41–42, 45–47); his mention of the autoimmunity within autobiography (47); and the reference to Valery's serpent, speaking as an "I am" from the abyss (66–67). Derrida's analysis of Bentham (27–28) also captures something of this otherness within the self. For Bentham, as Derrida reads him, the question of our treatment of animals is not dependent on some faculty, power, or ability that animals are said to have (reason, language, etc.), but whether they can suffer. Derrida understands this "can" not as an ability, faculty, or power, but in its combination with the passivity of "suffering" as a certain powerlessness, an inability, a vulnerability, which we share with animals. In speaking of such shared suffering, Bentham can be said to point to the relation between life and death in both human and non-human animals:

> Being able to suffer is no longer a power; it is a possibility without power, a possibility of the impossible. Mortality resides there, as the most radical means of thinking the finitude that we share with animals, the mortality that belongs to the very finitude of life, to the experience of compassion, to the possibility of sharing the possibility of this nonpower, the possibility of this impossibility, the anguish of this vulnerability, and the vulnerability of this anguish. (28)

To conclude this section, it is interesting to note that the Greek myths (Prometheus), biblical narratives (*Genesis*), as well as modern accounts on the origin of the human being likewise speak of a certain lack or vulnerability, though a lack that differs from the "lack" identified in "the animal." As Derrida (20–21, 44–45) points out, at stake in these accounts with respect to the human being is an original sin, a fault, a lack, nakedness, shame, culpability, which then gets compensated by a certain power or ability (for example, fire, technology, clothes, ability to distinguish between right and wrong, which the animal is said to lack) that at the same time gives birth to the subject.[18] One thus can say that a certain impropriety in the human being gives rise to what is regarded as proper to the human being (45). For Derrida (43), what is perceived as an original sin or fault, and which is said to require a remedy in the form of an assumed power, is actually the dissimulation of a fault with respect to what is elsewhere referred to as an excessive demand or obligation (chapter 1 in this volume). By recounting the incident of his cat observing him naked in the bathroom, Derrida (57–61) is speaking of this demand by alluding to something unknown, which is felt as shame, modesty, and which certain animals also have access to. There is also a mirror in the bathroom, and at times more than one person, but this mirror is not the Lacanian mirror that captures the animal in the imaginary order and allows it no access to the symbolic order, to the unconscious, or to language (59–60). It is an abyssal mirror, which keeps on reflecting ad infinitum, and in the process interlinking desire, enjoyment (*jouissance*), and anguish (12, 58, 61).

The Civil Condition

After the analysis of the Kantian "I think," Derrida engages in a reading of certain passages toward the end of *Anthropology from a Pragmatic Point of View* in the chapter "Anthropological Characteristic" under the heading "The character of the species [*Gattung*]." At issue here is the distinction between the state of nature and the civil condition, the latter of which animals are said not to have access to. Derrida's approach is similar here: he first challenges the claim of a lack in the animal and then, second, raises the question of whether the human being can be said to possess the quality in its purity. Kant (327) refers here to a civil constitution, that is, the development of human society in its highest form, and notes somewhat enigmatically that under such a constitution "*animality* still manifests itself earlier and, at bottom, more powerfully than pure *humanity* [*ist doch die* Tierheit *früher und im Grunde mächtiger als die reine* Menschheit *in ihren Äußerungen*]." For Derrida, what is important here is the similarity that Kant points to between human and animal societies.[19] Kant appears to be seduced or tempted by this analogy, while at the same time resisting this idea (Derrida 2008, 96).[20] Kant (327) immediately switches from this mention of the animal still residing in man to the domestication of animals, noting that domestic animals are "only because of *weakening* [*nur durch* Schwächung]," more useful to human beings than wild animals). In Derrida's reading, human socialization is here made dependent on the taming of the beast (96). They in fact go hand in hand, together with the originary fault pointed to earlier, within the tradition of Western thinking (45). From the taming of the domestic animal, Kant moves back to the difficulties of the civil condition: left on his or here own, the human being strives for unconditional freedom and does not hesitate to engage in conflict with his or her neighbor, wishing to be independent of others and to subject even his or her equals to his or her will (Kant 2006, 327), thus acting like a wild beast (Derrida 2008, 96). Although Derrida does not explicitly say this here in his analysis (he will do so later), at stake seems to be not only the domestication of certain animals as a precondition for human society/a civil constitution, but also of the animal within the human being: the human being who, in the Kantian account, has to overcome or sacrifice his or her senses (Derrida 2008, 100). Civil society thus needs domestication, or taming of the beast in a double sense. The mechanism that works toward such domestication but, as we will see, never fully succeeds will be inquired into somewhat later. Derrida here simply points out that there is an inherent relation between animal domestication and (human) socialization, political constitution, and politics. For this reason, Kant needs to show that despite the similarities, there are also differences between human and animal societies, and, as we will see, he finds this in war.

Under the subheading "Main features of the description of the human species' character," Kant (330) notes that human society cannot be compared with a herd of cattle, that is, domesticated animals, but rather with a beehive. In both instances, that is, the bee and the human, there is a need to be a member of some or other civil society. The simplest way to establish such a society is by having a single ruler, that is, a monarchy. The analogy cannot, however, be taken too far, as the beehive remains in a bellicose state of nature: "many such hives next to each other will soon attack each other like robber bees (war); not, however, as human beings do, in order to strengthen their own group by uniting with others . . . but only to use by cunning or force *others'* industry for themselves" (330). The latter is of course exactly what, according to Kant, human beings may do with animals and, as we just saw, what the human being does to other human beings in striving for "unconditional freedom." The difference between human and animal wars is thus hard to detect with reference to this criterion.[21] Kant is here, as also elsewhere (2007, 8:24–25 ("Idea for a Universal History"), optimistic about human wars, which, as we saw earlier (para. 2), are destined to lead to a state of civil society:

> Therefore civil or foreign war in our species, as great an evil as it may be, is yet at the same time the incentive [*Triebfeder*, also "motivating force"] to pass from the crude state of nature to the *civil* state or condition [*zustande*]. War is like a mechanical device of Providence [*Maschinenwesen der Vorsehung*], where to be sure the struggling forces injure each other through collision, but are nevertheless still regularly kept going for a long time through the push and pull of other incentives [*durch den Stoss oder Zug anderer Triebfeder*]. (Kant 2006, 330)

Derrida (2008, 97) highlights here the providential machine that Kant speaks of, which is to be distinguished from the Cartesian animal machine, and which seems to be able to foresee how these two kinds of war, that is, animal wars and wars waged by the animal within the human being—the animal as we saw being prior to and stronger than the human, and remaining part of the human (Kant 2006, 327)—will end, and thus the use that evil can have.[22] Derrida furthermore points to the different, competing driving forces (*Triebfedern*) at stake in the Kantian account,[23] which function like a machine to eventually stabilize and regularize human society but not animal society. The question raised here by Derrida is "whether this criterion of stability and regularity alone would not be just as pertinent for describing so-called animal or savage societies."[24] In Derrida's reading, Kant (2006, 327–328n) seems to retract his statement about stability and regularization and thus to contradict himself when in a footnote he extends the possibility of evolution to certain primates. In the footnote, Kant (268) discusses the cry of a newborn child and the possible intention of nature with this seemingly self-destructive behavior, that is, drawing the attention of wild animals to its presence, which at the same time announces the child's freedom: "Even the child who has just wrenched itself from the mother's womb seems to enter the world with loud cries, unlike all other animals, simply because it regards the inability to make use of its limbs as constraint, and thus it immediately announces its claim to freedom (a representation that no other animal has)." Kant, insisting that the cry is not uttered in pain, but is due to irritation or annoyance (*ihm etwas verdriesst*), in response, postulates the existence of three different epochs: (1) where the child in the crude state of nature did not as yet cry; (2) where humankind enters a state of domesticity or culture, and the cry thus appears "without us knowing how, or through what contributing causes," but is thus protected. Kant then foresees the possibility, due to further disturbances in nature, that (3) in a third epoch yet to come, the chimpanzee and the orangutan might become human through the development of the necessary organs to walk, handle objects, and speak. They would thereby gain access to the "I think" and thus to understanding and would attain the rank and dignity of human beings. Derrida (2008, 98–99) points out that the evolutionary process as described here is somewhat improbable and naive and that it remains strongly anthropomorphic and anthropocentric. The future that is anticipated for the chimpanzee and the orangutan furthermore "retains the familiarity of a human structure" (99). The footnote is nevertheless interesting because Kant here no longer speaks about the animal in general, but "takes into account a structural difference between non-human types of animal" (99). It furthermore raises questions about the sustainability of the whole Kantian discourse, which, as we saw, takes its point of departure in the distinction between "the human" and "the animal" (98). Such an evolutionary process would further have the consequence that these primates should be granted the rights and responsibilities that Kant denies the animal in general in the *Metaphysics of Morals* (Derrida 2008, 99–100).

THE MORAL LAW

Derrida's analysis continues by pointing out the implications for the non-human animal under a civil constitution of Kant's (dominant) thinking, which were pointed to earlier: the supposed lack of the ability to say "I" on the part of the animal, that is, the absence of understanding and reason, translates into the absence of freedom and autonomy, and thus also the absence of a subject with rights and duties (Derrida 2008, 99). Compared with the human being, in Kant the animal (even the animal within the human being) has no end in itself, no dignity, and is therefore simply a means to an end (100). As noted earlier, Derrida (100), following Adorno, sees in this respect a direct correlation between the Kantian injunction to the human being to sacrifice his or her own sensible inclinations, that is, his or her own passions, affections, and pathological interests for the sake of the moral law, and the Kantian prescribed domination and consequent sacrifice of animals by human society.[25] There thus seems to be, as Nietzsche also noticed, an inherent cruelty in Kantian practical reason, the good (moral) will, as well as dignity (Derrida 2008, 100–1). Despite human beings' evolution toward the civil condition, they are in other words, and as noted earlier, still engaged in a war, a war against "the animal," a war that did not start with Descartes or Kant, but is at least as old as Greek mythology and as *Genesis* (20–21, 101).[26] As Derrida (101) puts it, "the man of practical reason remains bestial in his defensive and repressive aggressivity, in his exploiting the animal to death," and "bad will, even a perverse malice, inhabits and animates so-called good moral will." At the same time, the human being seeks to hide such violence, cruelty, and peculiar genocide from him- or herself (25–26). This war against "the animal" is furthermore not restricted to the animal located "outside," but also waged against the animal "within" the human being, inter alia by way of the death penalty, which Kant strongly defended (chapter 5 of this volume). Despite the human being's ability to think and reason, and in view of Kant's description of war (as evil), there thus appears to be something evil or perverse underlying the Kantian "I think," as its "other" or "unconscious" (101–2). Derrida wants us to understand this latter terminology beyond its Levinasian and Lacanian interpretations and limits, that is, rather in Freudian or Nietzschean terms. In the final paragraph of this section on Kant, Derrida invokes inter alia the question of evil and the idea of the providential machine in Kant, the Freudian unconscious, the Cartesian animal machine, and the Cartesian evil genius. The notion of *différance*, as outlined by Derrida (1987a, 399–405),[27] perhaps captures best what is at stake here. It expresses in a single "word" what Derrida refers to as the "unthought in the 'I think,'" or, as he also puts it, "it is the other that thinks me and the other that follows me where I am (following), that other which haunts in advance the 'I think that accompanies all my representations'" (2008, 102). This "other" likewise haunts the Kantian civil condition, at the national, international, as well as cosmopolitan levels, which, as we saw earlier, only gets established through a certain "repression" of unconscious forces.

Living Together

The preceding analysis calls for a rethinking of the Kantian position on freedom, the moral law, the virtues/ethics, as well as modern constitutionalism in general. Every aspect of Kant's thinking, as we saw, is based on a certain exclusion of "the animal." Kant (2006) can in summary be said to look at the animal in order to arrive at a certain property of the human being (to say "I"), but to not see the animal returning the gaze, or to have seen the gaze, but to have disavowed it (Derrida 2008, 14, 113). Kant fails thereby to acknowledge the otherness "within" or the abyssal limits of the human animal, which must be disavowed in order to arrive at the proper (12–14). Bentham's remark about the importance of suffering in contemplating the human-animal relation for Derrida by contrast points to a sharing of some "thing" between human and non-human animals, not of an ability, but of an inability, a lack of power, that is, our shared mortality. This points to another kind of "foundation" that precedes the indubitable certainty of the "I am" or "I think" (28).

Rethinking subjectivity, the "civil condition," and "morality" or justice, in view of the excessive responsibility that the analysis imposes, could clearly have important implications, in the first place, for the recognition of "entitlements" in the modern constitution. Traditionally, the modern constitution grants fundamental rights only to human beings, who as we saw are the only subjects of law with duties and responsibilities. This follows closely in the steps of Kant, for whom a subject of law is also a subject with rights and duties, with only a few exceptions: God (likewise the sovereign [Kant 1996b, 6:319]), who has only rights and no duties; and slaves, who have only duties, but no rights (Derrida 2008, 99–100; Derrida and Roudinesco 2004, 74). Animals have neither rights nor duties. The analysis by Derrida of subjectivity in Kant however considerably weakens the justification for the exclusion of animals from the protection of a constitution.[28] What the analysis nevertheless also makes clear is that animals cannot simply be turned into subjects with rights (Derrida 2008, 88). It is precisely the language of subjectivity that has during the whole of modernity been relied on to accelerate the war against non-human animals (Derrida and Roudinesco 2004, 64–65). This war of subjection includes among its practices the breeding, imprisonment, mutilation, fattening, catching, hunting, transportation, slaughter, and consumption of non-human animals in ever increasing numbers, as well as the exploitation of such animals for purposes of the adornment, health, benefit, and entertainment of human beings.

A different language would in other words have to be found for the claims to justice and dignity of non-human animals (Derrida 1995b, 255–87; 2002a, 246–47; 2005c, 60; Derrida and Roudinesco 2004, 74) and, arguably, for nature in general. In view of the earlier analysis, that is, in recognition of our "shared suffering," and through a radicalization of the Kantian moral law, our living together with non-human animals should have absolute hospitality as its point of departure (Derrida 2013; chapter 1 of this volume). In what can be read as a response to this demand, although seemingly motivated by a wide range of considerations, a number of state constitutions have recently started giving separate recognition to the duties and responsibilities owed by the state to non-human animals.[29] This has already led to certain improvements in their treatment (Eisen 2017, 911–24). This is undoubtedly an important development and a significant step taken toward a very different kind of "living together" of human and non-human animals, which should be extended not only to other state constitutions, but also to founding documents on the transnational and international level. Similar developments are taking place with respect to nature in general, with the Ecuadorian Constitution recognizing the "rights of nature" (Borràs 2016; Rühs and Jones 2016).[30] What about the existing fundamental rights of human beings or human rights, which are protected in the modern constitution? Although, as indicated, the notion of subjectivity is highly problematic because of its inherent link with the subjection of animals, these rights, which have thus far attained recognition and enforcement only partially, and often at great expense, should arguably remain protected in their present form, at least for the foreseeable future (Derrida 2003, 132–33).

The absolute hospitality invoked here would also have important implications for our understanding of democracy on the national, transnational, and international levels. We saw in chapter 3 how Nancy and Derrida reconceive freedom as no longer finding its privileged place of unfolding in the human being and consequently reconceiving democracy in terms of "the no matter who," the indeterminate "each one." Derrida's analysis thus appears to support the idea proposed in the recent literature that fundamental changes are required to the notion of political representation that underlies democratic theory, so as to cater to the interests of non-human animals.[31] His analysis also provides support for extending "democracy," insofar as it can or should still be referred to as such, in some or other form beyond human and non-human animals, to the non-living, as well as to plants, trees, forests, mountains, rivers, oceans, and so forth (*Rogues* 54).[32] A much wider range of "interests" must thus be represented, yet the question can also be raised whether such representation should be restricted to "interests" as traditionally conceived. Should representation not in the first place be connected to the suffering, or vulnerability, or mortality that we share with non-human animals and with nature in general,[33] or what was elsewhere referred to as a representation of the unpresentable, that is, of absolute hospitality? (De Ville 2017, 100), This unpresentable "interest," as the earlier analysis shows, can indeed be said to underlie all modern constitutions and similar kinds of founding documents on the transnational and international levels. Kant, as we saw, associates constitutions with leaving the state of nature, that is, entering the civil condition, which is the result of a subjection, both of non-human animals and of the animal in humankind, and arguably of nature in general. It is this "animal" or "beast" that continues to haunt constitutions and other, similar documents, in the formless form of absolute hospitality (De Ville 2017, 116–20) and consequently has to be accounted for in each of their iterations.

Chapter 5

Crime, Punishment, and Forgiveness

In the "Introduction" we saw that Kant's notion of human dignity has become central to modern constitutionalism since World War II. As criminal law in a broad sense[1] is subject to the bounds set by the modern constitution, Kant's thinking on human dignity has also been influential in determining the appropriate punishment for crimes committed (Ackermann 2012, 101, 126–27). As noted, Kant saw no conflict between human dignity and the imposition of the death penalty, a penalty that has today been outlawed in large parts of the world, frequently by virtue of (the constitutional protection of) human dignity. The notion of human dignity has not however as yet led to a widespread challenge of the founding principles of criminal law such as guilt and responsibility, which find their source in freedom.[2] Derrida's Death Penalty seminars, which ran from 1999–2000 and which have now been published in two volumes, challenge us to reflect again on our notions of crime and punishment. Kant's "Theory of Law" in the *Metaphysics of Morals* stands central in Derrida's analysis in the Seminars. The section titled "On the right to punish and to grant clemency" in Kant's "Theory of Law" deals with the power that the state has to punish the wrongdoer, the purpose of punishment, and the measure of punishment, specifically when the death penalty would be justifiable. Derrida provides a detailed analysis of this section, as well as of the section titled "Further Discussion of the Concept of the Right to Punish" in the appendix of the 1798 edition of the "Theory of Law," and in this chapter we follow him closely to highlight the most important aspects of his analysis. We will see that Derrida's quasi-psychoanalytical reading of Kant consists partly of a defense of Kant, partly of a critique and partly of a deconstruction. In

Derrida's Death Penalty seminars, Freud and Reik, as well as Derrida's own transformation of psychoanalysis in other texts, play an important role. Psychoanalysis was indeed influential in the criminal law field in certain jurisdictions during the late 1950s and early 1960s, that is, around the time of the appearance of the 1959 English translation of Reik's *The Compulsion to Confess* (Schmeiser 2007, 317–37). That influence has however been in decline, perhaps partly because of a realization that there would be no justification for criminal law should the claims of psychoanalysis be accepted (Schmeiser 2007, 318, 331). The same conclusion appears to follow from Derrida's seminars, which in broad terms show the tenuous nature of the basic principles of criminal justice as well as the need to thoroughly revisit their premises. As Derrida (2017, 9) puts it in the seminars, posing thereby a radical challenge to legal scholars: "Up until now, the law has forbidden itself or has been unable to integrate into its essential axiomatic a logic of the unconscious or the symptom."[3]

This chapter starts with an analysis of legal subjectivity and its relation to punishment.[4] Here we inquire into Kant's premise of freedom to establish criminal responsibility and show how this is undermined by the analysis of Reik, but even more so by Derrida in his analysis of a certain "sexual" desire as lying at the origin of all crime.[5] This is followed by an analysis of the relation between sovereignty and punishment as well as clemency. Here we see how Derrida, with reference to Nietzsche and Freud, shows the close relation between sovereignty, cruelty, and pleasure, thereby pointing to sovereignty's condition of possibility and its phantasmatic nature. With respect to the sovereign right to grant clemency, we inquire into its link with unconditional forgiveness. In looking at the purpose or theories of punishment, Kant, as we will see, rejects any kind of utilitarian argument in relation to punishment, specifically regarding the death penalty. For Kant, punishment follows by virtue of the categorical imperative in view of the human being's dignity, which he regards as having a value higher than life. Punishment, also the death penalty, is thus justified with reference to a certain concept of the human being, which Derrida traces back to political theology. We will see how Derrida seeks to explain what lies behind the abolitionist and pro-retention discourses on the death penalty, with reference to a conception of life that is not inspired by political theology. This is followed by an analysis of the measurement to be used with respect to punishment according to Kant. We will see here how Derrida, in a very close reading, shows that there is actually a tension in Kant between a certain noncalculability and calculation. Before concluding, a brief analysis is undertaken of the notions of "progress" and "advance" to be found in the thinking of Reik and Kant as well as its implications for criminal law. The chapter concludes by exploring the possibility of further reform of the principles of criminal justice in view of what can be referred to as its groundless ground, that is, unconditional forgiveness.

Legal Responsibility and Punishment

For Kant (1996b, 6:331), punishment follows (only) after a court has found that someone has committed a crime. Although Kant does not spell this out in detail here, responsibility for a crime and liability for punishment in his thinking are tied to the human being's noumenal nature, that is, his or her freedom from natural inclinations, and thus the freedom as subject to choose (consciously) whether or not to commit a crime, as well as subsequently to be held responsible and liable should he or she have done so (Kant 1997a, 5:100; Geismann 2012, 127–28).[6] Derrida (2017, 110) affirms this understanding of Kant and of modern criminal law in general, noting that "what gives meaning to the concepts of offense, crime, punishment, and in particular the death penalty" is—"responsibility, guilt, in other words, the freedom and consciousness of the subject, of the subject as 'I,' as a clear and unambiguous relation to its intention, to the intentionality of its acts, to its conscious will, to its power over itself, to the 'I can.' " In other words, as Derrida (210) also puts it, condemnation for a crime is tied to the notion of a free, responsible, and guilty individual.[7] The challenge posed to this Kantian account of *homo noumenon* comes primarily from psychoanalysis, which poses a radical threat to the credit we give to these concepts by questioning the self-identity of the subject, for example by showing the impact of the unconscious on consciousness, and, more specifically, by positing the notion of a death drive (Derrida 2017, 110). Theodor Reik contends in this regard that guilt or fault (in the form of *dolus* or *culpa*) does not only accompany the crime as supposed by Kant and by modern criminal law, but that it precedes the crime by virtue of the Oedipus complex as internalized in the superego, and thus motivates the crime. The criminal in other words wants to be punished (to ease his or her guilt and to satisfy his or her "masochistic sexual trend"), and therefore commits a crime (Freud 2001, 17:28; Reik 1959, 292–93; Derrida 2017, 38).[8] Reik (296–98) consequently proposes that legal punishment should be abolished and replaced with confession.[9] In the seminars, Derrida acknowledges the importance of this psychoanalytical explanation as well as of the inquiry into alternatives for legal punishment. He does not however find this explanation fully convincing and, as we will see, seeks to take Reik's analysis in a different direction.

Reik's account is attractive because of the challenge it poses to the Kantian notion of freedom by way of the Oedipus complex lodged in the unconscious. The (male) criminal, as we saw, commits a crime because he feels guilty, that is, he has an unconscious feeling of guilt (murder of the father, incest with the mother). The crime is in other words "reassuring for the one who feels guilty" (Derrida 2017, 181). In the words of Reik (1959, 292), "crime is felt as emotional relief because it can connect the unconscious feeling of guilt to something real, actual."[10] This account follows on the analysis of Freud (2001, 13: 125–26) in "Totem and Taboo" where he traced the origin of (criminal) law, and more specifically the taboos of murder and incest, back to the sons' killing of the father of the primal horde, and thus to the Oedipus complex. For Derrida (2017, 3–7), psychoanalysis raises fundamental questions about age, act, and desire. For example, what age should be relevant for deciding whether someone is criminally responsible? This is because it could very well be, assuming that Reik/Freud is right, that the crime is motivated by the unconscious Oedipus complex, which according to Freud develops in a child between the ages of three to five.[11] Criminal law is furthermore concerned only with (wrongful) *actions*, tied to conscious intentions (or negligence), and not unconscious wishes and desires, thereby disregarding the very prevalent unconscious desire to kill (Derrida 2017, 80). In other words, criminal law seems to attach no importance to the fact that we are all murderers in terms of the unconscious, which according to Freud is no less real than a conscious, intentional, actual act (Derrida 2017, 78–79). Should this not be central in thinking about crime and punishment? Derrida (170), as noted, is suspicious of the accounts of Freud and Reik, as the unconscious here appears to remain within a circular economy. Reik (1959, 425) specifically notes in this regard that "to the unconscious, gratefulness is as foreign as is forgiveness." The unconscious thus operates according to the talionic principle: it desires to punish, and to pay back; it knows no forgiveness and no mercy, no thanks, and no pardon (Derrida 2017, 170).

The questions of age, act, and desire; the notion of the unconscious; the idea of auto- or self-punishment and guilt, whether before, alongside, or after the crime, are arguably implicit in Kant (1996b, 6:331). This can be detected in the distinction he draws between external, legal, or public punishment by a court (*poena forensis*) and natural, inner, or self-punishment (*poena naturalis*), the latter of which he notes is of no interest to the legislator (Derrida 2017, 37). As Derrida (38–39) points out, the distinction between *poena naturalis* and *poena forensis* is undoubtedly an important one, but not one that is easy or possible to maintain in all rigor, especially not in view of Reik's analysis where, as we saw, guilt precedes the crime. Crime is therefore committed to give actuality to guilt, and self-punishment thereby becomes hetero-punishment. Conversely, the whole Kantian logic of legal rationality, whereby the laws enacted are supposed to be universally agreed to by citizens,[12] necessarily entails that hetero-punishment also becomes auto-punishment (Derrida 2017, 66–69, 98; Derrida and Roudinesco 2004, 150). We likewise see this logic reflected in Kant's description of punishment when he declares that "whatever undeserved evil you inflict upon another within the people, that you inflict upon yourself. If you insult him, you insult yourself; if you steal from him, you steal from yourself; if you strike him, you strike yourself; if you kill him, you kill yourself" (Kant 1996b, 6:332).[13] This convergence of auto- and hetero-punishment can furthermore play itself out in a variety of ways: the natural punishments that someone imposes on him- or herself can be more severe than the legal punishments, and can add to these or precede them (Derrida 2017, 38). Furthermore, someone may feel so guilty after a crime that he or she seeks legal punishment to alleviate the internal punishment (38).

Let us return now to the question of freedom in Kant as one of the foundational principles of criminal law.[14] It should already be clear from our analysis in chapter 3 and from the account thus far in the current chapter that things are not as simple as they seem. In *For What Tomorrow*, Derrida (152) casts doubt on the possibility of demonstrating, "in all Kantian logic, that the crime was committed freely, in a responsible and not a "pathological" way, in both the Kantian and the common sense of this word." We are not able to engage here in a thorough analysis of Derrida's reading of Freud and Reik, but, as already indicated, there are certain clear difficulties in their analyses. This is due inter alia to the circular economy that still characterizes the unconscious in Freud and Reik. We see this for example in Reik's positing of guilt because of Oedipal sexual desire as at the origin or as the motive of all crime (1959, 293). It is when the feeling of guilt becomes too intense that the criminal seeks a substitute, a peg, to hang the guilt on (Reik 1959, 292–93; Derrida 2017, 181–82).[15] Derrida (181) agrees with this idea—that every crime is a sexual crime—in principle, but not with Reik's understanding of sex in an Oedipal sense.[16] The Oedipal scene, as Derrida points out, incidentally also plays itself out in *The Metaphysics of*

Morals, with Kant (6:320) regarding the putting to death of the sovereign, through a formal process, parricide in other words (*parricida*, as Kant refers to it, "the attempt to destroy his fatherland"), as the supreme crime, the crime par excellence, which deserves death (Derrida 2017, 188).[17] The sovereign may thus not be judged or executed under any circumstances. This is because he is the source and foundation of law (Derrida 2017, 188). Kant (1996b, 6:320n) puts the feeling, a "feeling" that we already came across in chapter 1, and that arises as a result of such parricide in very strong terms:

> But how are we to explain this feeling, which is not aesthetic feeling (sympathy, an effect of imagination by which we put ourselves in the place of the sufferer) but moral feeling resulting from the complete overturning of all legal concepts [*Rechtsbegriffe*]? It is regarded as a crime that remains forever and can never be expiated (*crimen immortale, inexpiable*), and it seems to be like what theologians call the sin that cannot be forgiven either in this world or the next. . . .
>
> Like a chasm that irretrievably swallows everything, the execution of a monarch seems to be a crime from which the people cannot be absolved, for it is as if the state commits suicide.

Derrida (2017, 191) refers to this notion of the suicide of the state as "an autoimmune process," standing in tension with that which is immune, sacred, sovereign, untouchable. The formal execution of the monarch would be "the phenomenon or at least the symptom of an autoimmune disaster: absolute desacralization, blasphemy that attacks the sacral body—sacred and sacramental" (192). However, this abyssal suicide of the state never takes place as an actual event. As Derrida (192) puts it, "none of this takes place; it has no place taking place. None of this can actually happen. There can only be simulacra or phantasms of it." Derrida's comment follows in view of Kant's explanation that what motivates the (formal) parricide, the simulacra of a trial and punishment, is fear of the king returning to power and then taking vengeance on the people (Derrida 2017, 192). Similar to Freud and Reik, Kant thus seeks the motivation of this crime in a form of economic exchange (fear of castration/murder). At stake for Derrida in the "sexual" origin of all crime is however rather, as also alluded to by Kant, some "suicide" or force of self-destruction beyond the Oedipus complex, beyond parricide, an event that never takes place, of pleasure without end (Derrida 1987a, 397–402).

Insofar as guilt (a guilty conscience) is concerned, Derrida appears to accept the notion of guilt existing before the crime (rather than accompanying it as is supposed by criminal law), but for him this is not to be traced back to the Oedipus complex. At stake is again the force of self-destruction (primary masochism/sadism) that Freud invokes in "Beyond the Pleasure Principle," which doubles as a kind of ethics or prohibition preceding the guilt, thus making the latter possible (Derrida 2017, 126; De Ville 2011a, 92–93). This "ethics" entails a hyperethical demand or duty of absolute hospitality, the pure gift, forgiveness, which we are always already guilty of not complying with (Derrida 1995d, 52; 2001e, 43–44; De Ville 2011a, 92–93).[18] Guilt presents itself to psychoanalysis as Oedipal in nature, because it views the unconscious in economic terms (Derrida 2009a, 245; 2018, 44). Criminal law and its conception of guilt/fault is itself derived from this hyperethical demand.[19]

Freedom in the traditionally understood Kantian sense therefore cannot be accepted without qualification. This is, apart from the analysis in chapter 3, because of the inevitable merging of the noumenal and the phenomenal, or, in other words, the impossibility of human beings fully overcoming their phenomenal nature.[20] In Kant's *Metaphysics of Morals* (1996b, 6:336–337) there is an implicit recognition of this merging in the discussion of two exceptions to be made to the imposition of the death penalty in the event of murder: maternal infanticide in the case of an illegitimate child, and the killing of someone in a duel in defense of one's honor. For Kant (6:337) these are indeed killings, but not strictly speaking murders. He notes in this respect a disjuncture between the "incentives of honor in the people (subjectively)" and the measures that are (objectively) suitable for their purpose, which can be generalized (Derrida 2014c, 126–27). There is clearly an acknowledgement here of a remainder of the state of nature, or of *homo phaenomenon*, which can only be overcome when the ideal state of a congruence between the subjective and objective has been reached (and then the death penalty would no longer be required) (127). These exceptions, as Derrida (2014c, 125) notes, both undermine and lay bare the law on the death penalty. This does not however mean that Derrida prescribes to a complete (psychic) determinism,[21] as can also be seen in the reference to a hyperethical demand of absolute hospitality. One can however never be sure that one has complied with this command, that is, that one has really been "responsible" in the sense required here (Derrida 1997c, 68–69; 2017, 126–27; Derrida and Roudinesco, 2004, 52–53).

The Sovereign's Right to Punish and to Grant Clemency

Punishment

The analysis in the preceding section places in question the notion of "guilt" or "fault" as it operates in criminal law, which, if accepted, would necessarily imply that there is no justification for punishment. Let us however nonetheless look at the notion of punishment in Kant, and Derrida's analysis thereof in the Seminars to further underline this absence of justification. In the section dealing with the "Right to punish and to grant clemency," Kant (1996b, 6:331–37) sets out his views on the right of the state, the ruler (*des Befehlhabers*), to punish the wrongdoer. Kant (6:331) defines the right to punish as "the right a ruler has against a subject to inflict pain upon him because of his having committed a crime." The ruler cannot however himself (or herself) be punished; one can only withdraw from his (or her) dominion. In the appendix to the "Theory of Law," Kant (6:363) further elaborates on the concept of the right to punish. He starts off by noting again that "the mere idea of a civil constitution among human beings carries with it the concept of punitive justice belonging to the supreme authority (*der obersten Gewalt*)." In his analysis of this section, Derrida (2017, 87) points out that this power—to punish, but not to be subject to the law oneself—is fully in accordance with Schmitt's definition of the sovereign as he who decides on the exception as well as with Benjamin's description of the state as ensuring that it holds a monopoly on violence.[22] A number of limitations on sovereign power have of course been imposed in recent years, including term limits for heads of state, the possibility of impeachment, as well as the possibility of prosecution (Derrida 2017, 88–89). One could add to these the limitations imposed on sovereignty by transnational and international legal orders, the possibility of judicial review, which exists in certain countries in relation to these sovereign powers, as well as the abolition of the death penalty as a criminal sentence in the majority of countries around the world. Derrida (2014c, 2–3) specifically emphasizes the importance of visibility in relation to the imposition of the death penalty, whether or not in the form of a public spectacle. It is in seeing the condemned being put to death that the nation-state sees itself, becomes aware of its own sovereignty, and thus returns to itself, in what Derrida refers to as its *ipseity*.[23]

As he does in a number of other texts, such as *Rogues*, *Sovereignties in Question*, and *The Beast & the Sovereign*, Derrida in the Death Penalty Seminars closely analyzes the concept of sovereignty, here specifically the sovereign right to punish. The aim of this deconstruction is not to abolish sovereignty, but to show its phantasmatic nature, and in this way to expose its actual structure (2017, 171–72). In the first volume, this takes place with reference to the notion of cruelty, and in volume two, with reference to Freud's primal horde. The focus in the present section is on the relation between sovereignty and cruelty, specifically in Kant. Of relevance here is Nietzsche's reading of Kant in the *Genealogy of Morals* as well as Freud's analysis of the death drive in "Beyond the Pleasure Principle."

In the *Genealogy of Morals*, Nietzsche (2003a, 41) famously refers to Kant's categorical imperative as reeking of cruelty.[24] At stake here is Kant's reference to the law of punishment/penal justice (*das Strafgesetz*) and more specifically of the obligation to impose the death penalty in the case of an unlawful killing as a categorical imperative (1996b, 6:336). The latter is of course to be distinguished from a hypothetical imperative, which is subject to the calculation of ends and means, and which involves pathological interests or utility (Derrida 2017, 90; Kant 1997b, 4:413–17). Kant, as we will see in the further discussion, vehemently opposes utilitarian approaches that would either oppose or support the death penalty because of, for example, the greater good of society. In the "Theory of Law," Kant criticizes Beccaria, who argued in favor of abolishing the death penalty on utilitarian grounds. For Kant, utility and example (deterrence) cannot play any role in relation to the imposition of the death penalty. The human being has to be treated as an end in him- or herself, and not as a means toward an end (Derrida 2017, 21). Kant speaks in this regard of the interest of pure reason, which would be beyond any empirical or phenomenal interest (Derrida 2014c, 141). Invoking Nietzsche, Derrida (141) however raises the question of the interest lying behind the pure interest or the disinterest of pure reason. Following upon his comment on the categorical imperative, Nietzsche (2003a, 73) inquires into the alleged disinterest of assessments of the beautiful in Kant's *Critique of Judgment*: " 'That is beautiful,' says Kant, 'which pleases *without interest*.' Without interest! ['*Schön ist,*' hat Kant gesagt, '*was* ohne Interesse *gefällt.' Ohne Interesse!*]." Nietzsche here pokes fun at Kant's statement about naked female statues, which, if they are beautiful, can be looked at by men without interest. Nietzsche (75) therein detects a resistance to sensuality on the part of the philosopher in general, while being attracted by the beautiful. The philosopher typically negates the world and adopts a stance of hostility toward life and toward the senses (83). In the ascetic ideal the philosopher finds his faith as well as his power, his interest; his right of existence can be said to lie in this ideal (83). By positing this ideal, the ascetic philosopher shows a disgust in himself, the world, and all of life, causing himself "as much hurt as possible out of a pleasure in hurting—perhaps [his] one and only pleasure" (84). Nietzsche (84) concludes that at stake here is a certain tendency of life to turn against itself:

> It must be a necessity of the first order which makes this species, *hostile*, as it is to *life*, always grow again and always thrive again.—*Life* itself must certainly *have an interest* in the continuance of such a type of self-contradiction. For an ascetic life is a self-contradiction: here rules resentment without parallel, the resentment of an insatiate instinct and ambition, that would be master, not over some element in life, but over life itself, over life's deepest, strongest, innermost conditions; here is an attempt made to utilise power to dam the sources of power. . . . All this is in the highest degree paradoxical: we are here confronted with a rift that *wills* itself to be a rift, which *enjoys* itself in this very *suffering*.

The ascetic ideal is thus for Nietzsche (74) not at all characterized by an absence of interest, but "in fact, [by] the strongest and most personal interest of all, that of the victim of torture who escapes from his torture" (Derrida 2014c, 144). This idea is later also to be found in Freud (2001, 7:157–60; 18:53–54), who traces the phenomena of sadism and masochism back to an originary sadism/masochism, that is, a self-destructive drive. Applying these insights to Kant's stance on punishment, specifically the death penalty, Derrida (2014c, 145, trans. modified) contends that

> just as much as the abolitionist [this is Baudelaire's argument: those who oppose the death penalty feel guilty of a mortal sin and are scared of losing their own necks (Derrida 2014c, 129–30)], the proponents of the death penalty as categorical imperative are afraid for themselves [*ont peur pour eux*]; they seek to be delivered from a condemnation or from the threat of a verdict—and from the torture which this threat constitutes.

Derrida remains however interested in and seeks to explore further the notion of the cruelty of the categorical imperative, specifically in its relation to life and sovereignty. Nietzsche finds it particularly problematic that Kant's cruelty is a "cruelty that does not speak its name, a hypocritical cruelty that gives itself airs of keeping its hands clean" (Derrida 2014c, 148).[25] Central here is Nietzsche's second essay in the *Genealogy of Morals*, where he writes about the infliction of pain through the ages in ensuring that the human being gains a memory. From this Nietzschean genealogy of cruelty, Derrida (149) concludes that cruelty is the essence of life: "Life knows how to make itself suffer in order to keep itself, and to keep itself from forgetting, to keep itself in memory." At stake in cruelty, as Derrida (155–56, 159–60, 163–64) further points out, is the inevitability of a certain pleasure in causing suffering through the exercise of power, reminding us of Freud's analysis in "Beyond the Pleasure Principle" of the death drive, and its relation to the drive to dominate as well as to sadism and to masochism.[26] Kant therefore cannot escape from cruelty, and neither can Beccaria, seeing that cruelty has no opposite, for example, non-cruelty (Derrida 2014c, 147–48).[27] Life is in other words cruel in itself, in order to maintain itself. Therefore there are only "different ways, different modalities, different intensities, different values (active or reactive) of being cruel, only a differ*a*nce, with an *a*, in cruelty, a differant cruelty" (168).[28] Should one thus, Derrida (168) asks, simply accept cruelty as a fatal misfortune (whatever one does, it will be cruel), or alternatively (and this alternative splits in two), continue to believe, contra Nietzsche, in the possibility of not being cruel, that is, "to proceed from a place that is still protected by some innocence or some immunity or indemnity . . . or else [the second alternative] is it already, already and always, contaminated, overtaken by the contagion of this cruelty that it comprehends in advance?."

The relation between sovereignty and cruelty is further explored by Derrida in "Psychoanalysis Searches the State of Its Soul." There Derrida (2002d, 241, 258) links together very explicitly sovereignty, the drive to mastery, as identified by Freud (2001, 18:16), and cruelty. The latter, Derrida contends, is indissociably linked to the drive for sovereign mastery. There is no escape from this drive: the drive for sovereign power cannot be eradicated. Yet this drive always already involves a reaction to, a binding of, a certain force beyond measure (Derrida 1987a, 399–404). The latter arguably is another name for the impossible unconditionality that Derrida (2017, 172) has in mind as the condition of possibility of and a certain beyond to sovereignty and cruelty. At stake here for Derrida is another kind of interest than, or another figure of interest compared to, the disinterest that Kant for example speaks of, as well as of the other interests at stake in favor of and against the death penalty (Derrida 2014c, 255). The interest, as appears in the later discussion, is an "interest," if one can call it that, in the incalculability of the "to come," which is conditioned by my finitude (256). The death penalty, on the other hand, seeks to master this incalculability by seemingly putting an end to finitude, making the instant of death calculable (258).

CLEMENCY

Kant, in the second part of the same section "On the right to punish and to grant clemency," also briefly touches on the sovereign right to pardon the criminal by lessening or by canceling punishment. This power over life and death, similar to the power to impose punishment, stems from sovereignty, and Schmitt's analysis, referred to earlier, thus applies here as well (Derrida 2014c, 86; 2017, 56). Kant (1996b, 6:337) describes this right as "the slipperiest" (*das schlüpfrigste*) for the sovereign to exercise, as this is to be done "to show the splendor of his majesty." It can also lead to great injustice. According to Kant, the sovereign is therefore not entitled to pardon crimes of one subject against another, but only crimes against the sovereign himself (*crimen laesae maiestatis*), and furthermore only if such pardon would not endanger public security. Derrida does not analyze this section of the *Metaphysics of Morals* in the Death Penalty Seminars, although he does refer in the Seminars to the power to pardon in general.[29] The specific section in the *Metaphysics of Morals* is referred to in other texts of Derrida—dealing with forgiveness—where he points to the exceptional and unconditional nature of the pardon as a concept. According to Derrida (2001c, 25, 32–33, 45; 2001e, 21–22; 2014c, 45, 47), the pardon in its strict sense entails an unconditional forgiveness, a forgiveness that forgives the impossible, the unforgivable, which does not calculate, does not partake in economic exchange, makes no sense, and is foreign to law, specifically criminal law. The pardon in this pure and unconditional sense cannot however appear as such. In its appearance it is always conditioned, for example, by the requirement of repentance or apology, and by that which it seeks to bring about, that is, reconciliation or redemption (Derrida 2001c, 36; 2001d, 52–54).

The sovereign's right to pardon, as we saw in Kant, likewise stands above the law as its foundation and guarantee (2001c, 45–46). As Derrida (45) points out, this exception to the law is inscribed in the law itself—it inscribes in the law a power beyond the law. One can also say that this right to forgive is "what interrupts, in the juridical-political itself, the order of the juridical-political" (Derrida 2001e, 33). This right or power is politico-theological in nature, stemming from divine right; it involves an "exercise in the name of the State [of] a forgiveness that transcends and neutralises the law" (Derrida 2001c, 45–46). It is a right (*droit*) beyond right or law (*droit*) (46). In its manifestation, this right is however inevitably subject to conditions, that is, coupled with a calculation of interests, as also indicated by Kant in the *Metaphysics of Morals* (Derrida 2001c, 46–47; 2001e, 33; 2017, 62–64). The right to pardon thus only manifests itself as conditional forgiveness. We saw earlier that the sovereign right to pardon seems to find its origin in God. What Derrida's analysis however shows is that this presumed "origin" is itself preceded by and made possible by the "desire" or "thought" of unconditional forgiveness, which would be without sovereignty (Derrida 2001c, 59–60; 2001d, 53–54). If we should retain the language of theology, we would have to refer not to a sovereign and all-powerful God, but a God without power, without sovereignty (Derrida 2005c, 114). This unconditional forgiveness undermines the presumption of sovereignty and thus the right to decide over the life and death of others. At the same time, it imposes an infinite responsibility, to negotiate with the unconditional (Derrida 2001d, 58–59).

The Purpose of Punishment

Insofar as the purpose underlying punishment is concerned, Kant, as we saw, rejects any kind of utilitarian justification.[30] Punishment cannot be inflicted for the good of the criminal or that of society, but only because the criminal committed a crime. According to Kant (1996b, 6:331), as we saw earlier, the law of punishment/penal justice (*das Strafgesetz*) is a categorical imperative. Applying utilitarian principles in this context would, according to Kant, mean that the criminal is treated as a means to an end and not as an end in him- or herself. Justice here stands central for Kant, and it would be thwarted should any kind of means-ends argumentation be applied in this respect. This rejection by Kant of utilitarianism applies specifically to the death penalty, both in opposition to and in support thereof (Derrida 2017, 42). The penalty itself must likewise be an end in itself and not a means toward an end (39). The punishment is in other words not supposed to serve any purpose, and even if it serves no purpose, it must still be imposed (39). This again applies specifically to the death penalty, which according to Kant has to be imposed on someone who was sentenced to death even if it would serve no purpose, for example, in an island society that decides to disseminate and is faced with the decision what to do with a prisoner who has been sentenced to death. For Kant, punishing someone does not amount to disposing of that person or to do with him or her as one pleases by instrumentalizing him or her (Derrida 2017, 41–42). Punishment is for Kant about respecting that person, honoring him or her as someone "worthy of being punished because his [or her] act is punishable" (41). It is thus for Kant about respect, respecting the dignity of the person being punished "and not because the punishment will repair a harm or serve as a deterrent or as an example or will ensure the security, the happiness, and the well-being of a society" (Derrida 2017, 40; Höffe 1995a, 241). Kant further distinguishes between the innate personality and the civil personality: the innate personality, that is, dignity, cannot be lost whatever the crime, but the civil personality can be lost (Derrida 2017, 90).

We saw earlier that Kant posits a link between the death penalty, the dignity of human beings, their reason, their ability to raise themselves above their pathological interests and above animal life, their being an end in themselves and not a mere means to an end. The death penalty as inscribed in law thus raises the subject above life itself (Derrida 2017, 25–26, 95–96). Derrida (26–27) invokes in this context the link identified by Benveniste between honor and punish (having the same etymological root: *timē*) and compares this with the link posited by Kant between the death penalty and human dignity.[31] The human being, as we saw, belongs to two worlds. It is because of his or her belonging to the noumenal world that the human being feels within him- or herself respect and reverence for the moral law. Should one abolish the death penalty, one would give up on that which constitutes the honor and dignity of the human being. Respect for dignity is thus worth much more than life itself (Derrida 2014c, 116). Life, the right to life, cannot be an absolute principle. Whereas *homo phaenomenon* clings to life, *homo noumenon* must raise him- or herself above this by providing for the death penalty in his or her laws (124). This demand is also imposed by justice, which, according to Kant, must be beyond calculation and not tied to a price, justice being worth more than life (Derrida 2014c, 270–71; 2017, 40). One could say that for Kant, a code of law that does not have the death penalty would not be a code of law (Derrida 2014c, 116). The idea of law for Kant is thus inherently tied to the dignity of the human being, to his or her sovereignty, to the notion that there is something more worthy than life. Life as such is in other words not sacred, and "must be liable to be sacrificed" (116). To fail to inscribe the death penalty in law would be unworthy of human dignity; it would amount to a "return to the state of nature and animality" (130).

What we find in the analysis of Kant is a certain conception of "man," of what is proper to "man," which we also find in some or other form throughout the whole history of Western philosophy. At stake in these conceptions is the traditional distinction between the human being and the animal and which in the case of the death penalty specifically (but also elsewhere) aligns philosophy (from Plato to Heidegger) with political theology (Derrida 2017, 248; Derrida and Roudinesco 2004, 147; chapter 4 of this volume). Philosophy in other words asks what it is in the human being—whether language, speech, reason, and so forth—that raises him or her above the animal, above animal life, above biological life. In Kant, as we saw, this distinction lies in freedom/dignity, which is what is supposedly proper to the human being. In Plato's thinking, characterized by the distinction between the ideal and the phenomenal world, there is likewise something worse than receiving the death penalty, that is, to be treated like a beast, not to be buried (Derrida 2014c, 8–9). For Heidegger, similarly, it is only Dasein who can die; the animal simply perishes. Being-toward-death is thus viewed by Heidegger as proper only to the human being (Derrida 2017, 219, 209–11).

Kant's notion of dignity clearly has theological overtones and can be described as an immortality beyond life, or as life beyond or greater than life (Trumbull 2015, 331; Naas 2012, 53). This notion of immortality or infinity is in turn aligned to sacrifice: life (human or animal) needs to be sacrificed for the sake of that which is greater than life (Derrida 2014c, 116; Naas 2012, 53). This sacrifice of life moreover provides the condition of possibility for law in Kant (Derrida 2017, 245; Derrida and Roudinesco 2004, 142, 145–46).[32] As Derrida (2017, 245) points out, "Kantian thought is sacrificial through and through; Kantian morality is a sacrificial morality." (Bloody) Sacrifice, one could perhaps also say, is the older logic, providing the basis for the *lex talionis* (Goldgaber 2017, 3), and it is in turn tied to the theological notion of sin: rather punish the guilty one, than have God punish all (Derrida 2017, 255). This sacrificial politics, as Derrida (256, 259) points out, is not restricted to Christianity, or to the Abrahamic religions, but is a characteristic of all cultures. Derrida (253) therefore contends that the death penalty only makes sense as long as there is a belief in God and the afterlife. Only then is the final judgment still coming and the death penalty not irreversible. Secularization must therefore inevitably lead to the abolition of the death penalty as well as of criminal law, of punishment, of law, and of the state (54, 262–64).

Having exposed the political theology that informs Kant's views on criminal law in general and capital punishment specifically, Derrida toward the end of *Death Penalty* I outlines the structure or "stricture" of Kant's principled argument in favor of the death penalty. Derrida does so while at the same time devising an alternative understanding of life (as survival), which is not informed by political theology. What belongs to life, according to Derrida (2014c, 256), is not immortality, but "to have a future, thus some life before it, some event to come"; and moreover, life entails that the moment of death is not calculable. What the death penalty however does is to make the moment of death calculable, amounting to "the interruption of the principle of indetermination, the ending imposed on the calculable chance whereby a living being has a relation to what comes, to the to-come and thus to some other as event, as guest, as *arrivant*" (256). As Derrida points out, it is precisely because my life is finite that I have this relation to incalculability as to the instant of my death. The death penalty on the other hand appears to deprive me of my finitude and makes death calculable through all kinds of machines: "the law, the penal code, the anonymous third party, the calendar, the clock, the guillotine or another apparatus" (257). In doing so, the death penalty seduces "fascinated subjects," both those who condemn and at times the condemned (257–58). This is because of the phantasm of the end of finitude, of incalculability, the anxiety before the future, which as we saw belongs to life. The death penalty thus creates the illusion of infinity; it seems, in the words of Gratton (2014, 4), "to master the future, to master death, and to put an end to finitude itself" and in this manner fascinates us: "What we are dreaming of, that is, what in a certain way we desire, namely to give ourselves death and to infinitize ourselves by giving ourselves death in a calculable, calculated, decidable fashion" (Derrida 2014c, 258). Proponents of the death penalty (like Kant) thus dream of mastering the future, whereas opponents fight against the calculating decision in the name of an incalculable future. The force of this phantasmatic truth, as Derrida (258) points out, makes it likely that there will always be proponents of the death penalty, and thus also abolitionists.[33]

The Measure of Punishment

We saw earlier that for Kant the *ius talionis* lies at the basis of criminal law, and punishment must consequently be meted out in line with this principle. Both Nietzsche and Reik, as we will see later in more detail, object to the *ius talionis* in Kant. For Nietzsche, there is no equivalence, no common measure between injury and pain, between wrong and suffering. He then traces the origin of the belief in such an equivalence to commercial law, that is, to the idea of credit, duty, debt, sale, exchange, the market. The equivalence was in other words invented; it does not exist, has never existed, and will never exist (Derrida 2014c, 151–52). For Reik (1959, 290), on the other hand, Kant is here simply rationalizing the talionic drive of vengeance that is lodged in the unconscious (Derrida 2017, 178–79). Derrida defends Kant against both Nietzsche and Reik. Although the *ius talionis* is usually associated with passionate or pathological vengeance, Derrida (91) points out that for Kant, the *ius talionis* is instead about a principle of calculation that avoids vengeance.[34] It is in other words about equity or equality: the punishment, which is to be meted out by a third party, that is, the state, instead of by the victim, should not escalate into an "uncontrolled unleashing of vengeance" (91). There is however another dimension to the *ius talionis*, which Derrida points to, partly in response to Nietzsche. The Latin *talio*, as Derrida (102) notes, derives "from *talis* (*tel* [such]), a demonstrative of quality (from *tel* [such] one moves to *quel* [which or what]: he has committed such a crime [*il a commis tel crime*], he will be punished in such a way or in an equal way [*il sera puni de telle ou d'égale façon*]), [so] that the enigmatic passage from quality to quantity under the schema of equality or equity is already inscribed in the word" (102). According to Derrida (102), the same thing happens in Kant because ultimately it is for Kant about dignity, honor, and respect, which have no price, that is, which are not calculable.[35]

When Kant (1996b, 6:332) therefore says that the same "undeserved evil you inflict upon another within the people, that you inflict upon yourself," at stake are two equivalences that actually escape calculation. The first is the evil done to another that is felt within the self (of the wrongdoer); and the second, between the wrongdoer and the victim, two persons of equal worth and dignity. The equality in the second instance does not enable calculation, because at stake are "two 'without measures,' two measureless or immeasurable dignities" (Derrida 2017, 92).[36] The incalculability of the first equivalence stems likewise from such immeasurable dignity, leading to the "immediate, rational interiorization of the suffering or the evil inflicted upon the victim" (92). According to Kant (1996b, 6:332), as we saw, it is not the victim, but a third party, that is, a court, that must determine the exact punishment ("the quality and the quantity of punishment") with reference to the *ius talionis*. Derrida (2017, 93) reads this as law being subject to a kind of ethics, the ethics of the *talio*. In Derrida's reading, quality dominates here, and this is shown by all the examples that Kant gives under the heading: an insult, theft, murder, and treason. Derrida

(102) summarizes the effect of Kant's examples as follows: "Everything is played out in the half-light of the relation between the quantitative and the qualitative, the calculable and the incalculable. And what Kant seems to prescribe, or what Kant seems to describe as to what rights, justice, and law should prescribe, is like a calculation of the incalculable, a rational and impersonal calculation of what eludes calculation."[37] In responding to Reik's accusation against Kant, Derrida (2017, 183–84)[38] similarly reads Kant's statement regarding the talionic law—that it is "by its form always the principle for the right to punish since it alone is the principle determining this idea *a priori* (not derived from experience of which measures would be most effective for eradicating crime)" (Kant 1996b, 6:363)—as giving "the idea of calculation," but that it "is not itself originally calculable."[39] There is thus here a distinction and a tension between a pure talionic law, or an Idea of punitive justice that remains foreign to calculation, and to any unconscious drive (Reik/Freud) or calculation of assurances, on the one hand, and (penal) law, on the other, which remains calculable (Derrida 2017, 184–85). This statement of Kant, which appears in the Appendix, precedes the discussion of the particular difficulty of applying the talionic law, that is, of determining the appropriate sentence for certain "sexual" or "perverse" crimes where it would be either impossible or a crime against humanity to do the same unto the criminal as he (or she) had done unto another. The examples Kant gives are of rape, pederasty, and bestiality. The punishment Kant prescribes are castration (for rape and pederasty) and expulsion from civil society in the case of bestiality. These punishments, Kant (1996b, 6:363) says, come closest to the *ius talionis*, if not in the letter, then at least in its spirit. Derrida (2017, 109) notes that a cutting is at stake in both types of punishment: in the first and second, the cutting is literal; in the third, the citizen is cut off from civil society. Whereas the tendency in psychoanalysis is to see castration as central, showing thereby its privileging of the phallus and thus its phallocentrism, and death as secondary, Derrida (130, 228–30) switches these concepts around and reads Kant's two proposed punishments as both signifying death (or the death penalty).

Derrida (2017, 158) further observes a certain remorse or discomfort on the side of Kant in having to calculate the noncalculable in these three instances. It is interesting, significant, and not coincidental that it is specifically sexual crimes that Kant mentions here for which it is so difficult to find an equivalent punishment or rather chastisement. For the punishments prescribed are indeed attempts to chastise, to make chaste, words with "a kind of sexual family likeness, a sexual subconscious lodged in the word"

(167). The chastisement at stake here, Derrida (168) further notes, "awakens or alerts us to a sexual world in which all this penal law and talionic law take on meaning." It further raises the question of "whether talionic law in general is not, first of all, in its very paradigm, a law of sexual exchange and substitution.[40] Properly or figuratively speaking" (168). Derrida points here to the biblical "an eye for an eye and a tooth for a tooth," and the fact that eyes and teeth in psychoanalysis are understood as phallic substitutes (169). He raises the following hypothesis, which we touched on earlier:

> According to this hypothesis, the sexual crime would first be, in a manner at once paradigmatic and archaic, the very mainspring of talionic law, the essence or the element of every crime and every punishment, of every castigation, of every castigating exchange in general. This is because the essence of crime, its quasi-transcendental mainspring or motivation, would be what is called—at any age, at the time of the desire, or at the time of the act—sex. (169)[41]

In the talionic law, we thus appear to again come across the stricture of *différance*, the death drive, pleasure, with all their abyssal detours. The penal justice of Kant, as Derrida (184 n29) points out in line with this stricture, specifically in relation to the death penalty, serves no purpose and is not supposed to serve any purpose; it amounts to an incalculable madness, as can be seen inter alia from the island example.[42] At stake in Kant's notion of justice can therefore in a sense be said to be a gift that gives measure or calculation, but remains foreign to the calculable (184).[43]

Progress

Reik sees a certain evolution in relation to punishment over time from retribution or vengeance (that is, the talionic law, which is closely tied to the unconscious) toward prevention and deterrence (Reik 1959, 290–96; Derrida 2017, 127–28). He views the latter theory of punishment as progress, as it "must be that people pre-consciously (*vorbewußt*) recognized that no deep gulf separates them from crime, that we all carry within us latently al the germs of the criminal" (Reik 1959, 291; Derrida 2017, 128). Reik acknowledges the need for punishment, yet he raises the question as to the need for or utility of specifically legal punishment in future (Reik 1959, 293; Derrida

2017, 129). As Derrida (129–32) reads Reik (297–98), legal punishment needs to be replaced by a culture of confession and repentance, which will be more and more free and spontaneous, and psychoanalysis should play a role in the acceleration of this evolution. In Kantian language, *poena forensis* should thus be replaced by *poena naturalis*. Derrida (132–33) however points out that with this movement toward *poena naturalis*, the *ius talionis*, for which Reik (290) criticizes Kant, would still dominate. Reik's solution does not therefore provide a break with the circular economy of the unconscious, unless one engages in a deconstructive reading of Reik's text, specifically by looking closely at the notions of "progress" and "development" that are employed there (Reik 1959, 296–98; Derrida 2017, 129–32, 227–28).

Reik (296) speaks in the latter regard of "a growing tendency toward the elimination of punishment" and that psychoanalysis endeavors to "advance this psychological development [*steht im Dienste dieser psychischen Entwicklung*]." As Derrida (179 n23) points out, there is something strange about this assertion of progress and the need for psychoanalysis to participate in this development, because Reik (290) at the same time views the principle of revenge as completely in line with the principle of the talionic law operating in the unconscious.[44] What therefore drives this progress, why seek to advance it, and in the name of what should this advancement take place (Derrida 2017, 130)? A clue is for Derrida to be found in Reik's (292) depiction of the unconscious as not knowing much caution. This understanding of the unconscious appears to be at odds or in tension with Reik's (425) depiction of the unconscious as not being acquainted with gratefulness/thanks or forgiveness/mercy. This lack of caution of the unconscious, as Derrida (129) points out, poses both a threat and a chance: "The unconscious is the chance that causes things to befall, to fall at the wrong moment, or to fall at the right moment, as the chance may be. Always the enigma of the calculation of the incalculable." Kant likewise believed in the progress of humanity, and he saw the French Revolution as a sign of such progress. Derrida's analysis in volume two of the Death Penalty seminars in this respect focuses on *The Conflict of the Faculties* where Kant (1979, 151) refers to the French Revolution as an event (*Begebenheit*), which is not to be viewed "as the cause of history but only as an intimation, a historical sign [*als hindeutend, als Geschichtszeichen*] (*signum rememorativum, demonstrativum, prognostikon*)." Kant is inquiring here into an experience of the human race, which, as event, demonstrates the tendency of the human race viewed in its entirety to proceed toward its own improvement in a moral sense, specifically the giving of a republican constitution to itself. At stake here is thus a certain "disposition" and "capacity" in humanity "to be the cause of its own advance toward the better, and (since this should be the act of a being endowed with freedom), toward the human race as being the author of this advance" (Kant 1979, 151; Derrida 2017, 202). Derrida (201) however reads this passage as involving something more than a power or possibility. The passage seems to refer to a peculiar sign that does not point to anything present or presently existing; it is thus not a sign of any being, but of nothing, of no thing, which reminds us that there is some future and a progress to come. The event, which the "sign" refers to, therefore does not happen or arrive in the present; it arrives in another way, and remains to come; it comes to pass "as promise and reminder" (201). This can be understood in view of Kant's perception of the Revolution as having been a failure, as it ended in the Terror (201). Kant, in Derrida's reading, was filled with both horror and enthusiasm[45] regarding the "event" of the French Revolution. As Derrida (204) puts it, the Revolution "at once destroyed law, cruelly threw the foundation (*Grund*) of law into the abyss (*Abgrund*) by executing the sovereign and generating the Terror, at once, then, destroyed the law and established the law, killed and resuscitated it again, refounded and recalled it, the law of a free people and the rights of man."

In the Seminars, Derrida (2014c, 179–80) links Kant's statements in the essay "An Answer to the Question: What Is Enlightenment?" on the Enlightenment, that is, that the time in which he lived was not as yet an enlightened age (*afgeklärter Zeitalter*), but an age of enlightenment (*Zeitalter der Aufklärung*), with the abolition of the death penalty, which Kant of course (in the age in which he lived) opposed in the name of human dignity. The Enlightenment could in other words be another name for this "progress" in relation to the abolition of the death penalty, especially if linked to another conception of dignity. Derrida (180) points here to Kant's (1996a, 8:42) statement at the end of the Enlightenment essay about governments finding that "they can themselves profit by [or 'have an interest in'—*zuträglich findet*] treating man, who is henceforth *more than a machine*, in a manner appropriate to his dignity." This passage can be read as envisaging the abolition of the death penalty, taking account of what Kant (1996b, 6:435; 1997b, 4:435) says elsewhere about dignity, that is, it speaks of the human being's value as being beyond calculable interest, beyond measure, value, and price, and of the human being as an end in him- or herself. In both Reik and Kant we therefore find a belief in progress that Derrida (2017, 171–72), in answer to Reik, ties to a force beyond the economic exchange of the unconscious, that is, to the impossible, hospitality, the gift, forgiveness, and a radical forgetting as condition of possibility. This same force finds expression in Kant as an abyssal event that is not fully present, and that remains to come.[46]

Calculating with the Incalculable

How should law, which is inevitably conditional and calculating, respond to the challenge posed by Derrida to take account of the unconscious and of the symptom in relation to specifically criminal law with respect to act, desire, and age? What should, in other words, in view of Derrida's analysis, happen with the basic principles, concepts, and stratagems of criminal law: *actus reus*, *mens rea*, punishment? How should the modern constitution, which, as we saw, sets the limits within which criminal law operates, be read in view of Derrida's analysis? Let us at this point look again at some of the more specific questions raised in Derrida's analysis under the headings of responsibility and punishment: First, *responsibility*—How can someone be found guilty of a crime if it cannot be proved that the person had the requisite freedom to decide what to do in the circumstances, that is, if there indeed is no such thing as freedom in the traditional Kantian sense; if we can never be sure that we are capable of or have in fact acted responsibly; and if the age of a person always consists of a variety of ages? Shifting the focus, how is the notion of guilt accompanying the crime reconcilable with a radically forgotten guilt because of a "sexual desire," which we all share and are subject to?; if the wrongdoer, by committing a crime, in fact is confessing to a guilt that existed beforehand?; if the wrongdoer seeks hetero-punishment so as to obtain relief from an overbearing sense of guilt?; when we all harbor aggressive and murderous thoughts, at least in the unconscious? Second, *punishment*—How can we continue to impose punishment as a society, if this is inevitably motivated by a cruel, sovereign drive?; if the notion of punishment (especially the death penalty) is intricately tied to political theology, to bloody sacrifice, to the instinct of self-preservation of a society? (Reik 1959, 290). How do we measure punishment in a justifiable way, when it involves a calculation with the incalculable? Third, with respect to *both* responsibility *and* punishment—Is a break possible with the circle of economic exchange that so clearly characterizes criminal law, making the latter an active part of the circle, being invoked by wrongdoers, as well as by the public in general, who seek punishment in its variety of forms

Crime, Punishment, and Forgiveness | 123

(auto-, hetero, yet unavoidably cruel)? These are uncomfortable questions that challenge the very foundations of criminal law, both its assumptions and its justice.

Seeking to minimize the cruelty of punishments (abolition of the death penalty and corporal punishment, prison reforms, alternatives to incarceration, etc.), under the influence of human rights declarations, are undoubtedly progressive advances.[47] Even more so would be the replacement of hetero-punishment with confession, with auto-punishment, as Reik (297–98) proposes. We already see isolated examples of the latter in the Truth and Reconciliation process of a country like South Africa, where legal punishment was for a period suspended on the condition of a full disclosure of all the relevant facts relating to the (political) crime, as well as in the "confessions" by heads of state or heads of government of atrocities committed in the past of a nation (Derrida 2001c, 28–32; 2001e, 25–26). With attempts to minimize cruelty, with "amnesty," subject to certain conditions, and serving the aim of "national reconciliation," as well as confessions that serve certain political and economic interests, we however remain within the circle of economic exchange, of "forgiveness" viewed in economic (Reikian) terms. "In principle," as Derrida (2001c, 27) notes, "there is no limit to forgiveness, no measure, no moderation, no 'to what point?'" At stake in this unconditional forgiveness is, as we saw, something excessive, mad, hyperbolic (Derrida 2001c, 39), something that lies beyond the space of the legal order, beyond punishment and penalty, beyond legal calculation, even beyond the sovereign power to pardon (Derrida 2001c, 39, 45; 2001e, 25, 33). Forgiveness in this unconditional sense goes beyond the reciprocity implied by repentance, atonement, reconciliation, and confession (Derrida 2001e, 27–29). Today, in the twenty-first century, we still live in the age of Enlightenment, which is also the age of deconstruction, the age in which sovereignty is increasingly showing signs of dissolution (abolition of the death penalty in a majority of countries in the world, the prosecution of and limits placed on the powers of presidents). We see a certain (Kantian) "progress" here, a (Reikian) "advance," which signals the end of criminal law, of punishment, and thereby also of the ordinary course of historic temporality (Reik 1959, 296; Kant 1979, 151). It is in the name of the (French) Revolution, the (Kantian) Enlightenment, as an event that remains to come, in the name of an uneconomical and unconditional forgiveness, in the name of absolute hospitality, the perfect gift, justice, that criminal law reform must be accelerated, that is, economic exchange should be broken with, to become more hospitable, forgiving, giving. A negotiation is in other words called for between the unconditional and the conditional (Derrida 2001d, 58). This demand remains a categorical imperative, even though law may never be able to escape from economic circularity.

Chapter 6

Perpetual Peace

We saw in the "Introduction" how human dignity has, especially after World War II, come to play a foundational role in national, transnational, and international legal orders with the aim of securing peace. It is generally acknowledged that Kant's thinking had a significant influence in this development. We further saw in chapter 3 that Kant lay the foundations of freedom in the *Critique of Pure Reason*, which is closely tied to the moral law. In his politico-legal writings he explores the implications of freedom and the moral law for the modern constitution as well as the international and cosmopolitan legal orders. Today Kant's politico-legal texts continue to play an important role in the development of global or multilevel constitutionalism. A central essay in this regard is Kant's "Toward Perpetual Peace," which is the main focus of the current chapter.

Kant's 1795 essay *Zum ewigen Frieden* was published shortly after the conclusion of the treaty of Basel on April 5, 1795, between the revolutionary French republic and monarchic Prussia.[1] In terms of this treaty, all territory to the west of the Rhine was ceded by Prussia to France.[2] Kant's essay can be read as responding to this treaty and its implications, as well as to the debates at the time about the possible ways of securing peace between European powers.[3] These debates related inter alia to the question of whether peace could be achieved between monarchies or only between republican states, as well as the possibility of establishing a federation of European states (Krause 2013, 11). Apart from the historical context, it is also important to note that Kant's essay follows after his three Critiques, and it therefore needs to be read in line with the insights developed there with respect to especially practical reason (Rimoux 2015, 16–17; chapters 1–3 of this volume).

We saw in earlier chapters that, according to Kant, before the establishment of a civil condition (*bürgerlichen Zustand*) that regulates the scope and protection of everyone's external freedom, human beings find themselves in a state of nature and thus in a potential state of irresolvable conflict with others. Practical reason prescribes that the state of nature be transcended and that a civil condition regulated by public law (a republican constitution) be established. Here the external freedom of each individual is limited by general laws so as to be compatible with the freedom of others (Kant 1996b, 6:230–31). The public law so established can also be enforced. The freedom of the individual, even when secured within a republican state, however remains threatened by the lawless state of nature within which sovereign states still find themselves. For Kant, reason stands opposed to war, and in the Perpetual Peace essay he therefore makes a number of proposals—as dictated by reason—to secure peace between sovereign states by way of public law.

The essay "Toward Perpetual Peace" itself takes the literary form of a peace treaty[4] and consists of a preface, six preliminary articles, three definitive articles, as well as two supplements and two appendixes.[5] Kant's prescriptions in the preliminary articles respond specifically to the political conditions existing at the end of the eighteenth century. These prescriptions include a definition of peace as perpetual, with the consequence that a temporary armistice or halting of hostilities would not be valid as a peace treaty; the gradual abolition of all standing armies; a prohibition in relation to existing states being inherited, exchanged, purchased, or offered as gifts; the prohibition of states incurring debt with respect to the waging of war; the prohibition of states interfering with the internal affairs of other states; and the prohibition of certain actions during the waging of war so as not to make future peace impossible.[6] These actions include assassination, poisoning, breach of agreements, and the instigation of treason. In the definitive articles, Kant prescribes a republican constitution containing a separation of powers so as to secure the autonomy of individuals.[7] However, as noted previously, wars between states still pose a threat to such autonomy. On the level of international law (the law of nations), Kant therefore prescribes a voluntary and ever-expanding association of states (the nature of which is, as we will see, contested) to secure peace. With respect to cosmopolitan law,[8] which Kant understood as the law relating to human beings and to states as world citizens (*Weltbürgerrecht*), he prescribes a limited right of foreign visitors to be treated with hospitality in the states they visit.[9]

Derrida engages with Kant's essay on Perpetual Peace in a great number of his published texts as well as in a number of interviews. He focuses specifically on the preface, the first preliminary article where Kant gives a definition of peace, as well as on the definitive articles where Kant prescribes the essential conditions for securing peace with respect to international law and cosmopolitan law. Derrida's discussion of Kant's essay on Perpetual Peace in the texts referred to earlier is mostly to be found within the context of a discussion of hospitality. The latter concept, as Derrida analyzes it, has been extensively commented on in the literature,[10] whereas less attention thus far has been given to Derrida's discussion of Kant's notion of perpetual peace as well as to the relation between hospitality and perpetual peace. In what follows, Derrida's analysis of Kant's essay is discussed with the aim of rethinking the notion of peace and its implications for international law and cosmopolitan law, presuming for the moment that these can and should still be regarded as separate categories or fields of law.

Preface

The preface of Kant's "Toward Perpetual Peace" starts with a reference to the "satirical inscription" on the signboard of a Dutch innkeeper, which reads "Toward Perpetual Peace [*Zum ewigen Frieden*]," along with the picture of a graveyard. Derrida discusses the preface of Kant's essay inter alia in *Adieu*, where Emmanuel Levinas's texts are the main focus. Here Derrida comments on a certain intersection between Kant and Levinas. In *Totality and Infinity*, Levinas (1969, 306) appears to allude to Kant's preface when he notes that "peace therefore cannot be identified with the end of combats that cease for want of combatants, by the defeat of some and the victory of the others, that is, with cemeteries or future universal empires." Similarly, in the preface to *Totality and Infinity*, Levinas (22) condemns the peace of empires, which would be achieved through war (Derrida 1999a, 97). In his discussion of this Kantian-Levinasian intersection, Derrida (100) emphasizes the fact that the signboard, referred to in Kant's preface, belongs to an innkeeper (*Gastwirt*) who takes in guests and gives them shelter, in other words, to someone who offers hospitality. The reader is thus welcomed already at the start of the text "under the sign of a sign of hospitality"

(100). This signboard at the same time could be read as attesting to the wit or the ill humor of the innkeeper and thus serve as an introductory warning addressed to the reader. The words on the signboard serve at the same time as the title of Kant's essay,[11] and Derrida (100) points out that the title thereby announces a place (a refuge, the inn) and at the same time "promises, greets, dedicates: *Zum Ewigen Frieden* ('to or toward perpetual peace' or 'for perpetual peace')." Derrida (100) reads Kant's preface as "the ambiguous promise of a perpetual or eternal peace," which, as we will also see later, he equates with "the equivocal or hypocritical promise of a hospitality without restriction." The preface, Derrida further notes, warns us against the confusion between two types of peace: that of the refuge and that of the cemetery. Kant (1996a, 8:343) issues this "warning" in the following words: "It may be left undecided whether this satirical inscription on a certain Dutch innkeeper's signboard picturing a graveyard was to hold for human beings in general, or for heads of state in particular, who can never get enough of war, or only for philosophers, who dream that sweet dream." In Derrida's reading, Kant in the Preface rejects the peace of the cemetery, which he associates with the actions of heads of state, and he also rejects the "sweet dream" of the pacific philosopher (100–1).[12] This dream amounts to "an idealistic and impotent utopia, an oneiric irenism" (101). Kant proposes in response to these two alternatives, as Derrida (101) puts it, "a law and cosmopolitics of hospitality" consisting of "a set of rules and contracts, an interstate conditionality that limits . . . the very hospitality it guarantees."

Kant's preface appears to be alluded to again by Derrida in *Of Hospitality* (Derrida and Dufourmantelle 2000, 121–31), in "Hostipitality" (2006c, 208), and in *Adieu* (1999a, 43). In all three of these texts, Derrida reads Kant's "Toward Perpetual Peace" together with Klossowski's *Roberte ce Soir*. At stake in the latter text is also a certain "signboard," here in the form of handwritten pages under glass and framed, which the uncle of the narrator had placed above the bed in the spare room, kept for visitors. These "laws of hospitality" read as follows:

> The master of the house, having no greater nor more pressing concern than to shed the warmth of his joy at evening upon whomever comes to dine at his table and to rest under his roof from a day's wearying travel, waits anxiously at the gate for the stranger he will see appear like a liberator upon the horizon. And catching a first glimpse of him in the distance, though he be

still far off, the master will call out to him, "Come in quickly, my happiness is at stake." (Klossowski 2002, 12)

This text of Klossowski, in Derrida's reading, speaks of unconditional hospitality, that is, of the host becoming the guest, and the guest becoming the host of the host, of the guest welcoming and inviting the host in his own home; and moreover of the host becoming the hostage of the guest, and thus relinquishing his own sovereignty.[13] This is all made possible by woman (here, in the figure of Roberte, the aunt of the narrator) being there first (Derrida 1999a, 43). As we will see in the discussion that follows, something similar is at stake in Levinas's texts, also in the latter respect, when he speaks of the feminine being in terms of a pre-originary welcome and as the welcome par excellence, as well as in Derrida's reading of the rest of Kant's essay on perpetual peace. In the preface to Kant's essay, a link is in other words already established between peace, which Kant reserves for the living, and hospitality. Is this simply a conditional hospitality, or can it, similar to the hospitality in the texts of Klossowski and Levinas, be understood as unconditional in nature?

Defining Peace

The first preliminary article of Kant's essay on Perpetual Peace reads as follows: "No conclusion of peace that secretly reserves issues for a future war shall be held valid [*Es soll kein Friedensschluß für einen solchen gelten, der mit dem geheimen Vorbehalt des Stoffs zu einem künftigen Kriege gemacht worden*]." Kant (1996a, 8:343) explains that in such a case "it would be a mere truce, a suspension of hostilities, not *peace*, which means the end of all hostilities [*ein bloßer Waffenstillstand, Aufschub der Feindseligkeiten, nicht* Friede, *der das Ende aller Hostilitäten bedeutet*]." Derrida (1999a, 85–86) starts his analysis of this preliminary article, which he connects with Kant's introduction to the definitive articles, by noting that war and peace cannot in Kant's essay (or in general) simply be opposed to each other. In both Kant, and in Levinas, as we will see, one of the two terms of the "opposition" becomes originary, with inevitable consequences for any supposed symmetry. Derrida refers in this respect to Kant's statement that the state of nature (*Naturstand, status naturalis*) is a state of war (*ein Zustand des Krieges*), noting that Kant thus views war as natural, or, as Derrida (86) also puts it, "everything in nature begins with war." With respect to peace, Kant notes that it has to be formally instituted or established *(muß also gestiftet werden)*. Peace is thus for Kant not natural, but institutional and therefore juridical-political.[14] Peace, as is clear from the preliminary article and Kant's commentary, is furthermore not simply the cessation of hostilities, the abstention from war, or armistice. Kant insists that it has to be instituted as *perpetual* peace. The word "perpetual" or "eternal," as Derrida (86) notes, is not here to be understood as a utopia,[15] as an empty word, or as a supplementary predicate attached to peace. Kant contends that by the nature of the concept itself, peace of necessity has to be eternal. If peace is made with war or hostility remaining a possibility in the future, there would be no peace (Derrida 1999a, 86–87).[16] This may mean that peace in the strict sense could never be attained, as, according to Kant, "a threat of war, a simple pressure—whether symbolic, diplomatic, or economic—is enough to interrupt the peace" (Derrida 1999a, 88). Derrida (88) understands the prohibitions attached to this conception of peace as including potential or virtual hostility, and adds that "every virtual allergy,[17] whether unconscious or radically forbidden, [would be] contradictory to peace." Peace as elaborated by Kant (as eternal) can thus be understood as beyond political peace, even though Kant here prescribes the juridical-political as remedy (87).[18] Eternal peace in Kant can in other words be understood as both political and beyond the political, showing that the concept of the political is not adequate to itself (87).[19] From this it also follows that (Kantian) institutional peace is both pure and impure, containing within itself both the promise of an eternal peace and at the same time the trace of a threat, the threat of war (Derrida 1999a, 89; Kant 1996a, 8:349).

To further understand what is at stake in the notion of eternal peace and its relation to war, we have to turn to Derrida's reading of Levinas in *Adieu*. Derrida (1999a, 19–20) here explores the relation between an ethics of hospitality, to be found, for example, in Levinas's texts, with a law or a politics of hospitality, to be found, for example, in Kant's texts.[20] Derrida focuses here on the Levinasian notion of a "pre-originary declaration of peace,"[21] and Derrida (48–49) speaks in this respect of "an extremely complex relation with the Kantian legacy." At first sight there seems to be a great difference between these two authors regarding how they understand peace, but Derrida (87, 96–97) ultimately concludes that they can be read as saying something very similar, or at least as being not too far apart despite their differences.[22] One can perhaps say that Derrida reads Levinas along with Kant so as to open up another reading of Kant in line with Levinas's thinking. For Levinas, peace is not natural, institutional, or politico-legal (90). We saw earlier that this can to a certain extent also be said of Kant's conception of peace. Levinas (2007a, 195) suggests in this regard that perhaps "peace is a concept that goes beyond purely political thought." In Derrida's reading of Levinas, which is again to similar effect as his reading of Kant, this implies a division or partition in the concept of peace: "in sum, without being at peace with itself, such a concept of peace retains a political *part*, it *participates* in the political, even if another part of it goes beyond a certain concept of the political" (Derrida 1999a, 80). For Levinas, peace furthermore precedes nature (90). The apparent difference with Kant is minimized when Kant's notion of "eternal peace" is understood, as indicated earlier, in both a politico-legal and an unconditional sense. What about the other differences? With respect to war and peace, Kant and Levinas appear to have different points of departure (49). Whereas for Kant the starting point is the natural state of war, for Levinas it is peace, of which he says there can only be an eschatology (and which is not to be understood in a teleological sense). These different points of departure are not however of cardinal importance, in view of Derrida's notion of the double bind that operates with the idea of a pre-origin and where chronology makes place for a disjuncture in time.[23] Another seeming difference between Kant and Levinas, but which ultimately amounts to the same, is that for Levinas, war would at all times still retain a trace of hospitality (88, 90).[24] War thus derives from and still testifies to hospitality, to peace (95). For Kant, as we saw earlier, peace always still contains the trace of war, which can again break out at any moment because of human nature (88).[25]

To understand more about the nature of the peace that Derrida detects in the texts of Levinas and Kant, we would have to turn to other texts of Derrida, specifically those on Freud. In "Psychoanalysis Searches the State of Its Soul: The Impossible Beyond of a Sovereign Cruelty," Derrida for example employs the language of "cruelty," of which what Levinas and Kant call "war" would be a manifestation. Derrida here discusses Freud's *Why War?*, where Freud (2001, 22:203), in discussion with Einstein, indissociably links together what he calls a cruelty drive, an aggressive drive, a hatred drive, a destructive drive, and even a death drive[26] with the drive for sovereign mastery (the "I can").[27] According to Freud, these drives cannot be eradicated, yet he seeks methods of *indirectly* diverting these drives so as to minimize the risk of war (for example, by encouraging friendship between nations) (Derrida 2002d, 271). The invocation by Freud of the "indirect," which Derrida (241, 275–77) reads as an attempt at delay or deferral, prompts him to take a step beyond Freud's text, that is, to invoke a certain beyond to these drives (as well as beyond the pleasure and reality principles), a beyond to cruelty. Freud alludes to this "beyond" in other texts, for example, "Beyond the Pleasure Principle" in his analysis of the death drive.[28] In *Without Alibi*, Derrida (254) refers to this "beyond" inter alia by way of the language of hospitality, referring to it as "a hospitality of visitation and not of invitation." Kant's solution to war, that is, juridical-(cosmo-)political peace, would thus in the language of Freud still be in close alliance with the drive for sovereign mastery and the destructive drive. At the same time, insofar as it shares certain features with Levinas's notion of a pre-originary peace, it alludes to the impossible possibility of a beyond to these drives.

The non- or beyond-political conception of peace at stake in Kant's "Toward Perpetual Peace" can also be expressed in the language of hospitality, which Derrida analyzes with reference to Levinas's texts in *Adieu*, and which is the focus of the section that follows. "To be at peace with" would in other words involve the extension of an unconditional welcome to some other, for example, another state, nation, or group (Derrida 1999a, 85). As we saw earlier, peace understood thus would involve both a promise and a threat. It would go hand in hand with an abdication of (the drive for) sovereignty. Eternal peace, similar to unconditional hospitality, may not be possible, yet it remains an absolute and immediate imperative. It does not invoke a stability that has been attained or that can be attained or infinitely approximated, but a peace that is called for urgently and that needs to be continually negotiated and thus invented.[29] In "Hostipitality," Derrida (2006c, 213) speaks in this respect of peace as involving "a promise of indefinite, and therefore eternal, renewal." This is an imperative that places a demand on all states as well as associations of (free) states, even though, ultimately, they can only condition peace, in the same way that they can only limit hospitality, refuge, and asylum (Derrida 1999a, 89–90). Lest this demand be understood as conditioned by (the chance of) reciprocity, Levinas (1969, 306) insists that "peace must be my peace."[30] This promise and/or imperative is moreover to be heard against the background of the classical concept of war, understood in the first place as interstate war, but also as civil war and partisan war, with the nation-state as its focus, losing its pertinence today (Derrida 2003, 100–7; 2005c, 123–24). The "wars" being fought today, if they can still be called such, are all "world" or "worldwide" wars. There are no more local or national wars, on the assumption that there ever were (Derrida 2011, 259). At stake in these wars is consequently also the end of the world, both in the sense of its appropriation for a specific goal, purpose, or end, and its destruction (Derrida 2005c, 155–56; 2011, 259). Derrida (2005c, 156; 2003, 101–2, 105–6) thus refers to the violence that is being unleashed today as a result of technological developments, as characterized to an ever greater extent by deterritorialization as well as by autoimmunity. The threat of total self-destruction posed by the logic of autoimmunity nevertheless at the same time gives a chance, the "perhaps" of eternal peace.

Public Law

In the *Metaphysics of Morals*, Kant (1996b, 6:355) notes that peace is the "entire final end" of the theory of law within the limits of pure reason. The path toward perpetual peace is to be pursued on three levels: constitutional law, international law, and cosmopolitan law.[31] By distinguishing between these three levels of law, Kant creates a new category of law, distinct from international law, the latter of which in his understanding only concerns the relationship between states (Walters 2004, 441, 449). The aim of the recognition of this new category is to protect the individual as belonging to a general or universal state consisting of human beings (*allgemeiner Menschenstaat*).[32] Whereas international law concerns itself directly only with states, and with individuals only indirectly in their status as state citizens, cosmopolitan law, as we saw, can be understood as concerning itself directly with human beings (as well as states) as world citizens.[33] The tendency today is however to view either international law or cosmopolitan law as all-encompassing vis-à-vis the other. One such approach would be to regard international law as broad enough to encompass the human rights norms set out in the UN Declaration and in international treaties, which can be said to have been adopted under the influence of Kant's cosmopolitan law (Tesón 1992). Another approach would be to regard classical international law, which dealt with the relation between states, as having been transformed in the twentieth century into a form of cosmopolitan law, which now concerns itself with individuals not only as state citizens, but as citizens of a politically constituted world society.[34] The existing world legal order would, in terms of the latter view, be regarded as a transitional stage from international law toward cosmopolitan law, as a still very imperfect form of cosmopolitan law (Habermas 1988, 183; 2003, 38). Derrida does not draw a rigorous distinction between these two "categories" of law.[35] He usually mentions international law by name in analyzing the structure, role, and powers of existing international institutions. In principle, he supports the attempt, through international law, particularly the United Nations, to limit state sovereignty in the name of humanitarian considerations (1994b, 104–5). At the same time, he is acutely aware of the limits of the "humanitarian," its potential abuse, the domination of international institutions by certain powerful states, which refuse to have their own sovereignty limited, and therefore the need for the reform of these institutions (Derrida 1994b, 104–6; 2006d, 261). He similarly stands ambivalent toward the idea of cosmopolitan law, which as we saw in its Kantian version is tied to the notion of hospitality, but remains subject to a variety of limits (Derrida 1999a, 87): on the one hand, he believes that the spirit of the tradition of cosmopolitan law must be cultivated, but on the other hand, as noted and as we will see later, Derrida wishes to transform the (ideal) category of cosmopolitan law. He notes in the latter respect that its limits should be adjusted today "by questioning the ways in which they have been defined and determined by the ontotheological, philosophical, and religious discourses in which this cosmopolitan ideal was formulated" (2003, 130). This attempt at transformation takes place through a reading of that which, as we saw, Kant places at the center of cosmopolitan law—hospitality—as an unconditional demand placed on public law in general. Derrida consequently calls for something beyond cosmopolitan law or a cosmopolitan constitution, and beyond international law: absolute hospitality, *khōra*, the democracy to come, or the New International.[36] This "beyond" serves as an urgent call for the transformation of the current institutions of international law as well as of the notion of and instruments to bring about world citizenship.

INTERNATIONAL LAW

Kant's second definitive article of a perpetual peace reads as follows: "The Law of Nations Shall Be Founded on a *Federation* of Free States" (Das Völkerrecht soll auf einen *Föderalism* freier Staaten gegründet seyn). In his discussion of this article, Kant states that, for the sake of their own security, each state could or should require of other states that they join a league of peoples (*Völkerbund*), which should nonetheless not be a state of peoples (*Völkerstaat*).[37] According to Kant, the latter solution would be contradictory insofar as the premise here is the law relating to peoples vis-à-vis each other (*das Recht der Völker gegen einander*). Such a single state of peoples would entail the disappearance of individual states and thus also the disappearance of international law.[38] Kant furthermore takes the view that states cannot be forced against their will to join such a league. Whereas this is indeed permissible with respect to individuals living in the state of nature (to subject themselves to public laws within a republican state), states already find themselves internally regulated by a legal constitution. States thus have no right to subject each other to a more extensive legal constitution in accordance with their own legal concepts (*Rechtsbegriffen*). As we saw earlier, reason, as the highest legislative moral power, nevertheless absolutely condemns war as legal recourse and makes the condition of peace an immediate duty. This can only be founded and secured through a treaty between states. A league of a special kind is therefore called for, which can be referred to as a league of peace (*Friedensbund, foedus pacificum*), and that does not simply seek to bring an end to a particular war as would a peace treaty (*Friedensvertrag, pactum pacis*), but to all wars. Kant insists here on states retaining their sovereignty by arguing that such a league should not, like a state would, attain any (sovereign) power of its own, and that the member states should not (like individuals in a state) be subjected to the coercion of public laws.[39] The aim of the league is the preservation and safeguarding of the freedom, that is, the sovereignty of the member states of the league. This league of states is furthermore to be extended gradually so that it eventually includes all states and thus leads to perpetual peace.

Toward the end of the discussion of the second article, Kant again raises the matter of a state of peoples (*Völkerstaat*). He refers here to such a (world) state, which would subject all individual states to public coercive laws, as the only rational way to escape from the lawless and warlike state of nature. He however immediately seems to abandon this "positive idea" of a world republic (*Weltrepublik*) because of the unwillingness of sovereign states "according to their present conception of international law" to subject themselves to such a state, and settles for the "negative surrogate" of an ever-expanding league to avert war (1996a, 8:357). With reference to Vergil's *Aeneid*,[40] Kant warns in language that reminds one of Freud (2001, 22:197–215) in *Why War?* that although such a league may halt the stream of law-defying, hostile inclination (*den Strom der rechtscheuenden, feindseligen Neigung*), the threat of its breaking out again would remain. In the First Supplement, Kant again expresses a preference for a federal coalition or association (*föderative Vereinigung*) rather than the merging of states under a universal monarchy. Laws would according to Kant lose their impact in such a large area, and the result would be a soulless despotism, eventually anarchy.

Much has been said about Kant's seeming inconsistency with respect to the alternatives of a federation of states and a world state, not only within "Toward Perpetual Peace," but also across different texts.[41] At least three readings can be detected in the literature:[42] The first and seemingly most obvious reading of the article and of Kant's discussion thereof is that Kant expresses a preference for a federation of states and that, at least in "Toward Perpetual Peace," he rejects any kind of world state.[43] This preference, it is argued, would be perfectly in line with his moral and political theory.[44] A second reading is to the effect that Kant's own arguments, for example, with respect to the state of nature, point in the direction of a world republic rather than a federation of states, which he seems to opt for.[45] For pragmatic reasons, Kant nevertheless settled for a federation of states, although reason prescribes a world state.[46] A third reading can be assembled from the analysis of a number of authors to the effect that Kant rejected only the idea of a universal monarchy,[47] in the form of a unitary state,[48] which would force other states into submission.[49] The federation of states would in terms of this reading be only a preliminary stage, and a world republic a final stage or ideal in the progression of reason.[50] This world state would have a federal, republican structure and its members, which need not be republican states, would voluntarily give up their external sovereignty as states.[51]

In his discussion of this specific article in "Toward Perpetual Peace," Derrida (2005c, 81) does not engage in a close reading of Kant, and also does not engage in any detail with the earlier-mentioned controversy. He appears to adopt the first of these readings, that is, that Kant rejects the notion of a world state and settles for a federation of sovereign states. A possible reason for Derrida's approach here might be that the most important issue for him is not so much what form of political structure Kant proposed, but instead to contemplate "something" *beyond international law and beyond the (cosmo-)political,* which corresponds with the notion of perpetual peace in the strict sense as analyzed earlier and its nonsynonymous substitutes, that is, the democracy to come, absolute hospitality, and justice beyond law. The issue for him in short is that of the relation between democracy, sovereignty, and the state. Let us first look at the issue of democracy. In this respect, Derrida (81) points out that "the democratic paradigm does not govern the tradition of Kant's treatise *Perpetual Peace*." He refers specifically to the concept of a world republic (*Weltrepublik*), which is mentioned (and as we saw, according to some, ultimately "preferred") by Kant, and notes that this "is not a democracy" (81). Derrida also refers here to Kant's statement in the second definitive article that the notion of the "majesty," or as Derrida translates it, the "sovereignty" of the people, is an absurd expression. Only a state can have sovereignty (81).[52] One can add to this Kant's comment in the first definitive article referred to earlier that democracy inevitably leads to despotism (1996a, 8:352).[53]

Derrida (2003, 115, 120, 123; 2005b, 133) categorically rejects the idea of a world state. This is most likely because of the inherent relationship between the state and sovereignty and the fact that even if such a world state were to be democratic in nature, that is, a cosmopolitan democracy, it would still involve a return to the self (Derrida 2005c, 18). Democracy as traditionally conceived, in other words, refers to the power, the force, the sovereignty of the people. This notion, Derrida (2005c, 10–12; 2009a, 66–68) contends with reference to Benveniste's analysis of hospitality, becomes possible by virtue of a circular movement toward the self, the recognition of oneself as a self, a master, a subject, a sovereign, a gathering of the self-same, which can be expressed by the notion of *ipseity*. From the latter is derived the (democratic) idea of giving oneself one's own law as well as the idea of the sovereignty of the state, the monarch, and the people (Derrida 2005c, 10–12).[54] A major concern for Derrida is the problematic nature of the notion of self-identity. He shows, for example in his reading of Husserl, Heidegger, and Freud that the self is instead divided in itself and haunted by a force of self-destruction (De Ville 2011a, 13–37; chapter 3 of this volume). In the earlier analysis of the concept of hospitality, we similarly saw how hospitality "radically" places in question and exposes the subject, that is, makes of the subject or of the host a hostage. In *Rogues*, Derrida (24–41) likewise shows that there is a certain indetermination and freedom at the heart of the concept of democracy, as well as a force of self-destruction or autoimmunity. The notion of the "democracy to come" gives expression to this lack of essence of the concept of democracy (chapter 3).

What would the notion of democracy to come entail in the context of interstate and trans-state relations? Derrida (2003, 134; 2005c, 84, 88, 92–93) describes the democracy to come in various terms, which tie in very closely with the notions of perpetual peace and unconditional hospitality: as beyond meaning, as a *demos* without *kratos* and thus without sovereignty, as the impossible, as unconditional, as a promise, as event, as in alliance with a justice beyond law, as a self-destructive, autoimmune force, in terms of an absolute and unconditional urgency, and as "what is most undeniably *real*." Derrida (2005c, 83–85; 2003, 133–35) thereby seeks to clearly distinguish the democracy to come from the Kantian regulative idea, the latter involving the following of a rule and thus a question of knowledge, possibility (some "I can"), that is, some ideal possible that is indefinitely deferred. In contrasting the democracy to come with cosmopolitanism, Derrida refers to the democracy to come as preceding the state, citizenship, and the cosmos. At stake here for Derrida (2003, 130) is "what lets singular beings (anyone) 'live together' there where they are not yet defined by citizenship, that is, by their condition as lawful 'subjects' in a state or as legitimate members of a nation-state or even of a confederation or world state."[55] He speaks in this regard of an "alliance beyond the 'political,'" which would stand up against injustice (1994b, 106–7; 2003, 130).[56] It is in other words ultimately a question of unconditional hospitality, of excluding no one (Derrida 2005c, 86). It calls for equal treatment in an absolute sense as well as for the recognition of the freedom and dignity of everyone, also by providing those in need with the basic necessities of life (Derrida 1994b, 106; 1995d, 86; 2005c, 86). It remains in close alliance with the idea of human rights, while it continues to question this tradition with its inherent limitations (Derrida 2003, 132–33).[57]

The democracy to come, alongside unconditional hospitality, perpetual peace, and justice (heterogeneous to law), calls urgently for the political transformation of international law, and would continue to place in question the limits of any transformation and democratization of international institutions. Derrida's criticism of the existing structure of international law and his proposals for change should be understood as so inspired. He argues in this respect, not that different from other scholars,[58] for the transformation of international law, for example, through the extension of international law to include "the *worldwide* economic and social field" (1994b, 105–6).[59] This would require reforms to, inter alia the WTO, the IMF, and the OECD, to bring an end to their domination by certain powerful states and interests.[60] He furthermore criticizes the takeover of other international institutions by powerful nation-states and capitalist interests, as well as the selective enforcement of and limits imposed on human rights (1994b, 104; 2009b, 125–27). He expresses his support for the extension of human rights through international treaties as well as for the creation of the International Criminal Court, which places significant restrictions on state sovereignty (2003, 132–33; 2005c, 87–88). Derrida further argues in favor of moving the UN headquarters from New York (2006a, 410; 2006b, 305; 2007b, 23) and calls for the strengthening of international law and its institutions by way of the granting of autonomous powers of enforcement to a reformed Security Council and International Court of Justice (2002b, 385; 2003, 114–15; 2006a, 410). At stake here for Derrida is the question of the unity between law and force, which Kant insisted on (2002c, 47;

2002d, 251; 2005c, 93). This has to be coupled with the democratization of international institutions, seeing that the political no longer has a "place," and can therefore today less than ever before be restricted to the state (Derrida 2009b, 121). There is in other words a need for the creation of an international juridico-political space, which, although not completely doing away with sovereignty—a concept that is necessarily linked to an enemy (Derrida 2009a, 77)—continuously invents new forms of distribution and sharing of sovereignty as a condition of peace (Derrida 2002d, 251; 2005c, 87; 2009b, 129).

Cosmopolitan Law

Kant's third definitive article of a perpetual peace reads as follows: "*Cosmopolitan law shall be limited to conditions of general or universal hospitality*" (*Das* Weltbürgerrecht *soll auf Bedingungen der allgemeinen* Hospitalität *eingeschränkt sein*). In elaborating on this article, Kant lays down a right for every person to present him- or herself to another state so as to enter into relations with the native inhabitants.[61] Sovereignty however remains in place, as a state can as a rule refuse permission for such a visit, unless this would lead to the demise (*Untergang*) of the person concerned. A visitor may furthermore not be treated with hostility as long as he or she behaves in a peaceful manner. A certain reciprocity is thus at stake here in the offering of hospitality (Höffe 2006, 140). Kant nevertheless specifies that this is not a right to be treated as guest (*Gastrecht*), that is, for the visitor to take up residence, but only a right to visit (*Besuchsrecht*), which everyone is entitled to offer.[62] Kant derives this right to visit from natural law, more specifically from the common possession by mankind of the surface of the earth, which as a globe limits the possibilities of dispersion. In view of this right, there is thus a need for mutual toleration (*sich doch neben einander dulden müssen*), and Kant condemns inter alia the inhospitable actions of those living in coastal areas who plunder ships and enslave stranded seafarers as well as the actions of the colonial powers at the time who, on the pretext of visiting them, conquer foreign territories. At stake in this article is thus a limited right to visit that Kant ties to world citizenship, a form of citizenship that is complimentary to state citizenship (Rimoux 2015, 120; Höffe 2006, 140, 201).

In defining this article, Kant seems to have drawn upon both the ancient idea of cosmopolitanism to be found in the Stoics and St. Paul, and the modern tradition of international law as elaborated on at the time in

Vattel's Law of Nations (1758) (Rimoux 2015, 114).[63] In his commentary on this article, Derrida (2001c, 17–18) also links the right to hospitality and the notion of cosmopolitanism as elaborated on by Kant to another source: that of the Biblical Cities of Refuge. Derrida refers here specifically to Levinas's commentary on the cities of refuge, which ties in closely with his own analysis. In chapter 3 of Beyond the Verse ("Cities of Refuge"), Levinas contends that the biblical passages that relate to cities of refuge make it clear that there is no absolute distinction between causing the death of someone intentionally (subjectively) or through negligence (objectively).[64] The cities of refuge were nevertheless created for the latter category, to provide for temporary refuge against the avenger "with heated heart" (although no crime was committed, such vengeance was not prohibited) until the high priest of the city of refuge dies (Levinas 2007a, 39). Levinas (40) extends this reasoning to the twentieth century and the high standard of living enjoyed in general by those in the West and the (unintentional) suffering this causes elsewhere. He raises the question of whether "these advantages, one thing leading to another, are not the cause, somewhere, of someone's agony?" (40) As Derrida (1999a, 108) points out in commenting on these passages, Levinas reminds us

> that there is no real discontinuity between voluntary and involuntary murder. Sometimes invisible, always to be deciphered, this continuity forces us to infinitize our responsibility: we are also responsible for our lack of attention and for our carelessness, for what we do neither intentionally nor freely, indeed, for what we do unconsciously—since this is never without significance. Further on, there appears a more radical formulation: "there would be only one race of murderers, whether the murder is committed involuntarily or intentionally."[65]

According to Levinas (52), the cities of refuge are indeed a progression, a political and legal civilization, where subjective innocence is protected and objective guilt is forgiven. It is to be preferred to a condition where "men are ready to swallow each other alive." Levinas nevertheless expresses the view that the cities of refuge are still to be surpassed by the earthly Jerusalem, where a new humanity will show itself, where there will be a more conscious consciousness, where there will be absolute vigilance, complete justice, a new attentiveness to the other, no avengers of blood, and not even the negligent or accidental causing of death.[66] In his reading of Levinas's

"Cities of Refuge," Derrida (1999a, 105–6) reminds the reader of the fact that Jerusalem is spoken of in the Bible as a woman, and thereby links what Levinas says here to absolute hospitality, that is, of the feminine being as the welcoming par excellence.[67]

Kant's third definitive article is the focus of a number of Derrida's published texts and interviews. In "Hostipitality," Derrida (2006c, 209) notes that in the wording of Kant's article, the question of conditional and unconditional hospitality already presents itself. He further notes that two words are highlighted by Kant in this article, as can be seen from the earlier quotation: cosmopolitan law [*Weltbürgerrecht*] and hospitality [*Hospitalität*]. The question of hospitality to be addressed here, as Derrida (209) points out, is thus a question of law, and not of ethics or politics. The article prescribes and anticipates the adoption of a treaty between states to establish the conditions of a cosmopolitan law (209). Kant speaks here of general or universal hospitality (*allgemeinen Hospitalität*), the latter word being of Latin origin, as Derrida notes. He describes this origin as "troubling" because—as shown by the analysis of Benveniste (1973, chapter 7)—it carries its own contradiction (*hostis*: guest, enemy, stranger) within itself. The word "hospitality," Derrida further notes, carries within itself this undesirable guest. This remark ties in with our earlier discussion, where we saw that in absolute or unconditional hospitality, the host becomes the hostage of the guest, as well as the close relation that exists between hostility/war and hospitality/peace.[68] Derrida notes in addition that Kant translates the word hospitality as *Wirtbarkeit* (landlord, host). With reference to Kant's insistence that at stake here is a question of law (*Recht*) and not philanthropy, Derrida (209–10) points out that this does not mean that the right (to be treated with hospitality) should be misanthropic or an-anthropic. This right is a human right, which raises the question of the anthropocentric limits of the right of hospitality extended here. He in other words raises the question of offering hospitality to the stranger as god (as in the Bible), as animal, and as plant (210). At least two limits thus already appear here: the right to hospitality at stake here is limited to a question of law, and it is to be restricted to human beings (210; chapter 4 of this volume).

With respect to Kant's comment that hospitality "means the right of a stranger not to be treated with hostility when he arrives on someone else's territory," Derrida (210) notes the opposition posited here by Kant between hospitality and hostility, which we also came across earlier in the analysis of the relation between war and peace, as well as in the reference to the etymological origin of the word "hospitality." As noted, Kant refers to *Wirtbarkeit* as the equivalent of hospitality, and Derrida in view thereof proceeds to explore words closely related to *Wirtbarkeit*, such as *Wirt*, *wirtlich*, *Wirtshaus*, and *Wirtschaft*. He comments that all these words point to another limitation on the hospitality to be offered in this article, that is, they point to an owner, landlord, or master who determines the conditions of the welcome or the gift to be offered in his house, inn, café, cabaret, restaurant, hotel, city, or state (210–11). There can under these circumstances be no unconditional welcome (210). Kant, as Derrida (1999a, 87) points out, continues to impose further limits on the hospitality offered: the stranger may be turned away if this does not cause his death; as long as he behaves in a peaceful manner, he should not be treated with hostility; the right to be treated with hospitality is not a right to be treated as a guest, but only a right to visit (*Es ist kein Gastrecht . . . sondern ein Besuchsrecht*)—the stranger in other words does not have the right of residence, unless there is an agreement in place to this effect between states. The latter limitation, Derrida (1999a, 87; 2001c, 22) notes, makes the right of residence subject to the sovereignty of states and something that can be extended only to state citizens.

A further limitation of hospitality appears from Kant's derivation of the right to hospitality as a right to visit from "a right to the earth's surface which the human race shares in common." As Derrida (2001c, 20–21) points out, this implies that the right of hospitality does not extend to what is built on, erected, or constructed on the earth's surface, or to what sets itself up above the soil. The state, habitat, culture, and institution are not unconditionally accessible to newcomers. This can be contrasted with Levinas's analysis of the territory on which a nation resides, as not natural, but allotted, entrusted, or assigned, and which the national occupant therefore cannot possess or own. "The earth," Derrida (1999a, 93) notes in commenting on this analysis, "gives hospitality before all else, a hospitality already offered to the initial occupant, a temporary hospitality granted to the *hôte*, even if he remains the master of the place. He thus comes to be received in "his" own home."[69] A final limitation appears from Kant's statement that the peaceful relations between continents should eventually be regulated by public laws, thereby bringing the human race ever closer to a cosmopolitan constitution. As Derrida (1997a, 105–6; 1999a, 87) notes, universal or unconditional hospitality is thus to be instituted gradually and to be approached indefinitely, not approached in terms of what he elsewhere refers to as "the singular urgency of a *here and now*."[70]

Yet, returning again to the wording of this third definitive article, it appears that while Kant imposes a number of limitations on the hospitality to be offered to strangers, one can also catch a glimpse of a universal hospitality without limit, as "the condition of perpetual peace between all men" (Derrida 2001c, 20). In other words, only thus—by way of universal or unconditional hospitality—can (perpetual) peace in Kant's view be attained. Kant's concept of hospitality in Derrida's reading thus imposes a double or contradictory imperative, both of which are valid and remain in tension with one another: In the first place, unconditional hospitality, which would entail a welcome without reservations or calculation; an unlimited display of hospitality to the new arrival, and to those excluded in the interior, before knowledge.[71] Hospitality would furthermore not be restricted to human beings (Derrida 2002a, 363; chapter 4 of this volume). Second, conditional hospitality, which inevitably involves restrictions in order to protect one's home, property, and belongings. Conditional hospitality is thus necessary for there to be hospitality in practice. What is called for then is a negotiation between these two imperatives, an attempt to make the laws of hospitality as well as their implementation as hospitable as possible.

Peace as Absolute Hospitality

Why engage in a reading of Kant by way of Derrida in contemplating the notion of perpetual peace? Would it not be enough to simply pursue peace within multilevel constitutionalism as proposed by Kant, albeit with pragmatic adaptations within the present context, as Habermas and others have, for example, proposed? Perhaps the answer lies in a certain realism. In spite of claims to the contrary, as Derrida (1999a, 91) notes, the juridico-cosmopolitanism in Kant "could never succeed in interrupting an armed peace, peace as armistice, and with the laborious process . . . that would still organize war by other means." We should perhaps give some credit here to Schmitt, who showed already early in the twentieth century how (cosmopolitan) concepts such as humanitarianism are employed hypocritically by hegemonic nation-states in the waging of war (Schmitt 2007, 54–55; Derrida 2009a, 71–74).[72] Schmitt was particularly critical of the notion of the unjust enemy, which Kant introduces in the *Metaphysics of Morals*, as it opens the door to unlimited violence against such an enemy. This is because the enemy is in this way effectively turned into a criminal, and action against such a state is viewed as police action, as events in the twentieth century have shown (Schmitt 2006, 168–71).[73] Through such a designation, a powerful state or alliance of states claims for itself or for themselves the position of "man" (fighting for the sake of humanity, human rights, cosmopolitanism, et cetera), declares another state a "wolf," and unleashes unlimited violence against it (Schmitt 2006, 147).[74] The principles, concepts (including "peace"), and institutions of international and/or cosmopolitan law, even if democratized and provided with the necessary means of enforcement, are subject to the same risk, a risk that Kant was clearly not unaware of. This is ultimately the risk posed by the drive to sovereignty, whether of an individual, a nation-state, an empire, a world state, or even of states sharing their sovereignty under a cosmopolitan constitution. This drive, as we saw, cannot be eradicated (Derrida 2002d, 251–52). The solution does not however lie in the abandonment of the Kantian ideal of perpetual peace and its replacement with a Schmittian *grossraum*-politics or with a neoliberal imperial power imposing its vision of a global market society on the rest of the world in the name of globalization. Both these "solutions" would simply perpetuate the principle that the strongest always has right (Derrida 2005c, 12, 69–70). The answer rather lies in the recasting of the Kantian ideal, which is what is at stake in Derrida's reading of Kant. We saw in the earlier analysis how Derrida, through a reading of Kant alongside Levinas, recasts peace as absolute hospitality. Kant is thus taken seriously when he insists that peace is to be understood in a rigorous sense, even if this means having to go beyond Kant. As we saw, juridical-(cosmo-)political peace cannot suffice as peace, as it will inevitably retain sovereignty and will still amount to another manner of waging war. The transformation and democratization of international and/or cosmopolitan law will in other words inevitably only be a conditional response to the Law, the Law beyond laws, of absolute or unconditional hospitality. Peace therefore has to be understood as beyond the political, as a total exposure of the self, as absolute hospitality. The host, the subject, the sovereign, as Levinas's analysis shows, is a hostage; the host is welcomed in his or her own home, which does not belong to him or her.

Kant after Derrida

In the discussion thus far, we have engaged in a close reading of a number of Kant's texts that are foundational to modern constitutionalism. The aim of this discussion has not been in the first place to present Kant's thought in a coherent and unitary manner, but instead to look for tensions and contradictions in his texts, to find traces there of a force without economy, and thus beyond metaphysics. Kant was acknowledged as a cofounder of modern constitutionalism, and it was noted that his thinking still determines to a large extent the way we think today about inter alia justice, reason, freedom, self-government, democracy, human rights, the human-animal relation, criminal responsibility, peace, and state sovereignty. Through our reading of Heidegger and Derrida, it became clear that a question mark needs to be placed behind many of these foundational concepts and ideas because of the problematic assumptions on which they are based. These concepts and ideas are namely, in line with metaphysical thinking, conceived as returning to the self in a circular economy within modern constitutionalism. We have nevertheless become so used to these foundational concepts and ideas that attempts at questioning their assumptions often meet with fierce resistance, especially when psychoanalysis comes into the mixture. However, the injustices flowing from modern constitutionalism, such as its failure to stem inequality, conflict, exploitation, oppression, violence, and climate change, are becoming increasingly clear and undeniable. This may facilitate efforts to rethink its foundations. *Deconstructive Constitutionalism* seeks to bring to the fore the abyssal nature of the foundations of modern constitutionalism to give another, more just constitutionalism a chance. Chapters 1 to 6 of this volume have made an attempt to reread Kant with this aim in view, primarily through the lens of Derrida. As indicated, Derrida poses a radical challenge to metaphysical thinking, without illusions as to our ability to escape fully therefrom. In what follows, some of the main findings of *Deconstructive Constitutionalism* are recapped, and the discussion concludes with a few thoughts on the prospects of addressing the challenges of today.

Abyssal Foundations

Deconstructive Constitutionalism started its analysis in chapter 1 with the moral law because, as we saw, according to Kant, the legal system is derived from this law. To be able to understand fully what happens with the moral law in Derrida's reading, let us however first proceed to chapter 3, where, in the analysis of Heidegger's reading of Kant on freedom in *The Essence of Human Freedom*, we saw that Kant is able to identify the moral law because of the tendency of human beings to construct maxims for the will (Heidegger 2005, 196, 198). Kant's own formulations of the categorical imperative are in Heidegger's reading attempts at giving form to the moral law. Heidegger (197), however, points to the contingency of this attempt at formalization, which "belongs to the Age of Enlightenment, to the time of the Prussia of Frederick the Great." Heidegger consequently draws a distinction between the moral law, the "existence" of which he does not deny, and Kant's attempt to give expression to it through the categorical imperative. Heidegger thus seeks to rethink the moral law in terms of the essence of the human being, that is, in its relation with Being. In chapter 1, we saw that Derrida similarly points to the historical determination of the moral law in Kant. This is not however done in an effort to differentiate between the moral law and the categorical imperative as Heidegger seeks to do, but to take a step further back by inquiring into the "origin" of the moral law itself, primarily with reference to Freud, and specifically with reference to the death drive. At stake here is at the same time a beyond to Being. The moral law as formalized by Kant, according to Derrida, involves the limitation of this much more excessive demand of self-sacrifice, or, in Heidegger's terminology, a "binding" of the self in response to a more originary "unbinding." Derrida further describes this "law" of the moral law as imposing a duty beyond duty, as exceeding all calculation, whether conscious or unconscious, and as beyond restitution and reappropriation. At stake here can also be said to be a law or a conception of justice that precedes moral conscience and involves a certain heteronomy, an interruption or a "trembling" of the self, in contrast with the autonomy of Kantian self-legislation. The law of law disrupts subjectivity, with the subject becoming a hostage.

For Derrida, although Kant's thinking on the moral law appears to remain inscribed within a circular economy, there are indications in Kant's texts of the recognition of a more excessive demand. We see this, for example, in Kant's discussion of the impossibility of knowing whether one has complied with the duty imposed by the moral law, in his designation of the demand imposed by the moral law as "unconditional," as well as in his ascription of the characteristics of "majesty" and "severity" to the moral law. Further indications of an interruption of metaphysics can be found in Kant's notion of a feeling of respect toward the moral law, and in Kant's mention of the sacrifice of the inclinations and of pathological interests, which is required by the moral law.

What would be the implications for modern constitutionalism if it is not derived from and subject to the Kantian moral law or to human dignity as foundational value, but instead derived from and subject to a "law of law," to a law or conception of justice that precedes the moral law, a law that demands the impossible, that is, absolute hospitality, a gift without exchange, perpetual peace understood in a rigorous sense? What would be the relation between this "law of law," or justice on the one hand, and modern constitutionalism, on the other? Because of the close relation between the moral law, freedom, and reason in Kant, we arrive at these same questions when we proceed by way of reason (chapter 2) and freedom (chapter 3).

The analysis in chapter 2 focused on the principle of reason (*nihil est sine ratione*) as formulated by Leibniz. Heidegger shows that the principle can be understood in two ways: first as a statement about beings, that is, stating that everything that exists has or must have a reason for existing and for the way in which it exists. Where does this demand to render reason, however, come from? To answer this, Heidegger contends that the principle must be heard in a different tonality. Heard as such, the principle of reason speaks not only about beings, but about Being, saying that Being itself is ground-like. The demand to render reason in other words happens through the sending of Being, which itself withdraws. According to Heidegger, even though Being is ground-like, it does not have a ground, and is itself groundless. Kant's reflections on theoretical and practical reason are consequently to be understood as a response to the claim of the principle of reason, and as ultimately concerning itself with the Being of beings. Kant's transcendental method namely shows how it is possible that beings appear to us. In Kant's thinking, this happens by way of subjectivity: a being appears if it can become an object for a subject conscious of him- or herself. Kant thereby reveals the way in which beings appear in modernity: through the sending and withdrawal of Being, reason thereby being reduced to calculation. Derrida's analysis focuses specifically on this withdrawal of Being, showing that reason ultimately finds its abyssal "origin" in the gift. The demand issuing from this withdrawal of Being necessarily precedes Kantian practical (and theoretical) reason. The gift is a stranger to reason and entails a certain madness, an interruption of subjectivity. It does not involve a circular return to the self, but instead imposes a duty beyond duty, a welcoming of the other, an infinite responsibility for the death of the other.

In chapter 3, the notion of freedom in Kant was discussed. It was noted that the notion of freedom in modern constitutionalism, as Schmitt showed, precedes the state, and in the thinking of Kant is primarily conceived of as human freedom, as giving rise to mastery, autonomy, subjectivity, sovereignty, and rights. In Heidegger's reading of Kant, freedom is rethought, first by way of Kant's notion of transcendental or cosmological freedom in the *Critique of Pure Reason*, an analysis that shows that human freedom is only one instance of cosmological freedom. Heidegger further shows that Kant's *Critique of Practical Reason* involves a radicalization of freedom. Here freedom is no longer understood in terms of causality, as happens in the *Critique of Pure Reason*, or as a property of the human being. Freedom here concerns the essence of the human being and thus Being itself, which finds it abyssal ground in freedom. What comes to the fore in this rethinking of freedom, which Heidegger renames "the Free," and which is radicalized further by Nancy and Derrida, is an unforeseeable and incalculable event, without power, an exposure beyond mastery, a gift beyond Being, absolute generosity. Only here a certain "freedom" from the circularity of economic exchange is to be found.

Toward the Democracy to Come

We saw in the "Introduction" and in chapter 3 that Kant furnishes the foundations for the modern constitution through the construction of an ideal republican constitution, which is founded, by way of reason, in freedom and the moral law. The aim of this constitution is to protect external freedom through the recognition of fundamental rights and the separation of powers, and thereby further to secure peace (chapter 6). If freedom, reason, and the moral law are however reconceived, what would be the consequences for democracy as it finds expression in modern constitutionalism? Democracy is traditionally restricted to those of the same kind, that is, to brothers, those capable of autonomy and self-rule, and is characterized by calculation and reciprocity (Derrida 1997c, 20, 23). Although there was progression in this respect in the twentieth century, this model returns vividly in recent instances of authoritarian populism gaining a foothold in "democracies." What would a democracy be like beyond what Derrida refers to as its traditional phallo-paterno-filio-fraterno-ipsocentric structure, when freedom is understood as without power; as an exposure beyond mastery, sovereignty, and autonomy; as absolute generosity; as the gift beyond Being; as a welcoming of the unforeseeable event; as an opening and welcoming to the other without the expectation of a return; an opening of the self to its own destruction? At stake here, following this understanding of "freedom," would be a transformation that goes against the dominant tradition, understanding the *demos* as without *kratos*, thereby exploding and rendering meaningless democracy as an inherited concept. Democracy in this understanding would involve not simply a return to the sovereign self, but a turn against the self. The *demos* would not simply rule, but would open itself to its own destruction. Democracy would thus be recognized as containing a certain structural weakness, as well as by mutability, plasticity, and indeterminacy, as a concept without concept (chapter 3). Conceived in this way, with its allusions to the Freudian death drive, democracy can no longer be restricted to the nation-state, to human beings, or to the living. The injunction of absolute hospitality belonging to the democracy to come, precedes and at the same time undermines all the traditional limits and exclusions imposed by modern constitutionalism.

In chapter 4, the focus was on the place of non-human animals within modern constitutionalism. Here we are still, despite some positive developments, operating under the shadow of Kant, who determined the point of departure of constitutionalism as the freedom and autonomy of the human being. Human beings' differentiation from animals with respect to thinking is for Kant in *Anthropology from a Pragmatic Point of View* a determining feature, which gives them subjectivity as well as power over the animal. In the *Groundwork*, it is human beings' capacity for morality, which gives them value and dignity. For Kant, the subject of morality is in fact constituted by way of the sacrifice of his or her natural or animal inclinations. The collective self is similarly characterized by a subjection of the animal in order to attain the civil condition, which only human beings have access to. Kantian morality thus appears to be implicitly marked by an inherent cruelty, both toward the animal within the human being, and in the external treatment of the non-human animal. Today this cruelty is to be seen in an industrialized system of mass breeding and slaughter to meet the needs of "civilized" society. Granting rights or legal personality to (certain) animals would possibly have some positive effects on their treatment, but this solution does not address the inherent link between the construction of the (human) subject and rights. It is precisely this subjectivity, which in the Cartesian tradition has led to the mastery over and subjection of as well as the treatment of "the animal" as machine, which cannot think, reason, speak, or respond to questions. It would be hypocritical and likely ineffectual to now simply accord subjectivity, personhood, and/or rights to (certain) formerly subjected animals. The notion of the subject with rights is in itself highly problematic and needs to be rethought. As long as it remains at the foundation of modern constitutionalism, the war of subjection against animals is likely to continue. A new starting point perhaps lies in a recognition of the suffering or vulnerability, that is, the finitude that the human being shares with animals. At stake here is an inability and lack of power rather than a (distinguishing) capability. From this "lack" or shared mortality, which imposes an unconditional demand, the human-animal relation can be rethought, also in respect of democracy. The democracy to come, understood in terms of the demand of absolute hospitality, would indeed require that non-human animals and perhaps also nature in general should in some way be included within the "demos."

In chapter 5, the focus was on crime and punishment, which, according to Kant, inherently forms part of the notion of a civil constitution. In Kant's thinking, human freedom and subjectivity—which make possible responsibility, and when the latter fails, leads to guilt and punishment—lie at the foundation of the criminal justice system. According to Kant, a criminal justice system must necessarily make provision for the death penalty, which amounts to a recognition of human dignity, that is, it makes the human being rise above mere life. We followed Derrida's analysis closely insofar as it touches on the notion of legal responsibility, the sovereign right to punish and to grant clemency, as well as the purpose and measure of punishment. Derrida poses a radical challenge to the foundational principles of criminal law and punishment and exposes the justification of the death penalty as politico-theological in nature. Insofar as responsibility is concerned, we saw that Derrida up to a point follows psychoanalysis, which places a question mark behind this notion through the invocation of the unconscious. The operation of the latter casts serious doubt on the assumption of the dominance of consciousness within the psyche as well as the assumed self-identity of the subject. Psychoanalysis raises the question of whether guilt indeed follows upon the crime, as is generally assumed, or whether it instead precedes and motivates the crime because of the Oedipus complex, which is lodged in the unconscious. Derrida further radicalizes the challenge posed by psychoanalysis by noting that the Freudian unconscious is still characterized by a circular economy. The notion of guilt needs to be rethought in view of the Freudian death drive as a force of self-destruction or of pleasure without end, from which issues an unconditional demand, of absolute hospitality, which in turn gives rise to guilt. Insofar as sovereign power is concerned, we see two contrasting forces at stake in the right to punish and the right to grant clemency. The sovereign right to punish follows from the drive to mastery, a drive that is inherently cruel, but nevertheless finds its condition of possibility in absolute hospitality. The sovereign right to grant clemency, on the other hand, stands above the law. It divides in two by alluding to unconditional forgiveness, even though its exercise inevitably involves calculation. In considering the purpose of punishment, we saw that Kant's notion of human dignity, which authorizes the imposition of the death penalty, is tied to political theology, to a belief in God, to the notion of sacrifice, to the self-preservation of society, and to the belief in a life beyond death. It is necessary to rethink life as necessarily entailing an incalculability concerning the moment of death, which the death penalty (unconsciously) seeks to bring to an end by making the moment of death calculable, and thus by mastering the future. Insofar as the measure of punishment is concerned, Derrida shows that the *ius talionis* in Kant is not tied to vengeance but an attempt to calculate with the incalculable, confirming the Nietzschean insight that there is no equivalence between the (evil imposed through the) commission of a crime and the imposition of punishment. Crime and punishment are moreover ultimately motivated by "sexual desire," which cannot be confined to age, that is, to space and time. Within constitutionalism, Derrida's analysis shows that criminal law and punishment require radical and continuous transformation. This transformation must take place in the name of an unconditional forgiveness, which goes beyond calculation, conditionality, and reciprocity, a forgiveness or justice that underlies the modern constitution.

We saw in chapter 6 how Derrida takes Kant's notion of perpetual or eternal peace to its logical limit by equating it with absolute hospitality. This notion should guide the transformation of constitutional law (chapters 3–5) as well as international and cosmopolitan law (chapter 6). In absolute hospitality, the host becomes the hostage of the guest, relinquishing his or her sovereignty and mastery. At stake here is a peace beyond political peace, and for peace in this strict sense to stand a chance, states must abandon their own sovereignty. Although eternal peace may not be possible, it remains an absolute and urgent imperative. A continuous negotiation is in other words required between peace in this strict, impossible sense and politico-legal peace, which will inevitably still lead to war. Insofar as transnational and international law is concerned, Derrida does not call for a federation of states, or a world state, but for a democracy to come, characterized by absolute hospitality, and thus excluding no one (chapters 3 and 4). This would require at a minimum the democratization of existing international institutions. The democracy to come would furthermore require a certain attitudinal change to focus on avoiding suffering and death caused not only intentionally, but also unintentionally (chapters 2 and 6). This is a call for "absolute vigilance" and "complete justice."

Reading Kant to Meet the Challenges of Today

An omnibus of challenges was referred to in the "Introduction," which modern constitutionalism need to address and seek solutions to today. These challenges include climate change, globalization, global health, global conflict, terror and oppression, authoritarianism, authoritarian populism, religious fundamentalism, migration, the nature and conditions of work, abuse of state powers, criminality, inequality, the treatment of non-human animals, as well as challenges posed to democracy by technological developments. Derrida's reading of Kant, often by way of Heidegger, has brought to the fore the abyssal nature of the foundations of modern constitutionalism, thereby "enabling" us to address these challenges in a new way. We saw this in Derrida's rethinking of the concept of democracy in terms of the demands of the "democracy to come," that is, the need for a more inclusive and welcoming democracy, and for its extension on multiple levels both within and beyond the limits of the nation-state. Derrida further challenges us to make fundamental changes with respect to the treatment of animals (and of nature in general) and their inclusion in some way as beneficiaries of modern constitutionalism, as well as fundamental changes to the criminal justice system. Finally, he calls for the transformation of international institutions, which would include a more extensive sharing of sovereignty. Derrida does not provide us with new foundations. Yet his analysis requires of us to take decisions, and responsibility, even in the absence of assured foundations (1999a, 21). Whether it is a question of wide-ranging constitutional reform, amendment of a constitutional text, drafting of new policies or legislation, or application in an individual case, a negotiation is in each instance called for. This negotiation is not in the first place between various possible or workable alternatives, but between the unconditional demand of absolute hospitality, the perfect gift, unconditional forgiveness on the one hand, and the always conditional and restricted possibilities of economic rationality on the other. This will have to involve singular decisions, dependent on context and circumstance and should not simply be a balancing act or a compromise, but an attempt at a solution as close as possible to justice understood as the perfect gift, as absolute hospitality.

Notes

Introduction

1. See, e.g., Rawls 1999a, 1999b, 2005; Habermas 1988, 1996.
2. For analysis, see De Ville 2011a, 141–64.
3. See Klare 1998, 152–53, 169; and Woolman and Davis 1996, 382–85.
4. See Bragyova (2011, 97–114); and Sweet and Palmer (2017, 377–411), who show the alignment of modern national constitutions in general with Kant's core thinking on constitutionalism. Sweet and Palmer extend this analysis also to the transnational and international/cosmopolitan levels; see further Sweet and Ryan 2018, 562–80.
5. See Ackermann 2012, 58–62; and see further Kant 1997a, 5:4; 1997b, 4:436.
6. See Stern 1984, 764–76; Schmidt-Aßmann 2004, 552–53; Blaau 1990, 76–96; Blaauw and Wolf 1996, 267–70; De Waal 1995, 4–5. Stern (1984, 769) specifically mentions the role of Kant in the development of the *Rechtsstaat*, with reference to texts such as "Idea for a Universal History with a Cosmopolitan Purpose" (1784) and Part I of *The Metaphysics of Morals* (Metaphysical First Principles of the Doctrine of Right) (1789).
7. See further chapters 1 and 3 of this volume.
8. See Häberle 2004, 318–19, 321–23, 338–39; Botha 2009, 170, 174–78; Chaskalson 2000, 1382; Ackermann 2012, 140.
9. See Botha 2009, 183–84, 207; Ackermann 2012, 54, 115–62; 2004, 633–80; Woolman 2014, 36-1 to 36-19.
10. See further later in the current chapter, and chapters 1 and 3 of this volume. In chapter 5, we nonetheless see that human dignity plays an important role in Kant's conception of criminal law and punishment, and that, in Derrida's reading, for Kant the idea of law is inherently tied to human dignity.
11. See further chapter 6.

12. See De Waal 1995, 1–29; De Vos and Freedman 2014, 49–52; Ackermann 2012, 10, 13, 116; Woolman 2014, 36–34; Blaauw and Wolf 1996, 267–96.

13. *S v Makwanyane* para. 329 (per J. O'Regan): "The recognition and protection of human dignity is the touchstone of the new political order and is fundamental to the new Constitution." See further Chaskalson 2000, 196, 204; De Vos and Freedman 2021, 562; Botha 2009, 197.

14. See, e.g., *Ferreira v Levin* para. 49–52; *MEC for Education* para. 63; Currie and De Waal 2013, 251. This also happened extracurially, see Ackermann 2004, 633–80; 2012, 54, 99–105. Other judges linked the notion of human dignity to the African notion of *ubuntu*: a human being is a human being because of other human beings; see *S v Makwanyane* para. 224, 311.

15. *Carmichele* para. 54; *Du Plessis* para. 94; O'Regan 2009, 6–10; Chaskalson 2000, 204; Woolman 2014, 36–62 to 36–75.

16. See *S v Dodo* para. 38; Ackermann 2012, 101.

17. See Ackermann 2012, 48–53, 74–76, 147; 2004, 649–50. Compare Bilchitz 2010, 267–300, and see further chapter 4 of this volume.

18. See Habermas 1988, 165–201; Werner and Gordon 2016, 505–25; Koskenniemi 2007, 9–36; Rauber 2009, 49–76.

19. See, e.g., Peters 2009, 397–411; 2015, 1–4; Habermas 2008, 444–55; 2014b, 5–12; De Wet 2006a, 611–32; 2006b, 53–76; 2007, 20–46; 2012, chapter 58; Somek 2020, 467–89.

20. See, e.g., Rauber 2009, 49–76; Qerimi 2019, 227–69; Habermas 1988, 165–201; 2014a, 226–38; Brown 2009; Capps and Rivers 2010, 229–57; Corradetti 2016, 105–21; Sweet and Ryan 2018; see further chapter 6 of this volume.

21. Migration of course raises important questions for democratic theory; see, e.g., Botha 2013, 837–69; Le Roux 2009, 370–99; 2011, 117–37; 2015, 263–83. See further chapter 3 of this volume.

22. As I am finalizing the manuscript, Russia is continuing its invasion of Ukraine, with uncertain consequences.

23. See Ramose 2018, 326–41; Modiri 2018, 300–25. Recently an (unsuccessful) attempt was made to amend the Constitution to provide for expropriation of property, specifically of land, without compensation. Defenders of the current constitutional dispensation do not believe that the fault lies with the Constitution itself, but rather blame the lack of progress on government inaction, corruption, and maladministration.

24. Kant's opposition to colonial conquest should be noted here; see later in the current chapter, and see further "Toward Perpetual Peace" (Kant 1996a, 8:358–59).

25. See, somewhat similarly, Modiri 2018, 307–8.

26. See Derrida 2014a, 9–30; De Ville 2011a, 113–40; 2017, 104–20. The notion of *ubuntu* can potentially play a pivotal role in this respect, if understood in a certain way; see Meylahn 2010, 1–9; Ramose 2005a, 35–46; 2005b, 270–80; and De Ville 2011b, 333.

27. See, e.g., Klare 1998, 146–88; Albertyn and Davis 2010, 188–216; Davis and Klare 2019, 27–43.

28. See further De Ville 2011a, 3–8; De Ville 2017, 9–73; and chapters 3 and 6 of this volume.

29. See, e.g., Stone, Wall and Douzinas 2012, 1–7; Douzinas 2014, 187–98.

30. See Maris and Jacobs 2011, 342–52; De Ville 2011a, 2017.

31. Compare, e.g., Balkin 1987, 743–86; Cornell 1992; Van der Walt 2019, 166–80; Van der Walt and Botha 2000, 341–62; and see further Legrand 2009; and Goodrich et al. 2008.

32. See De Ville 2011a, 20; 2017, 3–4; Maris and Jacobs 2011, 342–46.

33. It should be noted that gender-neutral language was not prevalent in the age in which Kant was writing, and it is thus somewhat artificial to use it in an exposition of Kant's thinking. Yet an attempt will be made to do so where possible.

34. See Kant 1996b, 6:312 (para. 44); Geismann 1996, 8, 11–13; Kersting 1992, 352; 2007, 28–29.

35. As Schmitt (2008, 255) points out, a republican constitution for Kant points to the *Rechtsstaat*, characterized by the separation of powers, and stands opposed to absolutism, whether monarchical or democratic. Principles of political form are relativized here into organizational means for the balancing of powers.

36. Maris and Jacobs (2011, 173) link this protection of external freedom to the freedom to pursue moral pursuits, whereas Geismann reads Kant as imposing a more rigorous distinction between law and ethics/virtue.

37. See Kant 1996a, 8:311–13, 8:357; 1996b, 6:350–53 (para. 61–2); Geismann 1996, 20–24; and Kersting 1992, 362. There are a number of different interpretations of Kant's views with respect to a global state; see chapter 6.

38. This section of the text is usually translated as "The Doctrine of Right" (*Der Rechtslehre*). *Recht* here can bear a variety of meanings, including right, law, and justice. "Theory of Law" is arguably a more lucid and contemporary name for the section, which captures sufficiently what is at stake here; see further Kersting 1992, 364–65 n1.

Chapter 1

1. Freud (2001, 19:167) refers to Kant's categorical imperative as the direct heir of the Oedipus complex.

2. See, e.g., Freud 2001, 21:122–23 ("Civilization and Its Discontents"), and 19:54 ("The Ego and the Id") where a link is posited between the death drive and the superego.

3. Lacan's analysis of ethics is elusive and has given rise to a variety of interpretations. He furthermore changed his position over the years; see, e.g., Evans (1996, 200–1) on the superego; Homer (2004, 81–91) on the Real; De Kesel (2009,

265) on desire, also in relation to the Oedipus complex, which early on remains tied to ethics, see, e.g., Lacan 1992; De Kesel 2009, 119.

4. Especially Lacan's *The Ethics of Psychoanalysis* seems at some points to correspond with Derrida's reading of Freud's "Beyond the Pleasure Principle." Even here, there are however important differences, such as with respect to "the Thing," which Lacan equates with the mother (85); and for commentary see Derrida 2014c, 161.

5. See, e.g., La Caze (2007, 781–805), who contends that Derrida confuses the requirements of the moral law with the virtues, that he transforms imperfect duties into perfect duties.

6. As indicated in the "Introduction," in Kant's thinking as set out in the *Metaphysics of Morals*, a distinction is generally drawn between a broader morality or the moral law on the one hand, and ethics or virtue and law on the other. Both ethics and the law are derived from this general morality.

7. In *Before the Law*, Derrida (2018, 33–34) refers to the fact that in an unpublished seminar on respect he deals with the distinction that Kant (1997a, 5:67–71) in the *Critique of Practical Reason* draws between the typic and the schematic of practical reason. It is not possible to anticipate that analysis here.

8. We do not discuss here the Kantian analysis of beauty and its relation to the moral law, as found in the *Critique of Judgment*, which Derrida (1987b; 1998c, 263–93) explores in texts such as *The Truth in Painting* and "Economimesis." Derrida's discussion of the moral law in those texts, which touches also on the imagination, the sublime, and pleasure, requires detailed analysis, and would be difficult to integrate here. It nevertheless does not contradict the analysis undertaken in the present chapter.

9. *Achtung* can be translated as respect, esteem, regard, deference.

10. The notion of respect for the moral law is further explored in the *Critique of Practical Reason* that is discussed later in the current chapter.

11. See later in the current chapter on the voice of the moral law and the way in which it forces evildoers to hide from its sight.

12. See later in the current chapter on Kant's reference to the gate and the guardian.

13. See Derrida Seminars Translation Project 1980–81 *Le Respect* (12 sessions), https://derridaseminars.org/seminars.html. As noted earlier, in *Before the Law*, Derrida (2018, 33–34) seemingly refers to this same seminar, and he mentions here specifically Heidegger's *Kant and the Problem of Metaphysics* (para. 30), where an analyses of the notion of respect for the law in Kant is undertaken.

14. See, e.g., Derrida 1992b, 2005a, 2018.

15. See also Beardsworth 1996, 28. For Derrida's reading of the *Genealogy*, see 2002b, 215–56 ("Nietzsche and the Machine"); 1995d, 112–15; and 2014c, 142–65.

16. See Freud 2001, 18:1–99 ("Totem and Taboo").

17. See also Derrida 2002c, 46 ("Privilege"), where in an analysis of Kant's *Metaphysics of Morals*, specifically the "Introduction to the Theory of Law," Derrida

points to a passage where Kant speaks of "consciousness of obligation [*Bewußtsein der Verbindlichkeit*]," which founds both morality and law/right (tied to coercion/force). This being-before-the law, Derrida notes, is at the same time moral and juridical, and furthermore precedes the distinction between the two laws. As Ghetti (2017, 76–91) shows in his analysis of this text, Kant in the *Metaphysics of Morals* seeks to draw a clear distinction between law and its "foundation," which as Derrida shows, does not succeed; see Ghetti (87), pointing with reference to Derrida's "Force of Law," specifically to the differential notion of force, which cannot be restricted to the legal domain.

18. See in the latter respect Kant 1997a, 5:75.

19. See Kant 1997a, 5:28: "Since the mere form of a law can be represented only by reason and is therefore not an object of the senses and consequently does not belong among appearances [*Erscheinungen*]."

20. See Kant 1997a, 5:163 on philosophy as the guardian of the science of morals.

21. See Kant (1997b, 4:419), noting that "it is impossible to settle by any example, i.e., empirically, whether there is any imperative [of morality] . . . ; we should rather worry that all imperatives that seem to be categorical may yet be hypothetical in some hidden way."

22. See Kant (1997a, 5:4) where he notes that "among all the ideas of speculative reason freedom is . . . the only one the possibility of which we *know* a priori, though without having insight into it, because it is the condition of the moral law, *which we do know* [emphasis added]."

23. See Kant (1997b, 4:402n): "we should see respect as the *effect* of the law on a person rather than as what produces the law"; and Kant 1997a, 5:72–89.

24. Derrida is possibly alluding here to Kant (1997b, 4:413): "All imperatives are expressed by a 'must' [*sollen*]. Thereby they mark a constraint."

25. See Kant 1997a, 5:4.

26. See also chapter 3 of Kant 1997a, 5:78, 81.

27. See also Derrida 1993c, 133: "the moral law never gives itself to be seen or touched."

28. See in this respect Freud 2001, 13:18–74 (chapter II). Derrida's *On Touching* can in a sense be read as a response to this text of Freud, which ascribes the taboos on touching as well as the self-imposed prohibitions on touching of compulsion neurosis to the repression of (Oedipal) desire.

29. Discussed in chapter 3 of *On Touching*.

30. Derrida refers in this regard to three texts of Nancy: "Psyche" *Première Livraison* no. 16 (1978), *The Gravity of Thought* (1997), and *Corpus* (2008).

31. The full note reads as follows: "Räumlichkeit mag die Projektion der Ausdehnung des psychischen Apparats sein. Keine andere Ableitung wahrscheinlich. Anstatt Kants a priori Bedingungen unseres psychischen Apparats. Psyche ist ausgedehnt, weiß nichts davon." (Freud 1991, 17:152 [Space may be the projection

of the extension of the psychical apparatus. No other derivation is probable. Instead of Kant's a priori determinants of our psychical apparatus. Psyche is extended; knows nothing about it—Freud 2001, 23:300].

32. See also Freud (2001, 12:289–301), specifically 300 n1 ("The Theme of the Three Caskets"), who notes that "the Psyche of Apuleius's story has kept many traits that remind us of her relation with death. Her wedding is celebrated like a funeral, she has to descend into the underworld, and afterwards she sinks into a deathlike sleep."

33. See further De Ville 2011a, 136–37; 2017, 121–38; and Van Gorkom 2009, 156–57.

34. Beardsworth (1996, 52) notes that in the *Critique of Pure Reason*, "the Idea of freedom was deduced negatively through the feeling of 'guilt.' In feeling guilt for a deed, wishing it to be 'undone' although it is irreparable, one shows that one is free. Freedom is freedom from the linear determination of *time*." In the *Critique of Practical Reason*, "this feeling is recast *positively* as the feeling of 'respect' before the moral law, from which is deduced the idea of freedom" (52).

35. See also Derrida (2017, 93–94); and see Freud (2001, 14:178), who notes that "in general, the use of the terms 'unconscious affect' and 'unconscious emotion' has reference to the vicissitudes undergone, in consequence of repression, by the quantitative factor in the instinctual impulse." There is however according to Freud strictly speaking no such thing as unconscious affects, different from the position with ideas. There may nevertheless "be in the system *Ucs*. affective structures which, like others, become conscious." The difference between ideas and affects "arises from the fact that ideas are cathexes—basically of memory-traces—whilst affects and emotions correspond to processes of discharge, the final manifestations of which are perceived as feelings"; see further Freud 2001, 5:460–87, and 19:19–27.

36. See also Derrida (2017, 93–94) noting (and referring implicitly to Kant 1997a, 5:79, 80) that the interest at stake here is "a *moral interest* . . . , a disinterested interest, as it were, an interest that is pure and independent of the senses, a non-pathological interest, an interest that comes from pure and simple practical reason."

37. See also later in the current chapter.

38. This is indeed what the notion of a categorical (as opposed to a hypothetical) imperative implies, as Kant (1997b, 4:416–17) points out in the *Groundwork*: "a categorical imperative is limited by no condition [*durch keine Bedingung eingeschränkt wird*] and can actually be called a commandment in the strict sense, being absolutely, though practically, necessary." Cf. chapter 3 of this volume, where we see that Heidegger describes the categorical imperative as a product of the Enlightenment and the Prussian state at the time.

39. See also the *Groundwork*, where Kant (1997b, 4:407) refers to the "strict command of duty [*das strenge Gebot der Pflicht*]" as often requiring "self-denial [*Selbstverleugnung*]."

40. See further later in the current chapter on the example.

41. Freud (2001, 18:62–63) speaks about the need for the binding of an immeasurable pleasure ("where pain and pleasure are no longer viewed in oppositional terms"—see De Ville 2011a, 36 n80) so as to ensure the dominance of the pleasure principle, whereas Kant (2007a, 5:77) speaks of the respect at stake here as involving neither a feeling of pleasure (*Lust*) nor of displeasure (*Unlust*), and elsewhere in the same text of the feeling of pain (*Schmerz*) or of displeasure (*Unlust*) produced in us by the moral law in thwarting our inclinations (5:73, 78).

42. Kant 2007a, 5:83–4: "if a rational creature could ever reach the stage of thoroughly liking to fulfil all moral laws, this would mean that there would not be in him even the possibility of a desire that would provoke him to deviate from them; for, to overcome such a desire always costs the subject some sacrifice [*Aufopferung*] and therefore requires self-constraint [*Selbstzwang*], that is, inner necessitation [*innere Nötigung*] to what one does not altogether like to do." Compare in this regard Freud, who in the final chapter of "Beyond the Pleasure Principle" summarizes his findings in the earlier chapters as follows: "We have found that one of the earliest and most important functions of the mental apparatus is to bind the instinctual impulses which impinge on it, to replace the primary process prevailing in them by the secondary process and convert their freely mobile cathectic energy into a mainly quiescent (tonic) cathexis. While this transformation is taking place no attention can be paid to the development of unpleasure; but this does not imply the suspension of the pleasure principle. On the contrary, the transformation occurs on behalf of the pleasure principle; the binding is a preparatory act which introduces and assures the dominance of the pleasure principle" (2001, 18:62).

43. See also Derrida (2018, 35 n43) where he notes that Kant, toward the end of the *Critique of Practical Reason* (5:163), "presents philosophy . . . as the guardian (*Aufbewahrerin*) of the pure science of morals; it is also the 'narrow gate' (*enge Pforte*) leading to the doctrine of wisdom."

44. Geismann 2009, 17–18 contends that the good will of such a being can never be a pure will ("a will motivated completely by a priori principles apart from any empirical motives"—Kant 1997b, 4:390), but is always *both* determined by such pure will *and* pathologically affected. The inclinations as motivating forces (*Triebfedern*) can and need never be completely excluded in determining the will, but they need to be subordinated to the moral law. Duty should in other words have the absolute priority over inclination.

45. *Schuldig* (adj.) means to be guilty, sinful, for something to be due, or to owe someone something.

46. Kant 1997a, 5:83: "Pflicht und Schuldigkeit sind die Benennungen, die wir allein unserem Verhältnisse zum moralischen Gesetze geben müssen (Duty and what is owed are the only names that we must give to our relation to the moral law)." *Schuld* (noun) can be translated as debt, guilt, fault, liability, owing, and *Schuldig* (adj.) as guilty, due, blameworthy (see note 45). See also the *Metaphysics of*

Morals, where Kant (1996b, 6:222) defines duty as "that action to which someone is bound [*zu welcher jemand verbunden ist*]."

47. One could say that Kant's terminology with respect to the roots of duty is suggestive also of a "pre-origin," i.e., an "origin" of duty preceding such personality.

48. In "Passions," Derrida (1992b, 27 n4) refers to Nietzsche's reflections in the *Genealogy* on guilt (*Schuld*), bad conscience (*Slechtesgewissen*), and such like, and with reference to, the long history of the origin of responsibility, suggests that the moral concept of guilt draws its origin from debt. Nietzsche furthermore detects in Kant's categorical imperative a smell of cruelty. See also Derrida (2017, 204–7), where he, with reference to Reik and Adorno, points to a causal relation between the (Kantian) ideal (as well as the moral law and the good will) and cruelty. See further chapters 4 and 5 of this volume.

49. Derrida (1992b, 27 n4) refers here to Heidegger's invocation in *Being and Time* of attestation/witnessing (*Bezeugung*), the call (*Ruf*), and an originary being-guilty (*Schuldigsein*); See further Derrida 1995d, 31–33; 1987a, 264 n10; 1995b, 275–76; 1993b.

50. Derrida (1992b, 27 n4) refers here to Freud's investigation of the origin of remorse and conscience, and the sacrifices required as well as his speculations on the religions of the father and of the sons of the primal horde.

51. For analysis, see inter alia Derrida 1994a, 27–28; 1995d, 31–33, 52 (on Heidegger's *Being and Time*); and 2018, 36–47 (on Freud's "Totem and Taboo"). See also Derrida 2014c, 144–45, where Nietzsche's *Genealogy of Morals* is read to show that what drives Kant to believe in the death penalty is an originary guilt (within himself).

52. This is also touched on by Saghafi 2016, 124–38.

53. See, e.g., Derrida 1993a, 16–17; 1999a, 7; 2001d, 66; 2002b, 351; 2003, 133; 2005c, 152; 2014b, 65; Derrida and Dufourmantelle 2000, 83.

54. This is how Derrida also speaks of absolute hospitality, as we see in chapter 6 of this volume; see Derrida and Dufourmantelle 2000, 83.

55. See also Kant 1997a, 5:79–80, who speaks of the "boundless esteem for the pure moral law stripped of all advantage—as practical reason, whose voice [*Stimme*] makes even the boldest evildoer tremble [*zittern macht*] and forces him to hide from its sight [*ihn nötigt, sich vor seinem Anblicke zu verbergen*]," referred to by Derrida 2017, 94–95; and see Kant 2004, 8:402 ("On a recently prominent tone of superiority in philosophy") on man who trembles upon hearing the brazen voice of duty; and Derrida 1993c, 132–33.

56. See also Derrida 1996, 222–23. Douzinas and Gearey 2005, 359 express this relation between autonomy and heteronomy strikingly as follows: "The modern subject is created in this double movement in which we are subjected to the law while we imagine ourselves as autonomous—as legislating the norms of our subjection." Theirs is a dominantly Lacanian reading, but in this respect at least it comes close to the reading undertaken here.

57. See also earlier in the current chapter, Derrida 1992b, 21, and Derrida 1993c, on the secret of practical reason.

58. See further in this regard Freud 2001, 18:48–59 ("The Ego and the Id"), 21:123–45 ("Civilization and Its Discontents"), and 22:109–10 ("New Introductory Lectures") on unconscious guilt and the unconscious need for punishment; also Derrida's Death Penalty Seminars (2014c, 129–30, 141–42, 144–45, 247–50; 2017, 37–39, 227) on the unconscious forces at stake with respect to the giving of death as punishment.

59. At stake here, also in Patočka, is a thinking of responsibility beyond action in accordance with conscience and knowledge, seeing that such action would amount to nothing more than the "technical deployment of a cognitive apparatus, the simple mechanistic deployment of a theorem" (24).

60. According to Husserl, as Derrida (78) points out, "the *alter ego* . . . can never be originally presented to my conscience and . . . I can apprehend only through what he calls *appresentation* and analogy"; see also Derrida 1995b, 263–64.

61. This is also true with respect to the passion of Christ, see Kant 1997b, 4:408–9; and for analysis, Derrida 1992b, 31–32 n10: "Kant quotes, but *against the example*, the very example of passion, of a moment of the sacrificial passion of Christ, who provides the best example of what it is necessary not to do, namely, to offer/give oneself as an example [*se donner en exemple*]. Because God alone—the best and only possible example?—remains, in Kant's eyes, invisibly secret and must put his exemplary value to the test of moral reason, that is, to a pure law whose concept conforms to no example"; see also Derrida 2014c, 283 on the example of Jesus). At stake here appears to be the structure of the law in relation to the example. Derrida seems to be suggesting that the (non-)relation to the law of law is absolutely singular. Therefore there is no rule or example that can tell me what to do. As Derrida (1995d, 60) says in *The Gift of Death*: "Abraham doesn't speak, he assumes the responsibility that consists in always being alone, retrenched in one's own singularity at the moment of decision" (also Derrida 2001b, 73–74 on the exemplary as the universalizable). I am therefore not fully convinced by the reading of Caputo (1997, 52), who contends that the issue here is that "it is not possible to decide, pace Kant, whether Jesus is an example of the Moral Law, or whether the Moral Law is an example we learn from Jesus; when we cannot tell which way the mimesis goes, whether empirical actions imitate the Idea or whether Ideas imitate factical life." Perhaps one could agree with Caputo insofar as one views the "examples" of Abraham and Jesus not as historical events (i.e., as "factical life"), but as narrative events announcing the possibility of literature (Derrida 1995d, 110; see further later in the current chapter on the "as if").

62. Iterability, which Derrida in *Limited Inc.* inquires into with reference to speech acts, thereby challenging the metaphysical privilege of presence, also functions within the field of ethics (as well as politics and law) (Derrida 1992b, 31 n10, 33 n12). As appears from the earlier analysis, at stake here is a (perverformative) call

that disrupts subjectivity (similar to the possible death of the author in the case of speech acts); the necessity of alteration through repetition, each time singular and in excess of any ideal ("there are no examples while at the same time there are only examples" (15)); as well as a division or contamination from the start (the ethical act can never be shown to be pure). The gift, hospitality, justice, forgiveness, the event, i.e., doing the impossible, can all function as "examples" in this respect; see, e.g., Derrida 2007a.

63. In German it reads: "handle so, als ob die Maxime deiner Handlung durch deinen Willen zum allgemeinen Naturgesetze werden sollte" (in italics, with "allgemeinen Naturgesetze" further emphasized).

64. See also *Before the Law*, where Derrida (2018, 46) refers to the possibility of pure reason being in league with an unconscious fantastic.

65. See also "Tense," where Derrida (1995c, 57–59) distinguishes with reference to Sallis between the *eikastic* and the phantastic imagination. The role of the imagination in Kant is also at issue here (65–67), as well as the Platonic notion of *khōra* that precedes the imagination and in a strange sense lies at its "origin" (73).

66. See further Derrida 2003, 135; 2005c, xiv–xv; 2011, 269–71; 1998c, 284 ("Economimesis") on the Kantian "as if" in other contexts; and see Derrida 1996, 212–26. See further Gaon 2014, 44–45.

67. See, e.g., Kant 1996b, 6:221; 1997a, 5:31.

68. We thus arrive here at the same point as we would should we have closely followed Derrida's reading of Levinas.

69. See further Derrida (1995d, 86) on how we allow others to die.

70. See further Cornell 2009, 20–22; Ackermann 2012, 2, 49.

71. See chapters 2 to 6 of this volume.

Chapter 2

1. Although Kant, Heidegger, and Derrida are referred to by Schlag, the main texts to be explored in this chapter, and which were published at the time of the publication of Schlag's *Enchantment*: Heidegger's *Principle of Reason* (1991), Derrida's "The Principle of Reason: The University in the Eyes of Its Pupils" (1983), later included in *Eyes of the University* (2004), as well as *Given Time* (1992), are not referenced. For Schlag (69–71), it should be noted, Derrida, Freud, and others simply provide different "perspectives" or "orientations" on the relation between reason and the unthought. The argument presented here, however, is that Derrida's thinking on reason by way of Heidegger and Freud is not simply a "perspective" and deserves to be taken more seriously, both philosophically and legally.

2. See likewise Schlag (1998, 23–25) on reason as determining "whether something is or is not law" (24).

3. See further De Ville 2011a, 19–21, 121–22.

4. The principle of reason is a translation of the German *der Satz vom Grund*. *Satz* can be translated as "sentence" and "principle," as well as "leap," as we will see in the further discussion, whereas *Grund* can be translated as "ground," "reason," and "cause."

5. The translation of *ratione* from Latin into English is relatively straightforward: reason; the translation from the German *Grund* into English is more difficult, as indicated earlier.

6. In lecture 13, Heidegger will contend that *ratio* (related to the verb *reor*: to reckon) which is translated as ground (*Grund*) and reason (*Vernunft*) in modernity (98) is itself a translation of the Greek *logos* (n.)/*legein* (v.), a word that is in turn affiliated with *einai* and *phusis*, both of which are words for Being (105–9). *Logos* itself is a name for Being (109). *Logos* contains within itself a variety of meanings, including that of gathering (*Sammeln*), reckoning (*Rechnung*), relation (*Relation*), saying or bringing to light (*Sagen, zum Vorschein bringen*), as well as that on which something rests, that is, ground (*Grund*).

7. See Derrida 2004b, 83–112 ("Mochlos, or The Conflict of the Faculties") for further analysis.

8. See further Gasché 1994, 108–10, 121–25.

9. The role and essence of the university are discussed at length in *Du Droit à la Philosophie* (1990), translated as *Who's Afraid of Philosophy?* (2002c) and *Eyes of the University* (2004b), and taken up again by Derrida in *Without Alibi* ("The University without Condition") (2002d) and "Unconditionality or Sovereignty: The University at the Frontiers of Europe" (2009b), although not specifically in relation to the principle of reason.

10. In "Force of Law: The Mystical Foundation of Authority," justice is likewise described as beyond reason and calculation, and with reference to the gift, as demanding a "gift without exchange, without circulation, without recognition or gratitude, without economic circularity, without calculation and without rules, without reason and without theoretical rationality, in the sense of regulating mastery" (2002a, 254). Derrida further associates justice with a certain madness, an event to come, and a responsibility without limits as well as before memory (247–49, 254–56).

11. Derrida (2017, 151) notes that it is only in Kant where the death penalty is not justified with reference to such utilitarian considerations.

12. Derrida (2017, 184) notes a similar structure in Kant, where Kant speaks of the pure talionic law which remains foreign to calculation; see chapter 5 of this volume.

13. In the seventh session, Derrida (172) invokes psychoanalysis in this regard, and, similar to *Given Time*, he refers here to the gift as belonging to a certain unconscious that goes beyond the Freudian conception thereof; see also chapter 1 of this volume.

14. See further chapter 4 of this volume.

15. As Derrida (2009a, 319, 338) points out, Heidegger's rendering of *logos* in its more originary sense as gathering is nonetheless itself accompanied by force,

seeing that such gathering seeks to prevent a dispersion. See further Marrati 2005, 87–96.

16. See also *Adieu*, where Derrida (1999a, 26), with reference to Levinas, points to the interpretation of reason as "hospitable receptivity."

17. See similarly Derrida (2011, 60) on the need of reason; and Derrida (2019, 24–25) on the interest of reason, which in Kant's *Critique of Pure Reason* (A804/B832–A806/B834) can be read as preceding both theoretical and practical reason, yet having a greater affinity with the practical than the theoretical. Derrida (2019, 25–28) further relates this interest of reason to the Kantian "What may I hope?," a question that belongs to both theoretical and to practical reason, and thus precedes them, and, by way of Kant's definition of hope, to the event, to what comes.

18. As argued in more detail elsewhere (De Ville 2017, 9–73), the notion of the political is philosophically somewhat more complex than is assumed by some critical legal scholars in their claim that law is politics; see e.g. Tushnet 1991, 1517.

19. See somewhat similarly Klare 2015, 445–70; Brand 2011, 614–38; Davis 2004, 47–66.

20. See further Derrida 2007c, 1–47; and see e.g. the argument of some critical legal scholars who argue against the employment of formalistic legal reasoning, as it does not allow for innovation and creativity; Klare 1998, 166–72; Davis 2019, 73–85.

Chapter 3

1. See further Blaauw-Wolf and Wolf 1996, 267–71; De Waal 1995, 6–10; Ackermann 2012, 102–5).

2. In line with the distinction between ethics/virtue (*Ethik/Tugend*) and law (*Recht*), Kant (2016, 19:155) distinguishes between internal freedom (to set ends for oneself) and external freedom (acting in line with one's ends in relation to others), respectively: "Morality (objective) is freedom in accordance with (under) laws. Freedom under inner laws is ethical obligation. Freedom under outer laws is juridical obligation. Law is the restriction of freedom through universal conditions of the consensus of freedom with itself."

3. Certain proponents of Critical Legal Studies detected a "fundamental contradiction" within this limitation of freedom. In the words of Kennedy (1979, 211–12), "individual freedom is at the same time dependent on and incompatible with the communal coercive action that is necessary to achieve it." As we will see, Derrida, in following and surpassing Heidegger's ontological analysis of freedom, finds a "contradiction" or "tension" elsewhere.

4. See Schmitt 2008, 235–39; and further Kersting 2009, 260–63.

5. See further Kant 1997b, 4:436; 1997a, 5:4.

6. See further Derrida 2009a, 301 on the close relation between freedom and sovereignty: "We must not hide from ourselves that our most and best accredited concept of 'liberty,' autonomy, self-determination, emancipation, freeing, is indissociable from this concept of sovereignty, its limitless 'I can,' and thus from its all-powerfulness. . . . Liberty and sovereignty are, in many respects, indissociable concepts."

7. See also Raffoul 2010, 59–60. Heidegger's reading enables us to move beyond the debate with respect to the link in Kant between the moral law and law (*Recht*), e.g., in Geismann 1996; see also chapter 1 of this volume.

8. See also Reath (1997, x–xiv) on these different approaches to establishing the "existence" of transcendental freedom.

9. See further Devisch 2009, 725–31.

10. See also Heidegger 1985, 61.

11. Kant 1997b, 4:446: "*Will* is a kind of causality of living beings insofar as they are rational, and *freedom* would be that property [*Eigenschaft*] of such causality that it can be efficient independently of alien causes *determining* it, just as *natural necessity* is the property of the causality of all nonrational beings to be determined to activity by the influence of alien causes." See further Reath 1997, xvi; Korsgaard 1997, xxvi; and Hill and Zweig 2002, 94.

12. See also Heidegger 1985, 162.

13. This passage (as is the case with similar ones in *Being and Time*) is not to be understood as a call for moral resoluteness, or for a decision understood as exercising a choice between alternatives. Such an understanding would make of freedom a mere capacity of the human being—see Heidegger 2012b, 69–70.

14. See further the "Introduction" and chapter 5 of this volume.

15. See similarly Heidegger 1985, 9.

16. See likewise Heidegger (1985, 162) where he notes that "the essence of all Being is finitude and only what exists finitely has the privilege and the pain of standing in Being as such and experiencing what is true as beings."

17. See also *Ponderings VII–XI* where Heidegger (2017, 219) speaks of the need for an originary meditation, which rescues us "into the plight." This plight, he notes, "compels in that it places on humans the excessive demand of freedom—to bear the abyss. This plight is being itself."

18. See, e.g., Heidegger 1971, 91; 1977, 25; 1991, 94; 1993, 247. See further Ruin 2008, 281, 295–97; Richardson 1967, 301–3; Nancy 1993b, 33–43; and see Derrida 2005c, 112–14 on *das Freie* in Heidegger, understood as the safe, the immune, which stands in tension with the unsafe, the disaster.

19. *Ereignis* provides a challenge to translation, and is rendered as (event of) appropriation, propriation, as well as enowning in different translations of Heidegger.

20. In *Schelling's Treatise*, Heidegger (1985, 9) similarly treats freedom as a determination of Being, rather than as preceding Being.

21. See also Heidegger 1985, 162.

22. Schmitt (2008, 125–29) contends that the modern constitution finds its source of authority in the people who exercise their constituent power, yet if we follow Derrida's argument, this construction in itself presupposes freedom, i.e., a notion of autonomy, of self-rule. One of Schmitt's main objections against Kantian (ideal) constitutionalism is that sovereignty in the form of constituent power is effectively dissolved once a constitution has been enacted (Schmitt, *Constitutional Theory*, 154–55). See further De Ville, *Constitutional Theory*, 74–89 on constituent power, and chapter 6 of this volume on the temporary hospitality granted by the earth to the "host."

23. See also Derrida and Roudinesco 2004, 48–49; and chapter 4 of this volume.

24. Understood thus, freedom does not stand opposed to equality, as it often does in constitutional discourse. Freedom in this sense stands in alliance with what Derrida (2005c, 48–9, 52–53) refers to in *Rogues* as incalculable, unconditional, or immeasurable equality, which is itself likewise tied to unconditional hospitality and the democracy to come.

25. De Tocqueville (2010, 97) speaks in this regard of society governing itself for itself, noting that "the people rule the American political world as God rules the universe. They are the cause and the end of all things; everything arises from them and everything is absorbed by them."

26. In *Beast & Sovereign* II, in the analysis of Defoe's Robinson Crusoe, it is a case of fear of being swallowed alive—by the earth, wild animals, and/or cannibals, which Derrida (2011, 77–78, 82) refers to as the fundamental phantasy (threat, compulsion, fear, terror, promise, desire) that gives rise to the reinvention of the (grinder's) wheel and to prayer (which similarly entails a movement toward the self when moving toward the other) by Crusoe.

27. See also Heidegger's analysis in *Schelling's Treatise* (1985, 124–37), where he engages in a very similar kind of analysis of Shelling's conception of God. According to Schelling, who seeks to find an explanation for the evil in man, a distinction is to be drawn between God and the ground of God, the latter nevertheless being active or present in God (*in Gott wesenden Grund*) (124). This ground, although it is within God, is not God himself and is not caused by God. All of existence, including the human being, ultimately find their origin in this ground (121). The nature (*Wesen*) of the ground of God is to be understood in terms of an eternal longing, yearning, or desire (*Sehnsucht*).

28. There is a clear echo here of Heidegger's statements in *The Essence of Human Freedom* that the inquiry into the essence of human beings poses a radical challenge: "It places the human being in question in the ground of his [or her] essence, i.e. it harbors within itself the possibility of an onslaught on the human being, which does not strike him [or her] from the outside, but rises up from the ground of his [or her] essence [*Es nimmt den Menschen im Grunde seines Wesens*

in die Frage, d. h. birgt in sich die Möglichkeit eines Angriffes auf den Menschen, der nicht von außen ihn trifft, sondern aus dem Grunde seines Wesens aufsteigt]" (2005, 89, translation modified); and "The leading question does not initially and directly pertain to the human being, but its questioning, if it is radical, asks about beings as such, turns on the human being, overtakes him [or her] in his [or her] ground [*fällt dem Menschen in den Rücken, überfällt ihn in seinem Grunde*]" (89).

29. Heidegger (2005, 26) confesses to something similar: "To once *again* ask this question of Plato and Aristotle—the question, in brief, of Western philosophy—means something else, namely to ask *more primordially* than they did. In the history of all essential questions, it is our prerogative, and also our responsibility, to become the murderers of our forefathers; indeed it is even a fateful necessity for us! [*daß sie zu Mördern der Vorfahren werden müssen und selbst unter dem Schicksal einer notwendigen Ermordung stehen*!]."

30. In the Preface to *Rogues*, Derrida (xiv) links this giving of place, this giving rise to the coming of the event, to the Platonic notion of *khōra* as explored in the *Timaeus*, and analyzed by Derrida (1995a) in the essay "Khōra." Similar to the "reality" or "actuality" (*Wirklichkeit*) which we encountered earlier in Heidegger (2005, 198), *khōra* is a placeless place, associated with expropriation, uprootedness, homelessness, dislocation, the dissolution of identity, and a total exposure and giving of the self; see further De Ville 2017, 104–20.

31. See further Derrida (2004a, 144–45) where the errant democrat without character in Plato's *Republic* is compared to writing (in contrast with speech). The approach followed by Derrida in *Rogues* is somewhat similar to that followed in his earlier texts with respect to the speech/writing opposition. He does not simply overturn the hierarchy (here: celebrate the licentious with respect to freedom and democracy), but posits something beyond the traditional opposition, which is nevertheless closely related to that which was previously "repressed." The "repression" of course happened because of a reason, hiding a more deep-seated fear and desire.

32. It was noted earlier that in Kant there are indications of a fear that freedom without constraint would lead to self-destruction.

33. The "logic" of this approach is set out partly in chapter 6 of *Rogues* where Derrida shows that the negative evaluation and exclusion of the rogue (the *voyou*, with its libidinal connotations), of lawlessness, take place because of the repression of some unconscious force or desire within the self, here by the "civilized" members of society. See further note 35 on the *roué*.

34. See likewise Kant 2007, 8:29 ("Idea for a Universal History"), who speaks of "the play of human freedom [*Spiele der menschlichen Freiheit*]," which eventually leads to the establishment of a republican state, a federation of nations, and cosmopolitan law.

35. Whereas in chapter 1 of *Rogues* the *roue* (wheel, nf) is the main focus, in chapter 2 it is the French adjective for being rogue-like, *roué*: sly, tricky wily, and its related noun *rouerie* (action, turn, or trick of someone who is *roué*). Somebody

who is *roué* is in other words a kind of rogue (*voyou*). The rogue seems to be the opposite of the sovereign: rogues are those who threaten (monarchical) sovereignty, by promoting license. The *roué* points to the kind of character who has a subversive disrespect for principles, norms, and good manners, for the rules and norms that govern the circle of decent, self-respecting people, of respectable, right-thinking society. He is both included and excluded from the closely policed circles of respectable society. The word *roué* in French political history announces in a sense decadence as well as the revolution, the beheading, the democratization of (monarchical) sovereignty, its self-destruction or autoimmune suicide (Derrida 2005c, 20).

36. Commentators like Rousseau likewise detect in democracy the tendency to frequently and forcefully change its form and to always be at risk of civil war or internal agitation. Despite this formlessness, the lack of an essence, there remains for Rousseau a desire for democracy and for freedom, even though they may not exist (Derrida 2005c, 74).

37. Derrida 2005c, 29, 85–90; 2000, 78 (with Dufourmantelle) insists on distinguishing the democracy to come from the Kantian regulative idea, specifically because of the lack of presence, the promise and injunction of urgency of the democracy to come, not only on the national level, but also on the transnational and international levels; see chapter 6 of this volume.

38. See also the distinction that Kant 1996b, 6:314–15 draws between active and passive citizens (including minors and women), the latter not having the "equal right to vote within this constitution, that is, to be citizens and not mere associates in the state."

Chapter 4

1. See further chapters 2 and 3 of this volume.

2. The terminology "human animal" and "non-human animal" which is prevalent in discourse today, was of course not such when Kant was writing in the eighteenth century. Derrida (2008, 47–48) furthermore uses the terms "the animal" and "the human/man" to analyze the way in which the tradition has dealt with this relation, and to rethink this relation inter alia through the neologism "animot." The somewhat inconsistent use of terminology in what follows should be understood in this light.

3. For a broader analysis of Derrida's texts dealing with the human-animal relationship, see De Villiers 2019.

4. See for example, Derrida 2008, 135.

5. See Kant (1996b, 6:223) for the definition of a person as compared to a thing. See further Kant 1997c, 27:344; 2016, 27:1322.

6. See similarly Kant 2007, 8:114 ("Conjectural beginning of human history"): "The fourth and last step that reason took in elevating the human being entirely

above the society with animals was that he comprehended (however obscurely) that he was the genuine *end of nature*, and that in this nothing that lives on earth can supply a competitor to him. The first time he said to the sheep: *Nature has given you the skin you wear not for you but for me*, then took it off the sheep and put it on himself (*Genesis* 3: 21), he became aware of a prerogative that he had by his nature over all animals, which he now no longer regarded as his fellow creatures, but rather as means and instruments given over to his will for the attainment of his discretionary aims." Kant continues by noting that the human being nevertheless realized that this is not something he or she could say to fellow human beings, who should be regarded as an equal with respect to the sharing of natural resources. In this way, the human being already saw from afar the restrictions that reason would impose on him or her to enter civil society.

7. Reference is made to the page numbers in the margins of this text.

8. See similarly Kant 1997c, 27:459–60.

9. See however Kant 2016, 19:476: "In the peaceful condition I am secure through my right. In the state of nature I am secure through nothing but my power; I must always be prepared for war, I am always threatened by others; thus this is a state of war *juridice* [juridically]." Kant is here not far from Hobbes's description of the state of nature where man is a wolf for man. See further Kant 1998b, 6:19–53 on the evil in humankind.

10. Schmitt 2006, 147 describes the state of nature among states as depicted by Kant and others with reference to Hobbes's dictum as one where human beings are wolves for each other ("im Kampf des Naturzustandes 'der Mensch dem Menschen ein Wolf' ist"). He compares this to a situation (prevailing especially after World War II) where states are turned into unjust enemies (something that was supported by Kant in his proposals for perpetual peace) and where a comparison is consequently drawn between human beings and opponents who are characterized as wolves.

11. Kersting (1992, 343) notes in this respect the following: "Human nature and history constitute the domain for the empirical application of the principles of morality and right. They contain the conditions of realization without attention to which pure practical reason remains powerless, and which must therefore be considered by a practical philosophy that is concerned with the realization of its own principles." Kant (1996b, 6:217) seems to provide support for this contention.

12. See likewise Kant 2016, 27:1320.

13. See similarly Kant 2007, 8:21 ("Idea for a Universal History").

14. See in this regard Kant 1998a, B132–36.

15. See also Derrida 2008, 49–50.

16. See also Derrida 2008, 50; 2020, 76–137.

17. See also Derrida 2008, 60.

18. In Lacan this "lack," e.g., finds expression in the prematurity at birth and the castration complex (Derrida 2008, 122, 139).

19. See also Derrida (1988, 136; and 2009a, 14–16) where he notes that the human being is not the only political animal, and that one also finds in many animal societies hierarchies of power and refined organization, including a prohibition on incest and instances of sovereignty.

20. We saw something similar earlier where Kant in the *Lectures on Anthropology* describes human nature.

21. See likewise Freud 2001, 21:122 ("Civilization and its Discontents"): "This struggle [between the instinct of life and the instinct of destruction] is what all life essentially consists of, and the evolution of civilization may therefore be simply described as the struggle for life of the human species."

22. See similarly Derrida 2011, 272–73 where he notes that war, despite the great ills it causes, is according to Kant indispensable in the perfection of human culture.

23. See also Derrida 2009a, 181: "the living being is divisible and constituted by a multiplicity of agencies, forces, and intensities that are sometimes in tension or even in contradiction."

24. See also Derrida 2009a, 31 where he points to Freud, who contends in "Civilization and its Discontents" that animal societies are in fact more stable/in stasis than human ones, thus more state-like.

25. See also Derrida 2002a, 247: "carnivorous sacrifice is essential to the structure of subjectivity, which is to say to the founding of the intentional subject as well and to the founding, if not of the law [*loi*], at least of right [*droit*], the difference between law and right [*la loi et le droit*], justice and right, justice and law [*loi*], here remaining open over an abyss." See further Derrida 1995b, 279–83 ("Eating Well").

26. Derrida (2008, 28–29) also refers to a war concerning compassion for animal suffering, which is probably an ageless war, but which has been waged with a renewed intensity over the past two centuries. This is a war between those who testify to animal suffering on the one hand, and those (mostly male [104]) who engage in violence against animals, and also against compassion for animals, on the other hand.

27. See also Derrida 1973, 129–60 ("Différance").

28. The same is true for nature in general, which, as some have argued, should be accorded rights, in a move away from anthropocentrism toward biocentrism; see Borrás 2016, 113–43; Rühs and Jones 2016, 1–19.

29. Further evidence of a movement away from the Kantian position in terms of which the proper treatment/protection of non-human animals is linked to human interests/values, toward a position where they are protected because they "are sentient beings that are capable of suffering and of experiencing pain," is to be found in court judgments (even in the absence of constitutional provisions that protect animal interests) such as *National Society for the Prevention of Cruelty to Animals v Minister of Justice and Constitutional Development and Another* [2016] ZACC 46 paras. 1, 54–61; see further Eisen "Animals in the Constitutional State" 918–24.

30. In chapter 7, see in particular article 71: "Nature or Pachamama, where life is reproduced and exists, has the right to exist, persist, maintain and regenerate its vital cycles, structure, functions and its processes in evolution."

31. See, for example, Eisen 2017, 930–32, 949–50; Garner 2017. As Donaldson and Kymlicka 2011, 153–54 argue, such representation should also not be restricted to legislatures, but should include administrative and judicial processes.

32. See also De Blic 2021.

33. See in this respect also Eisen 2017, 941–52; Kotzé 2019, 6796.

Chapter 5

1. The field of "criminal law" as referred to here includes the issue of punishment or sentencing, which in many jurisdictions is regarded as a separate question of criminal procedure. "Criminal justice system" has a similar broad meaning.

2. See further chapter 3 of this volume.

3. See also Derrida 2002a, 253–54.

4. See also chapter 4 of this volume, where subjectivity was explored with reference to the traditional human-animal distinction.

5. See also chapter 3 of this volume, where freedom was explored by way of Heidegger, and within the context of democratic constitutionalism.

6. See further chapters 1 and 3 of this volume.

7. See also Derrida 2017, 95.

8. Reik (1959) views the compulsion to confess and the closely related unconscious need for punishment as a general tendency, and thus detectable also beyond the field of criminal law. Examples would include a partner who is sexually unfaithful and leaves behind clues of his or her infidelity; a person who is constantly hostile toward relatives and friends, even though this causes suffering; and a child who acts naughtily, thereby seeking punishment.

9. See also Silving (1960, 23), who points to the link between imprisonment and the infantile state of dependence; as well as the possible effects of harsh measures adopted in the event of a crime wave, which do not actually prevent crime, but encourage it, as the treatment meted out is then viewed as an advance payment, a "credit" by a wrongdoer for the commission of future crimes.

10. See also Reik 1959, 474.

11. Derrida (2017, 10–13) adds to this the relevance of other ages: mental age, social age, the agelessness of the unconscious, as well as the ages of human and animal life in general; see also Derrida and Roudinesco 2004, 158–59.

12. See the "Introduction" to this volume, and see further Kant 1996a, 8:297 ("On the Common Saying") where he speaks about the Idea of reason, that is, "to bind every legislator to give his laws in such a way that they could have arisen from the united will of a whole people and to regard each subject, insofar as he wants to be a citizen, as if he has joined in voting for such a will."

13. Derrida (2017, 66–67) points out that this situation is portrayed well by Kafka in *America*.

14. Elsewhere in this chapter, it is noted that the sovereign is referred to by Derrida as the foundation of law, and the death penalty as the foundation of criminal law. As will be seen, freedom is closely linked to these foundations.

15. See likewise Freud 2001, 14:332–33 ("Criminals from a sense of guilt").

16. Derrida's stance toward the Oedipus complex can be found inter alia in *The Post Card* where he describes it as only one of the most restrictive effects of dissemination without return (1987a, 340–41).

17. See Freud 2001, 14:333: "We must remember . . . that parricide and incest with the mother are the two great human crimes, the only ones which, as such, are pursued and abhorred in primitive communities."

18. See, e.g., Derrida 2001e, 22: "I always have to be forgiven, to ask forgiveness for not giving, for never giving enough, for never offering or welcoming enough. One is always guilty, one must always be forgiven the gift."

19. See also Derrida (2009a, 39–43) where he, in a reading of Hobbes's *Leviathan*, analyzes the notion of fear as the basis of both crime and compliance with the law, as well as, ultimately, for the establishment of the state. It is not the fear of one's fellow man that is at stake here, but fear for the self, for the wolf inside the self; see further De Ville 2012.

20. In *For What Tomorrow*, Derrida (48) notes that the word freedom "often seems to me to be loaded with metaphysical presuppositions that confer on the subject or on consciousness—that is, on an egological subject—a sovereign independence in relation to drives, calculation, economy, the machine."

21. See *For What Tomorrow*, where Derrida (48–49, also at 58) speaks of "an excess of play in the machine."

22. See also Derrida 2014c, 83–88.

23. Ipse=self, which contains within itself the idea of force, power and mastery; see further chapter 3 of this volume.

24. See also Derrida (2017, 204–6) on the causal relation, which Reik posits between idealism and cruelty.

25. See likewise Reik (1959, 473) who, invoking Freud, notes that "punishment not infrequently offers, to those who execute it and who represent the community, the opportunity to commit, on their part, the same crime or evil deed under the justification of exacting penance."

26. See also Derrida 1987a, 367–68, 404–5.

27. One cannot therefore make a convincing argument either for or against the death penalty simply in the name of cruelty. We know that Beccaria, for example, argued for the abolition of the death penalty, as it was not cruel enough; see Derrida 2014c, 160–61. On the other hand, proponents of the death penalty at times seek through new inventions to make executions more humane and less cruel.

28. See likewise Foucault (1991, 15–16), who points to the bodily pain of imprisonment and the trace of torture that remains in modern systems of punishment, even though the primary site of concern has moved toward the offender's soul; and see Guttmacher 1958, 641 on the moralistic and religious principles that still underlie punishment; as well as Maruna, Matravers, and King 2004, 277–99.

29. The pardon was the theme of seminars by Derrida between 1997 and 2000 (Perjury and Pardon), volume one of which is scheduled to be published in English in 2022.

30. Geismann (2012, 133) contends that for Kant utilitarian arguments (e.g., prevention) are not completely irrelevant; they are simply subject to the primary principle, that is, retribution. The Appendix to the "Theory of Law" (Kant 1996b, 6:362) can possibly be read in this way. The main section in the "Theory of Law," however, seems to suggest the contrary.

31. This link between honor and punish is also reflected in Walter Benjamin's exposition of the feeling of the people toward the great criminal: on one (unconscious) level they admire him or her as someone who challenges the monopoly of violence of the state, and on another level they approve of the punishment. As Derrida (2017, 27, 46) points out, this is also reflected in more ancient cultures such as the Greek and the Latin, where, respectively, the *pharmakos* and the *sacer* were excluded, yet celebrated.

32. In *For What Tomorrow*, Derrida (142) points out that the death penalty is at the same time transcendental *and* internal. While it is an element of criminal law, that is, one punishment among others, it is also external, excluded: the foundation of criminal law, its origin.

33. The structure of the death penalty (or the relation between life and death, including the death penalty), as elaborated on here, is similar to the stricture of *différance* as it plays itself out in a variety of Derrida's texts, for example in the differantial relation between justice and law. We find in this structure on the one hand a drive toward the proper, a binding or stricture, a conditionality, a calculation, an economy; and on the other hand, though not in opposition to it, a certain unconditional, noncalculable force of self-destruction, an expenditure without reserve, which cannot be presented as such to experience; see further De Ville 2011a, 28–37.

34. See further chapter 2 on the principle of reason, also its analysis by Derrida in the Death Penalty Seminars.

35. See further Derrida 2002b, 324–26; 2005c, 133–34; Kant 1997b, 4:434–36. It is important at this point to note that Derrida (2017, 139–40) understands the noncalculable (sometimes referred to as the incalculable) as heterogeneous to the calculable, that is, purely qualitative in the sense that it "removes or subtracts itself from any calculability, any accounting or bookkeeping."

36. See also Derrida 2002b, 325.

37. See likewise Derrida (2017, 140, 144) on the *ius talionis* as "the necessary, the ineluctable passage from quality to quantity, from the in-calculable or the non-calculable to the calculable."

38. Note that Derrida (2017, 183) appears to contain an error (in both French and English) in the first sentence just after the quotation. Derrida's summary of the passage from Kant he had just quoted appears to be incorrect, and also to contradict Derrida's next sentence.

39. Derrida relies here on the distinction in Kant between form and content, the latter of which would, e.g., point to the "interests" at stake in other discourses on the death penalty.

40. As Dutoit (2012, 126) points out, the appendix in Kant (in response to the critique of Bouterwek of the first edition of the *Metaphysics of Morals*) adds itself to the original discussion, but shows itself to be originary in nature: The *lex talionis* is shown to be first of all the law of sexual exchange and substitution, that is, of spiritual rather than literal equivalence. A discussion of the substitute or supplement as originary is to be found in Derrida 1997a, 141–64.

41. "Sex" is of course not here to be understood in the ordinary sense, or in an Oedipal sense, as indicated earlier.

42. Further complicating Kant's stance on the death penalty is his statement in the *Metaphysics of Morals* that the (execution of the) death penalty "must still be freed from any mistreatment that could make the humanity in the person suffering it into something abominable" (1996b, 6:333). As Derrida (2014c, 273) points out, this requirement is impossible to comply with, making "both the condemnation to death and especially its execution" forever impermissible. Kant would thus *de lege* be a proponent of the death penalty, but de facto an abolitionist. See also Derrida and Roudinesco 2004, 152.

43. It can be noted in this regard that for Heidegger (similar to what Kant seems to be saying here), death "is the measure because it gives the measure, and giving the measure, it is not measurable" (Derrida 2017, 156).

44. As we saw earlier, deterrence and confession likewise ultimately remain within the circle of economic exchange characterizing the unconscious.

45. Kant (1979, 155) distinguishes the enthusiasm, which he as a spectator of the revolution has, from feeling in a pathological or empirical sense. He does so in the same way in which he speaks of the feeling of respect for the moral law, and of the feeling of horror in the face of the execution of a monarch; see Derrida 2017, 93–95, 190, 203. See further chapter 1 of this volume.

46. See Derrida 2007a, 441–61; 2002b, 343–70 ("'As if it were Possible, 'within such limits' . . .") where we find more detailed analyses of the event, the impossible, and the perhaps.

47. Something similar can be said of movements toward decriminalization of, e.g., prostitution, homosexuality, abortion, drugs, and petty offenses.

Chapter 6

1. The manuscript was submitted by Kant on August 13, 1795, and publication followed on September 29, 1795; see Kant 1991, 276 n1 (all further references to "Toward Perpetual Peace" are drawn from Kant 1996a); Hackel 2000, 17.

2. See Bohman and Lutz-Bachmann 1997, 1; Höffe 1995b, 5; Saner 1995, 43.

3. See Klenner 1996, 16; Saner 1995, 43; Patzig 1996, 14; Krause 2013, 11; Eberl and Niesen 2011, 98. As Gerhardt (1995, 70) points out, this was the first treaty signed between the German monarchy and the revolutionary French republic, recognizing thereby the latter's legal form and boundaries. The world-historical event of the French revolution was thereby recognized by one of the great monarchical powers of Europe. According to Gerhardt, Kant's essay links the historical event of this peace treaty with the liberal-republican impulse of the French revolution and gives it a global political perspective. Human rights were thereby recognized as at the foundation of any future politics. The influence of these events on Kant's essay is contested by inter alia Hackel (2000, 20).

4. Saner (1995, 44) points out that in peace treaties of the seventeenth and eighteenth centuries, a preliminary treaty would first be signed between the parties so as to reach consensus about the conditions of the termination of the state of war and for the conclusion of a final peace treaty. Kant's preliminary articles are analogous to such a preliminary treaty (containing the negative conditions for peace), and the definitive articles with the supplements and appendixes are analogous to a final treaty (containing the positive conditions for future peace and dealing with the dangers and safeguards of such peace).

5. The second supplement (secret article of a perpetual peace), which deals with the relation between philosophy and politics/law, was added in the second edition (1796); see Klemme 1992, XXXIX. Derrida (1993a, 84–86 n10) briefly comments on this secret article, pointing to its alignment with Kant's *Conflict of the Faculties* and noting that the secret and the philosopher are both granted a place that *precedes* the oppositions (public/private and law/savagery), which are at stake here.

6. See Krause (2013) on how each of these can be read as responding to conditions at the time. The prohibition on states being inherited, exchanged, purchased, or offered as gifts was, e.g., presumably at least partially in response to the partition of Poland in 1795 between Prussia, Russia, and Habsburg, Austria.

7. In Kant (1996a, 8:352), this separation of powers is between the legislature and the executive, whereas in Kant (1996b, 6:313 [para. 45]), this separation is between the legislature, the executive, and the judiciary.

8. See Bohman and Lutz-Bachmann (1997, 20 n2) on the terminology to be used here, i.e., "law" or "right."

9. Bischof (2004, 434) points out that Kant is the first modern political thinker to speak of hospitality as a right and thus as falling within the legal sphere, i.e., not to treat it simply as a matter of custom, morality, or ethics.

10. See, e.g., Westmoreland 2008, 1; Caputo 1997, 109–13; Still 2010; Mansfield 2018.

11. The words *Zum ewigen Frieden* appear both on the title page and just before the preface.

12. See similarly Levinas (2007a, 150–52), who is critical of those who would suggest that there is no alternative between "Realpolitik and the irritating rhetoric of a careless idealism, lost in utopian dreams but crumbling into dust on contact with reality or turning into a dangerous, impudent and facile frenzy which professes to be taking up the prophetic discourse."

13. Derrida also refers in his texts to other examples in the literature of the host becoming a guest, such as in Camus's *The Guest in Exile and the Kingdom* (Derrida 1999b, 117–22); *Oedipus at Colonus*; Lot in Sodom, who invites angels to visit his home; and the story of the Levite and his concubine in *Judges* 19 (Derrida and Dufourmantelle 2000, 107, 151–55); as well as Abraham, when God changes his name from Abram (Derrida 2002a, 372).

14. See nevertheless the First Supplement, where Kant (1996a, 8:361–68) contends that nature has a hand in securing peace. According to Kant, nature uses men's hostile inclinations to first disperse them around the globe, and then to bind them together again in law-like and peaceful relations, both as a protection against war and because of mutual self-interest (commercial trade).

15. See also Derrida (2006c, 213) where he notes that peace is not to be understood as a utopian concept projected into infinity.

16. Saner (1995, 50) points out that Kant is expressing a judgment here on the whole of human history, which thus far has indeed been one of either war or armistice, thus a history without peace in the strict sense.

17. For Levinas, ethics as first philosophy begins with the encounter of the face of the other, which places an unconditional demand on me and which he also refers to as hospitality. "Allergy" here would entail a refusal or forgetting of the face.

18. As Derrida (1999a, 82) points out, peace beyond the political is to be understood as neither simply political in the traditional sense nor simply apolitical.

19. See also Derrida (1997c) on the concept of the political, and for commentary, De Ville (2017, 9–73).

20. Ethics is not to be understood here as a domain distinguishable from the domains of law and politics, but as "preceding" these domains in the sense of a pre-origin.

21. This ties in closely with Levinas's notion of hospitality (as well as goodness and friendship) as the essence of language; see Levinas 1969, 305; Derrida 1999a, 10, 51, 91, 133.

22. Derrida (1999a, 68) nonetheless remains ambivalent about this.

23. See, e.g., Derrida (1999a, 33–35) on the relation between the face to face and the third in Levinas.

24. As Derrida points out here, war for Levinas is always against a face, but such war would nonetheless retain a trace of the pacific welcoming of a face.

25. Derrida (1999a, 87–88) seems to allude to another difference between Kant and Levinas when he notes that for Levinas peace is not something that should be postponed indefinitely or continuously approached, but something that must happen "now." Yet it would also be possible to refer to passages in Kant where peace is spoken of as an "an immediate or direct duty [*unmittelbaren Pflicht*]" (1996a, 8:356) and as an "irresistible veto [*unwiderstehliches Veto*]" being pronounced in us by morally practicable reason: "*there is to be no war* [Es soll kein Krieg sein]" (1996b, 6:354).

26. In "Beyond the Pleasure Principle," Freud (2001, 18:3–64) distinguishes between these drives.

27. See also chapter 5 of this volume.

28. See Derrida (1987a, 2020) for detailed analyses of Freud's "Beyond the Pleasure Principle."

29. See Derrida and Stiegler (2002, 81) on the relation between negotiation and invention. See similarly Shryock (2008, 418).

30. See also Levinas (1998, xv): "A responsibility without concern for reciprocity: I have to respond for an other without attending to an other's responsibility in regard to me."

31. An analysis of Derrida's reading of Kant's exposition of constitutional law is undertaken in the "Introduction" and in chapter 3 of this volume.

32. Kant uses this phrase in a footnote in the second section of "Toward Perpetual Peace."

33. Werner and Gordon (2016, 514) note that the two categories of law derive from different sources: "The right of hospitality . . . was derived from a cosmopolitan precondition, that 'all nations are *originally* members of a community of the land,' in which, by virtue of the shape of the globe, 'everyone has an original right to share,'" whereas "the 'pacific federation . . . derives from international right." They nevertheless view Kant as making a link between the two categories with the peaceful federation eventually developing into a cosmopolitan constitution (515–16).

34. See Habermas 2003, 38; 2012, 55; 2014a, 226–27.

35. See, e.g., Derrida 2002b, 333.

36. See Derrida 1994b, 105–7; 1997b, 4; 2003, 130–31; Derrida and Kearney 2004, 11.

37. See also Kant 1996b, 6:344 (para. 54).

38. See Geismann 1997, 333; Kleingeld 2012, 60; Rimoux 2015, 106.

39. See also Kant 1996b, 6:344 (para. 54).

40. "Furor impius intus—fremit horridus ore cruento: And godless Furor will sit/Inside on his frightful weapons, hands bound with a hundred/Brass knots behind him, and roar with bloody mouth" (Vergil 1963, 1:294–96).

41. See, e.g., Kant 2007, 8:24 ("Idea for a Universal History") where he proposes a league of peoples (*Völkerbund*), which he seems to understand as a union of states, with member states abandoning their own sovereignty, rather than a (looser) federation of states.

42. There are of course internal differences and overlaps between some of these readings, and the analysis undertaken here is not exhaustive. It merely seeks to sketch the background to Derrida's reading.

43. See, e.g., Brandt 2010, 138–41; Huggler 2010, 133–34; Gerhardt 1995, 94, 104; Scheid 2011, 838; Koller 1996, 220–22.

44. See, e.g., Tesón 1992, 87; Holland 2017, 614. Krause (2013, 16), e.g., contends that Kant was in favor of the idea of a world state before the French revolution because it could limit the power of monarchies. After the revolution, a federation between republican states became a real possibility coupled with a right to hospitality.

45. See, e.g., Lutz-Bachmann 1997, 60, 69–74; Höffe 2006, 193; Habermas 1988, 166–71; Pogge 1988, 407; Wood 1995, 59.

46. See Lutz-Bachmann 1997, 73; Hackel 2000, 76–82.

47. See Höffe 1995c, 130–31.

48. See Rimoux 2015, 112–13.

49. See Kleingeld 2012, 50–58.

50. See, e.g., Kleingeld 2004, 304; 2012, 44, 58; Habermas 2014a, 227; Rimoux 2015, 103–14; Geismann 1996, 1997.

51. See Rimoux 2015, 113; Geismann 1996.

52. See also Derrida 2009a, 230–31, noting the equation of majesty and sovereignty. This quoted statement of Kant about sovereignty, the state, and the people can arguably be read in various ways: as simply a statement as to where sovereignty lies (not with a people or an international association), as dismissive of (direct) democracy, or as only dismissive of democracy insofar as it is tied to sovereignty (which would be in line with Derrida's analysis undertaken here). See the later analysis in the current chapter, and chapter 3 of this volume.

53. See further chapter 3 of this volume.

54. We see this movement from freedom to self-legislation in its two forms clearly in Kant's thinking; see in this regard the "Introduction" and chapter 3 of this volume.

55. Derrida seems to be alluding here to Kant's notion of a "kingdom of ends" in the *Groundwork* (1997b, 4:433–434) and the "ethical community" at stake in Kant's *Religion within the Boundaries of mere Reason* (1998b, 6:95–100); see Höffe (2006, 15), who points to the connection between Kant's kingdom of ends and (moral) cosmopolitanism; contra Geismann (1996, 7), who sees a clear distinction between these notions.

56. This "alliance" is perhaps to be understood with reference to Derrida's analysis of the without-world, i.e., a lack of world, of cosmos, *Weltlosigkeit*, an abyss

of the without-world. We are without world (*weltlos*) in at least two senses of the term: (1) as singular beings we do not and cannot really share a joint world with others (Derrida 2011, 265–68); and (2) because of the extension of "war" to the whole "world," this world is constantly being threatened by self-destruction, i.e., the logic of autoimmunity (Derrida 2003, 98–99; 2005c, 155–56). In the words of Celan, whose texts are analyzed by Derrida in *The Beast & the Sovereign* I, and in *Sovereignties in Question*: "Die Welt ist fort, ich muss dich tragen." This "lack of world" can also be expressed through the notion of *khōra*, which Derrida (2005c, xiv) refers to as "a spacing from 'before' the world, the cosmos, or the globe." See also Derrida and Kearney 2004, 11: "*Khora* opens up a universality beyond cosmopolitanism. . . . An empty mutual space that is not the cosmos, not the created world, not the nation, not the state, not the global dimension, but just that: *khora*."

57. See further chapters 3 and 4 of this volume.

58. See, e.g., Habermas 1988, 2006, 173–74; Douzinas 2007.

59. The international regulation and enforcement of a fair system of taxation of global companies would presumably be a priority here.

60. See Derrida 1994b, 105–6, 2006a, 409; 2006b, 305; Habermas and Derrida 2006, 273.

61. Kant's text in this regard is at times read as referring (primarily) to a right to engage in trade relations with the members of another state; see, e.g., Höffe 2012, 293–94, 306–7; Höffe 2006, 140–41.

62. For a *Gastrecht* to be established, a generous treaty to become a temporary member of the household (*Hausgenossen*) would according to Kant be required. The surface of the earth is thus to be distinguished from what is constructed on it (e.g., a state), which does not belong to everyone.

63. See also Ossipow 2008, 357.

64. To be noted is that in Levinas's reading, in the "thou shalt not kill," the entire Torah is concentrated; e.g., Levinas 2007b, 111: "The life of others, the being of others, falls to me as a duty. In the thou of this commandment, the me is only begun: it is for the other in its innermost nucleus."

65. See also Derrida 1995d, 85–86. 2017, 76–80; and chapter 2 of this volume.

66. Levinas (2007b, 98) similarly speaks of a messianic order where a people accept foreigners who come to settle among them. This acceptance can be spoken of in terms of tolerance, only if tolerance is understood in terms of love (98), or, as Derrida (1999a, 72) puts it, "a 'love' without measure." This can be compared with Kant's association of hospitality with tolerance in "Toward Perpetual Peace" and his restriction of hospitality to a right to visit.

67. See also the earlier discussion in the current chapter.

68. The host-guest relation can also be described in other terms such as being placed in question, or being "contested, interpellated, implicated, persecuted, *under accusation*"; see Derrida 1999a, 56.

69. This ties in closely with the earlier analysis of "woman," as conditioning hospitality; see Derrida 1999a, 93.

70. Another limitation with respect to hospitality is to be found in Kant's insistence on speaking the truth, even if this would expose the guest to danger; see Derrida and Dufourmantelle 2000, 65–73.

71. The notion of unconditional hospitality clearly resonates with Levinas's statements about Jerusalem in *Beyond the Verse* referred to earlier.

72. See further Derrida (2001d, 70) where he notes that committing a crime against humanity is today viewed as unforgivable. The human being is thus regarded as divine, sacred, an inheritance from the Christian religion.

73. See also Derrida 2005c, 95–96; 2009a, 208–9.

74. Schmitt's analysis here of course ties in closely with his *Concept of the Political*, where he defines this concept in terms of the potential of a friend-enemy grouping, with war as the most extreme consequence of such a grouping. Schmitt (2007) here bemoans the disappearance of the enemy in the twentieth century, yet notes that enmity now paradoxically becomes more intensified. In his analysis of this text, and other texts of Schmitt on the concept of the political, Derrida shows that the concept of the political in Schmitt includes within itself a force of self-destruction; see De Ville 2017, 9–73.

Bibliography

Ackerman, Lourens W. H. 2004. "The Legal Nature of the South African Constitutional Revolution." *New Zealand Law Review*, no. 4: 633–80.

———. 2012. *Human Dignity: Lodestar for Equality in South Africa*. Cape Town: Juta.

Albertyn, Catherine, and Dennis Davis. 2010. "Legal Realism, Transformation and the Legacy of Dugard." *South African Journal on Human Rights* 26, no. 2: 188–216.

Aristotle. 1984. *The Complete Works of Aristotle*. Edited by Jonathan Barnes. Princeton: Princeton University Press.

Balkin, Jack M. 1987. "Deconstructive Practice and Legal Theory." *Yale Law Journal* 96, no. 4: 743–86.

Barnard-Naudé, Jaco, Drucilla Cornell, and Francois du Bois, eds. *Dignity, Freedom and the Post-Apartheid Legal Order: The Critical Jurisprudence of Laurie Ackermann*. Cape Town: Juta.

Beardsworth, Richard. 1996. *Derrida and the Political*. London: Routledge.

Bentham, Jeremy. 1843. *The Works of Jeremy Bentham*. Vol. 2, edited by John Bowring. Edinburgh: William Tait.

Benveniste, Émile. 1973. *Indo-European Language and Society*. Translated by Elizabeth Palmer. Florida: University of Miami Press. https://chs.harvard.edu/book/benveniste-emile-indo-european-language-and-society/.

Bilchitz, David. 2010. "Does Transformative Constitutionalism Require the Recognition of Animal Rights?" *Southern African Public Law* 25, no. 2: 267–300.

Bischof, Sacha. 2004. *Gerechtigkeit—Verantwortung—Gastfreundschaft: Ethik-Ansätze nach Jacques Derrida*. Fribourg, Switzerland: Academic Press Fribourg.

Blaau, Loammi C. 1990. "The *Rechtsstaat* Idea Compared with the Rule of Law as a Paradigm for Protecting Rights." *South African Law Journal* 107, no. 1: 76–96.

Blaauw-Wolf, Loammi, and Joachim Wolf. 1996. "A Comparison between German and South African Limitation Provisions." *South African Law Journal* 113, no. 2: 267–96.

Bohman, James, and Matthias Lutz-Bachmann. 1997. Introduction to *Perpetual Peace: Essays on Kant's Cosmopolitan Ideal*, edited by James Bohman and Matthias Lutz-Bachmann, 1–22. Baskerville: MIT Press.

Borradori, Giovanna. 2003. *Philosophy in a Time of Terror: Dialogues with Jürgen Habermas and Jacques Derrida*. Chicago: University of Chicago Press.

Borràs, Susana. 2016. "New Transitions from Human Rights to the Environment to the Rights of Nature." *Transnational Environmental Law* 5, no. 1: 113–43.

Botha, Henk. 2009. "Human Dignity in Comparative Perspective." *Stellenbosch Law Review* 20, no. 2: 171–220.

———. 2013. "The Rights of Foreigners: Dignity, Citizenship, and the Right to Have Rights." *South African Law Journal* 130, no. 4: 837–69.

Bragyova, András. 2011. "Kant and the Constitutional Review: Kantian Principles of the Neo-Constitutionalist Constitutionalism." *Acta Juridica Hungarica* 52, no. 2: 97–114.

Brand, Danie. 2011. "Judicial Deference and Democracy in Socio-economic Rights Cases." *Stellenbosch Law Review* 22, no. 3: 614–38.

Brandt, Reinhard. 2010. "Vom Weltbürgerrecht." In Höffe 1995a, 133–48. Berlin: Akademie Verlag.

Brown, Garrett Wallace. 2009. *Grounding Cosmopolitanism: From Kant to a Cosmopolitan Constitution*. Edinburgh: Edinburgh University Press.

———. 2010. "The Laws of Hospitality, Asylum Seekers and Cosmopolitan Right: A Kantian Response to Jacques Derrida." *European Journal of Political Philosophy* 9, no. 3: 308–27.

Capps, Patrick, and Julian Rivers. 2010. "Kant's Concept of International Law." *Legal Theory* 16, no. 4: 229–57.

Caputo, John D. 1997. *Deconstruction in a Nutshell: A Conversation with Jacques Derrida*. New York: Fordham University Press.

———. 1997. *The Prayers and Tears of Jacques Derrida: Religion without Religion*. Bloomington: Indiana University Press.

Chaskalson, Arthur. 2000. "The Third Bram Fischer Lecture—Human Dignity as a Foundational Value of Our Constitutional Order." *South African Journal on Human Rights* 16, no. 2: 193–205.

Christodoulidis, Emilios, Ruth Dukes, and Marco Goldoni, eds. 2019. *Research Handbook in Critical Legal Theory*. Cheltenham: Edward Elgar.

———. 2011. "Dignity as a Constitutional Value: A South African Perspective." *American University International Law Review* 26, no. 5: 1377–408.

Cornell, Drucilla. 1992. *The Philosophy of the Limit*. New York: Routledge.

———. 2009. "Bridging the Span toward Justice: Laurie Ackermann and the Ongoing Architectonic of Dignity Jurisprudence." In Barnard-Naudé et al. 2009, 18–46.

Corradetti, Claudio. 2016. "Kant's Legacy and the Idea of a Transitional *Jus Cosmopoliticum*." *Ratio Juris* 29, no. 1: 105–21.

Currie, Iain, and Johan de Waal. 2013. *The Bill of Rights Handbook*. 6th ed. Cape Town: Juta.
Davis, Dennis. 2004. "Socio-Economic Rights in South Africa: The Record after Ten Years." *New Zealand Journal of Public and International Law* 2, no. 1: 47–66.
———. 2019. "The Pigeonhole Dictated by *Logos*: Behind the Text in *Volks v. Robinson*." *African Yearbook of Rhetoric* 9: 73–85.
Davis, Dennis, and Karl Klare. 2019. "Critical Legal Realism in a Nutshell." In Christodoulidis et al. 2019, 27–43.
De Blic, Damien. 2021. "Representing Nature." *Eurozine*, January 12, 2021.
De Kesel, Mark. 2009. *Eros and Ethics: Reading Jacques Lacan's Seminar VII*. New York: State University of New York Press.
Derrida, Jacques. 1973. *Speech and Phenomena and Other Essays on Husserl's Theory of Signs*. Translated by David B. Allison. Evanston, IL: Northwestern University Press.
———. 1981. *Positions*. Translated and annotated by Alan Bass. Chicago: University of Chicago Press.
———. 1982. *Margins of Philosophy*. Translated, with Additional Notes, by Alan Bass. Chicago: University of Chicago Press.
———. 1983. "The Principle of Reason: The University in the Eyes of Its Pupils." Translated by Catherine Porter and Edward P. Morris. *Diacritics* 13, no. 3 (Autumn): 2–20.
———. 1986. "Foreword: *Fors*: The Anglish Words of Nicholas Abraham and Maria Torok." Translated by Barbara Johnson. In Nicolas Abraham and Maria Torok, *The Wolf Man's Magic Word: A Cryptonomy*. Translated by Nicholas Rand, xi–xlviii. Minneapolis: University of Minnesota Press.
———. 1987a. *The Post Card: From Socrates to Freud and Beyond*. Translated by Alan Bass. Chicago: University of Chicago Press.
———. 1987b. *The Truth in Painting*. Translated by Geoff Bennington and Ian McLeod. Chicago: University of Chicago Press.
———. 1988. *Limited Inc*. Edited by Gerald Graff. Evanston, IL: Northwestern University Press.
———. 1990. "Let Us Not Forget—Psychoanalysis." *Oxford Literary Review* 12, no. 1/2 (Psychoanalysis and Literature: New Work): 3–7.
———. 1992a. *Given Time: I. Counterfeit Money*. Translated by Peggy Kamuf. Chicago: University of Chicago Press.
———. 1992b. "Passions: 'An Oblique Offering.'" Translated by David Wood. In *Derrida: A Critical Reader*, edited by David Wood, 5–35. Oxford: Blackwell.
———. 1993a. *Aporias*. Translated by Thomas Dutoit. Stanford: Stanford University Press.
———. 1993b. "Heidegger's Ear: Philopolemology (*Geschlecht* IV)." In *Reading Heidegger: Commemorations*, edited by John Sallis, 163–218. Bloomington: Indiana University Press.

———. 1993c. "On a Newly Arisen Apocalyptic Tone in Philosophy." In *Raising the Tone of Philosophy: Late Essays by Immanuel Kant, Transformative Critique by Jacques Derrida*, edited by Peter Fenves, 117–71. Baltimore: John Hopkins University Press.

———. 1994a. "Nietzsche and the Machine." *Journal of Nietzsche Studies* (Spring), no. 7 (Futures of Nietzsche: Affirmation and Aporia): 7–66.

———. 1994b. *Specters of Marx: The State of Debt, the Work of Mourning and the New International*. Translated by Peggy Kamuf. New York: Routledge.

———. 1995a. *On the Name*. Edited by Thomas Dutoit. Stanford: Stanford University Press.

———. 1995b. *Points . . . Interviews, 1974–1994*. Edited by Elisabeth Weber. Stanford: Stanford University Press.

———. 1995c. "Tense." In *The Path of Archaic Thinking: Unfolding the Work of John Sallis*, edited by Kenneth Maly, 49–74. New York: State University of New York Press.

———. 1995d. *The Gift of Death*. Translated by David Wills. Chicago: University of Chicago Press.

———. 1996. "As if I Were Dead: An Interview with Jacques Derrida." In *Applying: To Derrida*, edited by John Brannigan, Ruth Robbins, and Julian Wolfreys, 216–26. Basingstoke: Macmillan Press.

———. 1997a. *Of Grammatology*. Translated by Gayatri Spivak. Baltimore: John Hopkins University Press.

———. 1997b. "Politics and Friendship: A Discussion with Jacques Derrida." Centre for Modern French Thought, University of Sussex, December 1, 1997. http://hydra.humanities.uci.edu/derrida/pol+fr.html.

———. 1997c. *Politics of Friendship*. Translated by George Collins. London: Verso.

———. 1998a. "Faith and Knowledge: The Two Sources of 'Religion' at the Limits of Reason Alone." Translated by Samuel Weber. In *Religion*, edited by Jacques Derrida and Gianni Vattimo, 1–78. Stanford: Stanford University Press.

———. 1998b. *Monolingualism of the Other, Or The Prosthesis of Origin*. Translated by Patrick Mensah. Stanford: Stanford University Press.

———. 1998c. *The Derrida Reader: Writing Performances*. Edited by Julian Wolfreys. Lincoln: University of Nebraska Press.

———. 1999a. *Adieu: To Emmanuel Levinas*. Translated by Pascale-Anne Brault and Michael Naas. Stanford: Stanford University Press.

———. 1999b. *Manifeste pour l'hospitalité*. Venissieux: Éditions Paroles d'aube.

———. 2001a. *Deconstruction Engaged: The Sydney Seminars*. Sydney: Power Publications.

———. 2001b. "I Have a Taste for the Secret." In Jacques Derrida and Maurizio Ferraris, *A Taste for the Secret*. Translated by Giacomo Donis, 1–92. Cambridge: Polity.

———. 2001c. *On Cosmopolitanism and Forgiveness*. Translated by Mark Dooley and Michael Hughes. London: Routledge.

———. 2001d. "On Forgiveness: A Roundtable Discussion with Jacques Derrida." In *Questioning God*, edited by John D. Caputo, Mark Dooley, and Michael J. Scanlon, 52–72. Bloomington: Indiana University Press.

———. 2001e. "To Forgive: The Unforgivable and the Imprescriptible." In *Questioning God*, edited by John D. Caputo, Mark Dooley, and Michael J. Scanlon, 21–51. Bloomington: Indiana University Press.

———. 2002a. *Acts of Religion*. Edited by Gil Anidjar. New York: Routledge.

———. 2002b. *Negotiations: Interventions and Interviews 1971–2001*. Edited by Elizabeth Rottenberg. Stanford: Stanford University Press.

———. 2002c. *Who's Afraid of Philosophy: Right to Philosophy 1*. Translated by Jan Plug. Stanford: Stanford University Press.

———. 2002d. *Without Alibi*. Translated and edited by Peggy Kamuf. Stanford: Stanford University Press.

———. 2003. "Autoimmunity: Real and Symbolic Suicides: A Dialogue with Jacques Derrida." In Borradori 2003, 85–136.

———. 2004a. *Dissemination*. Translated by Barbara Johnson. London: Continuum.

———. 2004b. *Eyes of the University: Right to Philosophy 2*. Translated by Jan Plug et al. Stanford: Stanford University Press.

———. 2005a. *On Touching–Jean-Luc Nancy*. Translated by Christine Irizarry. Stanford: Stanford University Press.

———. 2005b. *Paper Machine*. Translated by Rachel Bowlby. Stanford: Stanford University Press.

———. 2005c. *Rogues: Two Essays on Reason*. Translated by Pascale-Anne Brault and Michael Naas. Stanford: Stanford University Press.

———. 2005d. *Sovereignties in Question: The Poetics of Paul Celan*. Edited by Thomas Dutoit and Outi Pasanen. New York: Fordham University Press.

———. 2006a. "A Europe of Hope." *Epoché: A Journal for the History of Philosophy* 10, no. 2: 407–12.

———. 2006b. "Honesty of Thought." In Thomassen 2006, 300–6.

———. 2006c. "Hostipitality." In Thomassen 2006, 208–30.

———. 2006d. "For a Justice to Come: An Interview with Jacques Derrida." In Thomassen 2006, 259–69.

———. 2007a. "A Certain Impossible Possibility of Saying the Event." *Critical Inquiry* 33 (Winter): 441–61.

———. 2007b. *Learning to Live Finally: The Last Interview*. Translated by Pascale-Anne Brault and Michael Naas. Houndmills: Palgrave MacMillan.

———. 2007c. *Psyche: Inventions of the Other*. Vol. 1, edited by Peggy Kamuf and Elizabeth Rottenberg. Stanford: Stanford University Press.

———. 2008. *The Animal That Therefore I Am*. Translated by David Wills. New York: Fordham University Press.

———. 2009a. *The Beast & the Sovereign*. Vol. 1, translated by Geoffrey Bennington. Chicago: University of Chicago Press.

———. 2009b. "Unconditionally or Sovereignty: The University at the Frontiers of Europe." *Oxford Literary Review* 31, no. 2: 115–31.

———. 2011. *The Beast & the Sovereign*. Vol. 2, translated by Geoffrey Bennington. Chicago: University of Chicago Press.

———. 2013. "Avowing—The Impossible: 'Returns,' Repentance, and Reconciliation." In *Living Together: Jacques Derrida's Communities of Violence and Peace*, edited by Elizabeth Weber, 18–41. New York: Fordham University Press.

———. 2014a. "Admiration of Nelson Mandela, or The Laws of Reflection." *Law & Literature* 26, no. 1: 9–30.

———. 2014b. *For Strasbourg: Conversations of Friendship and Philosophy*. Edited and translated by Pascale-Anne Brault and Michael Naas. New York: Fordham University Press.

———. 2014c. *The Death Penalty*. Vol. 1, translated by Peggy Kamuf. Chicago: University of Chicago Press.

———. 2017. *The Death Penalty*. Vol. 2, translated by Elizabeth Rottenberg. Chicago: University of Chicago Press.

———. 2018. *Before the Law: The Complete Text of Préjugés*. Translated by Sandra van Reenen and Jacques de Ville. Minneapolis: University of Minnesota Press.

———. 2019. *Theory and Practice*. Translated by David Wills. Chicago: University of Chicago Press.

———. 2020. *Life Death*. Translated by Pascale-Anne Brault and Michael Naas. Chicago: University of Chicago Press.

Derrida, Jacques, and Anne Dufourmantelle. 2000. *Of Hospitality*. Translated by Rachel Bowlby. Stanford: Stanford University Press.

Derrida, Jacques, and Richard Kearney. 2004. "A Dialogue with Jacques Derrida." *Philosophy Today* 48, no. 1: 4–11.

Derrida, Jacques, and Elisabeth Roudinesco. 2004. *For What Tomorrow . . . : A Dialogue*. Stanford: Stanford University Press.

Derrida, Jacques, and Bernard Stiegler. 2002. *Echographies of Television*. Translated by Jennifer Bajorek. Cambridge: Polity Press.

De Tocqueville, Alexis. 2010. *Democracy in America*. Indianapolis: Liberty Fund.

De Ville, Jacques. 2011a. *Jacques Derrida: Law as Absolute Hospitality*. Abingdon: Routledge.

———. 2011b. "Mythology and the Images of Justice." *Law and Literature* 23, no. 3: 324–64.

———. 2012. "Deconstructing the Leviathan: Derrida's The Beast and the Sovereign." *Societies* 2, no. 4: 357–71.

———. 2017. *Constitutional Theory: Schmitt after Derrida*. Abingdon: Routledge.

De Villiers, Jan-Harm. 2019. "The Anthropomorphic Hegemony of Subjectivity: Critical Reflections on Law and the Question of the Animal." PhD diss., Leiden University. https://www.universiteitleiden.nl/en/research/research-output/

law/the-anthropomorphic-hegemony-of-subjectivity-critical-reflections-on-law-and-the-question-of-the-animal.

Devisch, Ignaas. 2009. "De 'Affaire' van de Vrijheid. Jean-Luc Nancy over het Vrijheidsbegrip bij Kant en Heidegger." *Tijdschrift voor Filosofie* 71, no. 4: 725–31.

De Vos, Pierre, and Warren Freedman, eds. 2014. *South African Constitutional Law in Context*. Cape Town: Oxford University Press South Africa.

———. 2021. *South African Constitutional Law in Context*. 2nd ed. Cape Town: Oxford University Press South Africa.

De Waal, Johan. 1995. "Comparative Analysis of the Provisions of German Origin in the Interim Bill of Rights." *South African Journal on Human Rights* 11, no. 1: 1–29.

De Wet, Erika. 2006a. "The Emergence of International and Regional Value Systems as a Manifestation of the Emerging International Constitutional Order." *Leiden Journal of International Law* 19, no. 3: 611–32.

———. 2006b. "The International Constitutional Order." *International and Comparative Law Quarterly* 55, no. 1: 51–76.

———. 2007. "The Emerging International Constitutional Order: The Implications of Hierarchy in International Law for the Coherence and Legitimacy of International Decision-Making." *Potchefstroom Electronic Law Journal* 10, no. 2: 20–46.

———. 2012. "The Constitutionalization of Public International Law." In *The Oxford Handbook of Comparative Constitutional Law*, edited by Michel Rosenfeld and András Sajó, chap. 58. Oxford: Oxford University Press.

Donaldson, Sue, and Will Kymlicka. 2011. *Zoopolis: A Political Theory of Animal Rights*. Oxford: Oxford University Press.

Douzinas, Costas. 2007. *Human Rights and Empire: The Political Philosophy of Cosmopolitanism*. Abingdon: Routledge-Cavendish.

———. 2014. "A Short History of the British Critical Legal Conference or, the Responsibility of the Critic." *Law and Critique* 25, no 2: 187–98.

Douzinas, Costas, and Adam Gearey. 2005. *Critical Jurisprudence: The Political Philosophy of Justice*. Oxford: Hart Publishing.

Dutoit, Thomas. 2012. "Kant's Retreat, Hugo's Advance, Freud's Erection; or, Derrida's Displacements in his Death Penalty Lectures." *Southern Journal of Philosophy* 50 (Spindel Supplement): 107–35.

Eberl, Oliver, and Peter Niesen. 2011. *Immanuel Kant Zum ewigen Frieden: Kommentar*. Berlin: Suhrkamp.

Ebert, Thomas. 2015. *Soziale Gerechtigkeit: Ideen—Geschichte—Kontroversen*. Frankfurt am Main: Druck- und Verlagshaus Zarbock.

Eisen, Jessica. 2017. "Animals in the Constitutional State." *International Journal of Constitutional Law* 15, no. 4: 909–54.

Evans, Dylan. 1996. *An Introductory Dictionary of Lacanian Psychoanalysis*. London: Routledge.
Freud, Sigmund. 1985. *The Complete Letters of Sigmund Freud to Wilhelm Fliess, 1887–1904*. Translated and edited by Jeffrey Moussaieff Masson. Cambridge: The Belknap Press of Harvard University Press.
———. 1991. *Gesammelte Werke: Chronologisch Geordnet*. 17 vols. London: Imago Publishing Co., Ltd.
———. 2001 [1886–1939]. *The Standard Edition of the Complete Psychological Works of Sigmund Freud*. 24 vols., edited by James Strachey. London: Vintage, 2001.
Foucault, Michel. 1991. *Discipline and Punish: The Birth of the Prison*. Translated by Alan Sheridan. London: Penguin Books.
Gaon, Stella. 2014. "'As If' There Were a 'Jew': The (non)Existence of Deconstructive Responsibility." *Derrida Today* 7, no. 1 (April): 44–58.
Garner, Robert. 2017. "Animals and Democratic Theory: Beyond an Anthropocentric Account." *Contemporary Political Theory* 16, no. 4: 459–77.
Gasché, Rodolphe. 1994. *Inventions of Difference: On Jacques Derrida*. Cambridge: Harvard University Press.
Geismann, George. 1996. "World Peace: Rational Idea and Reality—On the Principles of Kant's Political Philosophy." In *Kant. Analysen—Probleme—Kritik*, Bd. II, edited by Hariolf Oberer, 265–319. Würzburg: Königshausen & Neumann. http://www.georggeismann.de/.
———. 1997. "Kants Weg zum Frieden: Spätlese von Seels 'Neulesung' des Definitivartikels zum Völkerrecht." In *Kant. Analysen—Probleme—Kritik*, Bd. III, edited by Hariolf Oberer, 333–62. Würzburg: Königshausen & Neumann. http://www.georggeismann.de/.
———. 2009. *Kant und kein Ende*, Band 1: *Studien zur Moral-, Religions- und Geschichtsphilosophie*. Würzburg: Königshausen & Neumann.
———. 2012. *Kant und kein Ende*, Band 3: *Pax Kantiana oder Der Rechtsweg zum Weltfrieden*. Würzburg: Königshausen & Neumann.
Gerhardt, Volker. 1995. "Eine kritische Theorie der Politik. Über Kants Entwurf Zum ewigen Frieden." *WeltTrends: Zeitschrift für internationale Politik und vergleichende Studien* 9: 68–83.
———. 1995. *Immanuel Kants Entwurf "Zum ewigen Frieden." Eine Theorie der Politik*. Darmstadt: Wissenschaftliche Buchgesellschaft.
Ghetti, Pablo. 2017. *Constitutional Exposure: A Postulation for Democracy to Come*. Oxford: Counterpress.
Goldgaber, Deborah. 2017. "Review of Jacques Derrida, The Death Penalty, Volume II." *Notre Dame Philosophical Reviews*. October 22, 2017. https://ndpr.nd.edu/news/the-death-penalty-volume-ii/.
Goodrich, Peter et al., eds. 2008. *Derrida and Legal Philosophy*. Basingstoke: Palgrave Macmillan.

Goosen, Danie. 2010. "The Tragic, the Impossible and Democracy: An Interview with Jacques Derrida." *International Journal for the Semiotics of Law* 23, no. 3: 243–64.

Gratton, Peter. 2014. "Death and Derrida." *Berfrois*. April 7, 2014. https://www.berfrois.com/2014/04/deathand-derrida-by-peter-gratton/.

Guttmacher, Manfred S. 1958. "The Psychiatric Approach to Crime and Correction." *Law and Contemporary Problems* 23, no. 4 (Fall): 633–49.

Häberle, Peter. 2004. "Die Menschenwürde als Grundlage der Staatlichen Gemeinschaft." In *Handbuch des Staatsrechts der Bundesrepublik Deutschland*, Band II, edited by Josef Isensee and Paul Kirchhof, 317–67. Heidelberg: CF Müller Verlag.

Habermas, Jürgen. 1988. *The Inclusion of the Other: Studies in Political Theory*. Edited by Ciaran Cronin and Pablo De Greiff. Cambridge: MIT Press.

———. 1996. *Between Facts and Norms*. Cambridge: Polity Press.

———. 2003. "Fundamentalism and Terror—A Dialogue with Jürgen Habermas." In Borradori 2003, 25–43.

———. 2006. *The Divided West*. Edited and translated by Ciaran Cronin. Cambridge: Polity Press.

———. 2008. "The Constitutionalization of International Law and the Legitimation Problems of a Constitution for World Society." *Constellations* 14, no. 4: 444–55.

———. 2012. *The Crisis of the European Union: A Response*. Translated by Ciaran Cronin. Cambridge: Polity Press.

———. 2014a. "A Political Constitution for the Pluralist World Society?" *Journal of Chinese Philosophy* 40, no. S1: 226–38.

———. 2014b. "Plea for a Constitutionalization of International Law." *Philosophy & Social Criticism* 40, no. 1: 5–12.

Habermas, Jürgen, and Jacques Derrida. 2006. "February 15, Or What Binds Europeans Together: A Plea for a Common Foreign Policy, Beginning in the Core of Europe." In Thomassen 2006, 270–77.

Hackel, Volker Marcus. 2000. *Kants Friedensschrift und das Völkerrecht*. Berlin: Duncker & Humblot.

Heidegger, Martin. 1962. *Being and Time*. Translated by John Macquarrie and Edward Robinson. New York: Harper & Row.

———. 1971. *On the Way to Language*. Translated by Peter D. Hertz. New York: Harper.

———. 1977. *The Question Concerning Technology and Other Essays*. Translated by William Lovitt. New York: Harper.

———. 1985. *Schelling's Treatise on the Essence of Human Freedom*. Translated by Joan Stambaugh. Athens: Ohio University Press.

———. 1991. *The Principle of Reason*. Translated by Reginald Lilly. Bloomington: Indiana University Press.

———. 1993. *Basic Writings*. Edited by David Farrell Krell. New York: Harper.
———. 1997. *Kant and the Problem of Metaphysics*. 5th ed., enlarged. Translated by Richard Taft. Bloomington: Indiana University Press.
———. 1998. *Pathmarks*. Edited and translated by William McNeill. Cambridge: Cambridge University Press.
———. 2000. *Poetry, Language, Thought*. Translated by Albert Hofstadter. New York: HarperCollins.
———. 2002. *On Time and Being*. Translated by Joan Stambaugh. Chicago: University of Chicago Press.
———. 2005. *The Essence of Human Freedom: An Introduction to Philosophy*. Translated by Ted Sadler. London: Continuum.
———. 2012a. *Bremen and Freiburg Lectures: Insight into That Which Is and Basic Principles of Thinking*. Translated by Andrew J. Mitchell. Bloomington: Indiana University Press.
———. 2012b. *Contributions to Philosophy (of the Event)*. Translated by Richard Rojcewicz and Daniela Vallega-Neu. Bloomington: Indiana University Press.
———. 2013. *The Event*. Translated by Richard Rojcewicz. Bloomington: Indiana University Press.
———. 2017. *Ponderings VII–XI: Black Notebooks 1938–1939*. Translated by Richard Rojcewicz. Bloomington: Indiana University Press.
———. 2018. *Hölderlin's Hymn "Remembrance."* Translated by William McNeill and Julia Ireland. Bloomington: Indiana University Press.
Hill, Thomas E., and Arnulf Zweig. 2002. Editors' Introduction to *Groundwork for the Metaphysics of Morals*, by Immanuel Kant, 19–108. Translated by Arnulf Zweig. Oxford: Oxford University Press.
Höffe, Otfried, ed. 1995a. *Immanuel Kant: Zum ewigen Frieden*, Berlin: Akadademie Verlag.
Höffe, Otfried. 1995b. "Einleitung: Der Friede—ein vernachlässigtes Ideal." In Höffe 1995a, 5–29.
———. 1995c. "Völkerbund oder Weltrepublik?" In Höffe 1995a, 109–32.
———. 2006. *Kant's Cosmopolitan Theory of Law and Peace*. Translated by Alexandra Newton. Cambridge: Cambridge University Press.
———. 2012. *Kants Kritik der praktischen Vernunft: Eine Philosophie der Freiheit*. München: C.H. Beck.
———. 2014. *Immanuel Kant*. München: C.H. Beck.
Holland, Ben. 2017. "The Perpetual Peace Puzzle: Kant on Persons and States. *Philosophy and Social Criticism* 43, no. 6: 599–620.
Homer, Sean. 2004. *Jacques Lacan*. London: Routledge.
Huggler, Jørgen. 2010. "Cosmopolitanism and Peace in Kant's Essay on 'Perpetual Peace.'" *Studies in Philosophy and Education* 29: 129–40.
Kant, Immanuel. 1795. *Vorarbeiten zu Zum Ewigen Frieden*. https://korpora.zim.uni-duisburg-essen.de/kant/aa23/159.html.

———. 1979. *The Conflict of the Faculties*. Translated by Mary McGregor. New York: Abaris Books.

———. 1991. *Political Writings*. Edited by Hans Reiss. Cambridge: Cambridge University Press.

———. 1996a. *Practical Philosophy*. Translated by Mary J. Gregor. Cambridge: Cambridge University Press.

———. 1996b. *The Metaphysics of Morals*. Edited by Mary J. Gregor. Cambridge: Cambridge University Press.

———. 1997a. *Critique of Practical Reason*. Edited by Mary Gregor. Cambridge: Cambridge University Press.

———. 1997b. *Groundwork of the Metaphysics of Morals*. Cambridge: Cambridge University Press.

———. 1997c. *Lectures on Ethics*. Edited by Peter Heath and J. B. Schneewind and translated by Peter Heath. Cambridge: Cambridge University Press.

———. 1998a. *Critique of Pure Reason*. Edited by Paul Guyer and Allen W. Wood. Cambridge: Cambridge University Press.

———. 1998b. *Religion within the Boundaries of Mere Reason and Other Writings*. Edited by Allen Wood and George di Giovianni. Cambridge: Cambridge University Press.

———. 2002. *Groundwork for the Metaphysics of Morals*. Translated by Arnulf Zweig and edited by Thomas E. Hill and Arnulf Zweig. Oxford: Oxford University Press.

———. 2004. *Theoretical Philosophy after 1781*. Edited by Henry Allison and Peter Heath. Cambridge: Cambridge University Press.

———. 2006. *Anthropology from a Pragmatic Point of View*. Edited by Robert B. Louden. Cambridge: Cambridge University Press.

———. 2007. *Anthropology, History, and Education*. Edited and translated by Robert B. Louden and Günter Zöller. Cambridge: Cambridge University Press.

———. 2012. *Lectures on Anthropology*. Edited and translated by Robert B. Louden and Allen W. Wood. Cambridge: Cambridge University Press.

———. 2016. *Lectures and Drafts on Political Philosophy*. Edited by Frederick Rauscher and translated by Frederick Rauscher and Kenneth R. Westphal. Cambridge: Cambridge University Press.

Kennedy, Duncan. 1979. "The Structure of Blackstone's Commentaries." *Buffalo Law Review* 28, no. 2: 205–382.

Klare, Karl. 1998. "Legal Culture and Transformative Constitutionalism." *South African Journal on Human Rights* 14, no. 1: 146–88.

———. 2015. "Self-Realisation, Human Rights, and Separation of Powers: A Democracy-seeking Approach." *Stellenbosch Law Review* 26, no. 3: 445–70.

Kersting, Wolfgang. 1992. "Politics, Freedom, and Order: Kant's Political Philosophy." In *The Cambridge Companion to Kant*, edited by Paul Guyer, 342–66. Cambridge: Cambridge University Press.

———. 2007. *Wohlgeordnete Freiheit: Immanuel Kants Rechts- und Staatsphilosophie*. Paderborn: Mentis Verlag.

———. 2009. " 'The Civil Constitution in Every State Shall Be a Republican One.' " In *Kant's Moral and Legal Philosophy*, edited by Karl Ameriks and Otfried Höffe, 246–64. Cambridge: Cambridge University Press.

Kleingeld, Pauline. 2004. "Approaching Perpetual Peace: Kant's Defence of a League of States and His Ideal of a World Federation." *European Journal of Philosophy* 12, no. 3: 304.

———. 2012. *Kant and Cosmopolitanism: The Philosophical Ideal of World Citizenship*. Cambridge: Cambridge University Press.

Klemme, Heiner F. 1992. "Einleitung." In *Über den Gemeinspruch: Das mag in der Theorie richtig sein, taugt aber nicht für die Praxis/Zum ewigen Frieden*, edited by Heiner F. Klemme, VII–LIII. Hamburg: Felix Meiner Verlag.

Klenner, Hermann. 1996. "Kants Entwurf 'Zum ewigen Frieden': Illusion oder Utopie?" In *200 Jahre Kants Entwurf "Zum ewigen Frieden": Idee einer globalen Friedensordnung*, edited by Volker Bialas and Hans-Jürgen Häßler, 15–25. Würzburg: Königshausen & Neumann.

Klossowski, Pierre. 2002. *Roberte Ce Soir and the Revocation of the Edict of Nantes*. Translated by Austryn Wainhouse. Chicago: Dalkey Archive Press.

Koller, Peter. 1996. "Frieden und Gerechtigkeit in einer geteilten Welt." In Merkel and Wittmann 1996, 213–38.

Korsgaard, Christine M. 1997. Introduction to *Groundwork of the Metaphysics of Morals*, by Immanuel Kant, vii–xxx. Edited by Mary Gregor. Cambridge: Cambridge University Press.

Koskenniemi, Martti. 2007. "Constitutionalism as Mindset: Reflections on Kantian Themes about International Law and Globalization." *Theoretical Inquiries in Law* 8, no. 1: 9–36.

Kotzé, Louis J. 2019. "Earth System Law for the Anthropocene." *Sustainability* 11, no. 23: 6796. https://doi.org/10.3390/su11236796.

Krause, Joachim. 2013. "Kant und seine Zeit—die Schrift 'Zum ewigen Frieden' vor der Hintergrund der Französischen Revolution und der nachfolgenden Kriege." In *Kant's Project of Perpetual Peace in the Context of Contemporary Politics: Proceedings of International Seminar*, edited by Andrey Zilber and Alexei Salikov, 9–23. Kaliningrad: Immanuel Kant Baltic Federal University Press.

Lacan, Jacques. 1989. "Kant with Sade." Translated by James B. Swenson Jr. *October* 51 (Winter): 55–75.

———. 1992. *The Ethics of Psychoanalysis 1959–1960*: The Seminar of Jacques Lacan. Book VII. Edited by Jacques-Alain Miller. London: Routledge.

———. 1998. *On Feminine Sexuality: The Limits of Love and Knowledge*. The Seminar of Jacques Lacan. Book XX. Edited by Jacques-Alain Miller and translated by Bruce Fink. New York: W.W. Norton & Company.

La Caze, Marguerite. 2007. "At the Intersection: Kant, Derrida, and the Relation between Ethics and Politics." *Political Theory* 35, no. 6: 781–805.

Legrand, Pierre, ed. 2009. *Derrida and Law*. Farnham: Ashgate.

Le Roux, Wessel. 2009. "Migration, Street Democracy and Expatriate Voting Rights." *SA Public Law* 24, no. 2: 370–99.

———. 2011. "Economic Migration, Disaggregated Citizenship and the Right to Vote in Post-Apartheid South Africa." In *Citizens of the World: Pluralism, Migration and Practices of Citizenship*, edited by Robert Danisch, 117–37. Leiden: Brill.

———. 2015. "Residence, Representative Democracy and the Voting Rights of Migrant Workers in Post-Apartheid South Africa and Post-Unification Germany (1990–2015)." *Verfassung und Recht in Übersee* 48, no. 3, Special Issue: The Current State of Democracy in South Africa: 263–83.

Levinas, Emmanuel. 1969. *Totality and Infinity: An Essay on Exteriority*. Translated by Alphonso Lingis. The Hague: Martinus Nijhoff Publishers.

———. 1998. *Of God Who Comes to Mind*. Translated by Bettina Bergo. Stanford: Stanford University Press.

———. 2007a. *Beyond the Verse: Talmudic Readings and Lectures*. Translated by Gary D. Mole. Bloomington: Indiana University Press.

———. 2007b. *In the Time of the Nations*. Translated by Michael B. Smith. Bloomington: Indiana University Press.

Lutz-Bachmann, Matthias. 1997. "Kant's Idea of Peace and the Philosophical Conception of a World Republic." In *Perpetual Peace: Essays on Kant's Cosmopolitan Ideal*, edited by James Bohman and Matthias Lutz-Bachmann, 59–77. Baskerille: MIT Press.

Mansfield, Nick. 2018. "Hospitality and Sovereign Violence: Derrida on Lot." *Derrida Today* 11, no. 1: 49–59.

Maris C. W., and Jacobs F. C. L. M. 2011. *Law, Order and Freedom: A Historical Introduction to Legal Philosophy*. Translated by Jacques de Ville. Dordrecht: Springer.

Marrati, Paola. 2005. *Genesis and Trace: Derrida Reading Husserl and Heidegger*. Stanford: Stanford University Press.

Maruna, Shaud, Amanda Matravers, and Anna King. 2004. "Disowning Our Shadow: A Psychoanalytic Approach to Understanding Punitive Public Attitudes." *Deviant Behaviour* 25, no. 3: 277–99.

Merkel, Reinhard, and Robert Wittman, eds. 1996. *Zum ewigen Frieden": Grundlagen, Aktualität und Aussichten einer Idee von Immanuel Kant*. Frankfurt am Main: Suhrkamp.

Meylahn, Johann-Albrecht. 2010. "Poetically Africa Dwells: A Dialogue between Heidegger's Understanding of Language as the House of Being and African Being-with (*ubuntu*) as a Possible Paradigm for Postfoundational Practical Theology in Africa." *Verbum et Ecclesia* 31, no. 1: 1–9.

Modiri, Joel, M. 2018. "Conquest and Constitutionalism: First Thoughts on an Alternative Jurisprudence." *South African Journal on Human Rights* 34, no. 3: 300–25.
Mureinik, Etienne. 1994. "A Bridge to Where? Introducing the Interim Bill of Rights." *South African Journal on Human Rights* 10, no. 1: 31–48.
Naas, Michael. 2012. "The Philosophy and Literature of the Death Penalty: Two Sides of the Same Coin." *Southern Journal of Philosophy* 50, no. 1: 39–55.
Nancy, Jean-Luc. 1993a. *The Birth to Presence*. Translated by Brian Holmes et al. Stanford: Stanford University Press.
———. 1993b. *The Experience of Freedom*. Translated by Bridget McDonald. Stanford: Stanford University Press.
Nietzsche, Friedrich. 2003a. *The Genealogy of Morals*. Translated by Horace B. Samuel. New York: Dover Publications.
———. 2003b. *Thus Spoke Zarathustra*. Translated by R. J. Hollingdale. London: Penguin Books.
O'Regan, Catherine. 2009. "From Form to Substance: The Constitutional Jurisprudence of Laurie Ackermann." In Barnard-Naudé et al. 2009, 1–17.
Ossipow, William. 2008. "Kant's Perpetual Peace and Its Hidden Sources: A Textual Approach." *Swiss Political Science Review* 14, no. 2: 357–89.
Patzig, Günther. 1996. Kants Schrift "Zum ewigen Frieden." In Merkel and Wittmann 1996, 12–30.
Peters, Anne. 2009. "The Merits of Global Constitutionalism." *Indiana Journal of Global Legal Studies* 16, no. 2: 397–411.
———. 2015. "Global Constitutionalism." In *The Encyclopedia of Political Thought*, edited by Michael T. Gibbons et al., 1–4. Hoboken, NJ: Wiley-Blackwell. https://www.mpil.de/files/pdf5/Peters_Global_Constitutionalism__Encyclopedia_of_Political_Thought_20151.pdf.
Plato. 1997. *Complete Works*. Edited by John M. Cooper. Indianapolis: Hackett Publishing Company.
Pogge, Thomas. W. 1988. "Kant's Theory of Justice." *Kant-Studien* 79, no. 1–4: 407–33.
Qerimi, Qerim. 2019. "The Contents and Contours of Contemporary Cosmopolitan Constitution-making: Immanuel Kant in the Twenty-first Century." *Global Constitutionalism* 8, no. 2: 227–69.
Raffoul, François. 2010. *The Origins of Responsibility*. Bloomington: Indiana University Press.
Ramose, Mogobe B. 2005a. *African Philosophy through Ubuntu*. Harare: Mond Books.
———. 2005b. "The Philosophy of Ubuntu and Ubuntu as a Philosophy." In *The African Philosophy Reader*. 2nd edition, edited by P. H. Coetzee and A. P. J. Roux, 270–80. London: Routledge.
———. 2018. "Towards a Post-Conquest South Africa: Beyond the Constitution of 1996." *South African Journal on Human Rights* 34, no. 3: 326–41.

Rauber, Jochen. 2009. "The United Nations—a Kantian Dream Come True? Philosophical Perspectives on the Constitutional Legitimacy of the World Organisation." *Hanse Law Review* 5, no. 1: 49–76.
Rawls, John. 1999a. *A Theory of Justice: Revised Edition*. Cambridge: The Belknap Press of Harvard University Press.
———. 1999b. *The Law of Peoples*. Cambridge: Harvard University Press.
———. 2005. *Political Liberalism: Expanded Edition*. New York: Columbia University Press.
Reath, Andrews. 1997. Introduction to *Critique of Practical Reason*, by Immanuel Kant, vii–xxxi. Edited by Mary Gregor. Cambridge: Cambridge University Press.
Reik, Theodor. 1959. *The Compulsion to Confess*. New York: John Wiley & Sons.
Reiss, Hans. 1991. Introduction to *Political Writings*, by Immanuel Kant, 1–40. Edited by Hans Reiss. Cambridge: Cambridge University Press.
Richardson, William J. 1967. "Heidegger and the Quest of Freedom." *Theological Studies* 28, no. 2: 286–307.
Rimoux, Frédéric. 2015. "Kants Rechtstheorie vom Weltfrieden. Zwischen apriorischen Rechtsprinzipien und politischer Praxis." PhD diss., Eberhard Karls Universität Tübingen. https://publikationen.uni-tuebingen.de/xmlui/handle/10900/64242.
Rühs, Natalie, and Aled Jones. 2016. "The Implementation of Earth Jurisprudence through Substantive Constitutional Rights of Nature." *Sustainability* 8, no. 2: 174. https://doi.org/10.3390/su8020174.
Ruin, Hans. 2008. "The Destiny of Freedom: in Heidegger." *Continental Philosophy Review* 41: 277–99.
Saghafi, Kas. 2016. "The Master Trembles: Sacrifice, Hierarchy, and Ontology in Derrida's 'Remain(s).'" *Derrida Today* 9, no. 2: 124–38.
Saner, Hans. 1995. "Die negativen Bedingungen des Friedens." In Höffe 1995a, 43–67.
Scheid, Don. E. 2011. "Perpetual Peace: Kant." In *Encyclopedia of Global Justice*, edited by Deen K. Chatterjee, 836–41. Dordrecht: Springer.
Scheuerman, William E. 2019. "Donald Trump Meets Carl Schmitt." *Philosophy & Social Criticism* 45, no. 9–10: 1170–85.
Schlag, Pierre. 1998. *The Enchantment of Reason*. Durham: Duke University Press.
Schmeiser, Susan R. 2007. "Furnishing Guilt." *American Imago* 64, no. 3: 317–37.
Schmidt-Aßmann, Eberhard. 2004. "Der Rechtsstaat." In *Handbuch des Staatsrechts der Bundesrepublik Deutschland*, Band II, edited by Josef Isensee and Paul Kirchhof, 541–612. Heidelberg: CF Müller Verlag.
Schmitt, Carl. 2006. *The Nomos of the Earth*. Translated by Gary L. Ulmen. New York: Telos Press Publishing.
———. 2007. *The Concept of the Political*. Translated by George Schwab. Chicago: University of Chicago Press.
———. 2008. *Constitutional Theory*. Translated and edited by Jeffrey Seitzer. Durham: Duke University Press.

Shryock, Andrew. 2008. "Thinking about Hospitality, with Derrida, Kant, and the Balga Bedouin." *Anthropos* 103, no. 2: 405–21.

Silving, Helen. 1960. "Psychoanalysis and the Criminal Law." *Journal of Law and Criminology* 51, no. 1: 19–33.

Somek, Alexander. 2020. "Cosmopolitan Constitutionalism: The Case of the European Convention." *Global Constitutionalism* 9, no. 3: 467–89.

Stern, Klaus. 1984. *Das Staatsrecht der Bundesrepublik Deutschland*, Band I. 2nd ed. München: CH Beck'sche Verlagsbuchhandlung.

Still, Judith. 2010. *Derrida and Hospitality: Theory and Practice*. Edinburgh: Edinburgh University Press.

Stone, Matthew, Illan rua Wall, and Costas Douzinas. 2012. "Introduction: Law, Politics and the Political." In *New Critical Legal Thinking: Law and the Political*, edited by Matthew Stone, Illan rua Wall, and Costas Douzinas, 1–7. Abingdon: Routledge.

Sweet, Alec Stone, and Eric Palmer. 2017. "A Kantian System of Constitutional Justice: Rights, Trusteeship, Balancing." *Global Constitutionalism* 6, no. 3: 377–411.

Sweet, Alec Stone, and Clare Ryan. 2018. *A Cosmopolitan Legal Order: Kant, Constitutional Justice, and the European Convention on Human Rights*. Oxford: Oxford University Press.

———. 2020. "Kant, Cosmopolitanism and Systems of Constitutional Justice in Europe and Beyond." *Global Constitutionalism* 9, no. 3: 562–80.

Tesón, Fernando R. 1992. "The Kantian Theory of International Law." *Columbia Law Review* 92: 53–102.

Thomassen, Lasse, ed. 2006. *The Derrida-Habermas Reader*. Chicago: University of Chicago Press.

Trumbull, Robert. 2015. "Derrida and the Death Penalty: The Question of Cruelty." *Philosophy Today* 59, no. 2: 317–36.

Tushnet, Mark. 1991. "Critical Legal Studies: A Political History." *The Yale Law Journal* 100, no. 5: 1515–44.

Van der Walt, Johan. 2019. "Law and Deconstruction." In Christodoulidis et al. 2019, 166–80.

Van der Walt, Johan, and Henk Botha. 2000. "Democracy and Rights in South Africa: Beyond a Constitutional Culture of Justification." *Constellations* 7, no. 3: 341–62.

Van Gorkom, J. M. L. M. 2009. "The Third One: Imagination in Kant, Heidegger and Derrida." PhD diss., University of Tilburg. https://research.tilburguniversity.edu/en/publications/the-third-one-imagination-in-kant-heidegger-and-derrida.

Vergil. 1963. *Vergil's Aeneid*. Translated by L. R. Lind. Bloomington: Indiana University Press.

Walters, Mark D. 2004. "The Common Law Constitution and Legal Cosmopolitanism." In *The Unity of Public Law*, edited by David Dyzenhaus, 431–54. Oxford: Hart Publishing.

Westmoreland, Mark W. 2008. "Interruptions: Derrida and Hospitality." *Kritike* 2, no. 1: 1–10.
Wood, Allen W. 1995. "Kant's Project for Perpetual Peace." In *Cosmopolitics: Thinking and Feeling Beyond the Nation*, edited by Pheng Cheah and Bruce Robbins, 59–76. Minneapolis: University of Minnesota Press.
Werner, Wouter, and Geoff Gordon. 2016. "Kant, Cosmopolitanism, and International Law." In *The Oxford Handbook of the Theory of International Law*, edited by Anne Orford and Florian Hoffmann, 505–25. Oxford: Oxford University Press.
Woolman, Stuart. 2014. "Dignity." In *Constitutional Law of South Africa*. 2nd ed., edited by Stu Woolman and Michael Bishop, 36-1 to 36-71. Cape Town: Juta.
Woolman, Stuart, and Dennis Davis. 1996. "The Last Laugh: *Du Plessis v De Klerk*, Classical Liberalism, Creole Liberalism and the Application of Fundamental Rights under the Interim and the Final Constitutions." 12, no. 3: 361–404.
Zenkert, Georg. 1999. "Politik als Friedensstrategie: Kants Entwurf zum ewigen Frieden in der Diskussion." *Philosophische Rundschau* 46, no. 2: 97–115.

Case Law

Carmichele v Minister of Safety and Security (Centre for Applied Legal Studies Intervening) 2010 (5) SA 457 (SCA).
Du Plessis and Others v De Klerk and Another 1996 (3) SA 850 (CC).
Ferreira v Levin NO and Others; Vryenhoek and Others v Powell NO and Other 1996 (1) SA 984 (CC).
MEC for Education: KwaZulu-Natal and Others v Pillay 2008 (1) SA 474 (CC).
National Society for the Prevention of Cruelty to Animals v Minister of Justice and Constitutional Development and Another 2017 (4) BCLR 517 (CC).
S v Dodo 2001 (3) SA 382 (CC).
S v Makwanyane and Another 1995 (3) SA 391 (CC).

Index

Abraham, 28, 30, 32, 34, 35, 163n61, 178n13
Adorno, Theodor, 95, 162n48
animal. *See* non-human animal(s)
apperception, 67, 89
appresentation, 32, 163n60
Aristotle, 24–25, 26, 47, 69, 76–77, 79
as if, 15, 21, 33–34, 164n66
autoimmune/autoimmunity, 40, 58–59, 60, 79–80, 91, 106, 132–33, 137, 181n56. *See also* death drive; drive(s); self-destruction
autonomy/autonomous, 9, 13, 14, 19, 32, 71, 75, 82, 84, 90, 95, 126, 146, 148, 149, 162n56, 167n6, 168n22

beauty/beautiful, 109, 158n6
Beccaria, Cesare, 109, 111, 174n27
Being/Beyng (*das Sein/Seyn*), 9, 15, 39, 42–46, 47, 48, 49–50, 52, 53, 56, 58, 63–64, 65, 68–69, 72–74, 75, 81–82, 91, 146, 147–48, 149, 165n6, 167notes
being-toward-death, 55, 65, 77, 115
Benjamin, Walter, 2, 108, 175n31
Bentham, Jeremy, 37, 91, 97
Benveniste, Émile, 31, 114, 137, 141

capitalism/capitalist, 6, 138
categorical imperative, 11–12, 15, 19, 21, 33, 34, 69–71, 85–86, 102, 109, 110–11, 113, 124, 146, 157n1, 159n21, 160n38, 162n48
causal(ity), 10, 11, 12, 16, 20, 37, 64, 65–69, 72, 74, 76, 81, 148, 162n48, 167n11, 167n24
Cicero, 55
cities of refuge, 140–41
citizen(s): active/passive, 170n38; independence of, 3, 12, 62; world 127, 133
civil condition, 3, 12–14, 38, 85, 87, 92–95, 96, 97, 99, 126, 149
clemency, 16, 102, 112–13, 150, 151. *See also* pardon
colonial(ism), 7, 14, 139, 156n24
compulsion neurosis, 159n28
compulsion to confess, 173n8
confess(ion), 103, 120, 122, 123, 173n8, 176n44
conscience, 11, 19, 20, 23, 32, 35, 107, 146, 162n48 & n50, 163n59 & n60
constituent power 82, 168n22
cosmo-political, 136
cosmopolitan: constitution/law/order, 5, 14, 17, 63, 87, 125, 126–27,

201

cosmopolitan *(continued)*
    133–34, 139–43, 144, 151, 169n34, 179n33; democracy 137; ideal 134
cosmopolitanism, 138, 139–40, 143, 144, 180n55, 181n56
critique, Kantian notion of, 47
cruel(ty), 17, 26, 86, 95–96, 102, 109, 110–11, 121, 122–23, 131–32, 149–50, 151, 162n48, 174n24 & n27

Dasein/Da-seyn, 55, 65, 68, 69, 72–73, 74, 91, 115
death drive, 9, 15, 20, 21, 29, 58, 91, 103, 109, 111, 119, 132, 146, 149, 151, 157n2
death penalty, 5, 13, 54–57, 96, 101–23 passim, 150, 151, 162n51, 165n11, 174n14 & n24, 175n32 & n33, 176n39 & n42
democracy, 16, 76, 78–80, 82, 98, 136–38, 148–49, 150, 152, 170n36, 180n52; to come, 16, 17, 63, 65, 82, 134, 136, 137–38, 149, 150, 152, 168n24, 170n37
democratic, 6, 8, 12, 16, 58, 77, 78, 79, 80, 82, 98, 136, 137, 156n21, 157n35
demos, 80, 82, 137, 149, 150
Descartes, René, 41, 48, 90, 91, 96
desire, 20, 24, 26, 53, 76–77, 78, 92, 102, 104, 105, 113, 116, 119, 122, 151, 157–58n3, 159n28, 161n42, 168n26 & n27, 169n31 & n33, 170n36
différance, 23, 24, 74, 80, 96, 111, 119, 175n33
dignity, 3–5, 11–12, 15, 19, 21, 35, 56, 59, 61, 63, 83, 86, 89, 90, 95, 97, 101, 102, 114, 115, 117, 121, 125, 138, 147, 149, 150, 151, 155n10, 156n13 & n14

drive(s) 9, 15, 20, 21, 28–29, 57, 58, 64, 76, 77, 82, 91, 103, 109, 110, 111, 117, 118, 119, 122, 131–32, 144, 146, 149, 151, 157n2, 174n20, 175n33, 179n26. *See also* inclination(s); instinct(s); death drive
duty/duties, 11, 15, 19, 21, 28, 29–33, 35, 39, 51, 54, 59, 60, 61, 86, 95, 97, 98, 107, 117, 135, 146, 147, 148, 158n5, 160n39, 161–62notes, 179n25, 181n64

ego, 20, 26, 35; *alter*, 163n60; *cogito*, 48
Einstein, Albert, 131
end-in-itself. *See* means/end-in-itself
Enlightenment, 1, 3, 7, 17, 70, 121, 123, 146, 160n38
equality, 3, 8, 12, 62, 83, 117, 168n24
event, 16, 34, 53–54, 59, 64–65, 68, 74, 75, 78, 82, 91, 106, 116, 120–22, 123, 137, 148, 149, 164n62, 165n10, 166n17 & n19, 169n30, 176n46
evil, 88, 94, 96, 105, 117, 151, 168n27, 171n9, 174n25
evil genius, 91, 96
example, 21, 34, 163n61

fault, 31, 32, 91–92, 93, 103, 107, 108, 161n46. *See also* guilt
federation/league of states, 13–14, 63, 87, 125, 134–36, 152, 169n34, 179n33, 180n41 & n44
finitude, 65, 66, 68, 73, 77, 91, 112, 116, 150, 167n16
Fontaine, Jean de La, 57–58
forgiveness, 17, 57, 59, 102, 103, 104, 107, 112–13, 120, 122, 123–24, 151, 153, 164n62, 174n18
Foucault, Michel, 175n28

Free, the (*das Freie*) 49, 72, 73–74, 75, 148
freedom, 1, 2–4, 9, 10–14, 15–16, 17, 19, 20, 23–24, 30, 35–36, 37, 38, 47–48, 50, 53, 54, 61–82, 83, 86, 87, 93, 94, 95, 96, 98, 101, 102, 103–107, 115, 121, 122, 125, 126, 135, 137, 138, 145, 146, 147, 148, 149, 150, 157n36, 159n22, 160n34, 166n2 & n3, 167–70notes, 174n14 & n20, 180n54
French Revolution, 120, 121, 123, 170n35, 176n45, 177n3, 180n44
Freud, Sigmund, 9, 14–15, 17, 19–21, 22, 24, 25, 26, 28, 31, 33, 58, 59–60, 63, 77, 80, 91, 96, 102, 103–107, 109, 110, 111, 118, 131–32, 135, 137, 146, 149, 151, 157n1 & n2, 158n4, 159–64notes, 172n21 & n24, 174notes, 179n26

gift, 2, 15, 16, 32, 39–40, 53–54, 56–57, 59, 60, 74, 75, 82, 107, 119, 121, 123, 142, 147, 148, 149, 153, 164n62, 165n10 & n13, 174n18
good will, 29, 69, 161n44, 162n48
guilt, 5, 19, 20, 32, 57, 64, 101, 103–107, 122, 140, 150, 151, 160n34, 161n46, 162n48 & n51, 163n58. *See also* fault

Habermas, Jürgen, 1, 8, 133, 143
Heidegger, Martin, 1, 9, 15, 16, 27, 31, 37–82 passim, 83, 91, 115, 137, 145, 146–48, 152, 158n13, 160n38, 162n49 & n51, 164–69notes, 176n43
heteronomy, 32, 146, 162n56
Hobbes, Thomas, 86, 171n9 & n10, 174n19
Homer, 77

hospitality, 14, 17, 34–35, 59, 60, 63, 65, 80, 97–99, 107, 121, 123–24, 125–44 passim, 147, 149, 150, 151, 152, 153. *See also* welcome
host, 129, 137, 141, 144, 151, 168n22, 178n13, 181n68
hostage, 35, 129, 137, 141, 144, 146, 151
human being, essence of, 39, 43, 46, 50, 55, 56, 68, 69, 71, 72, 73, 74, 75, 81, 82, 89, 146, 148, 168–69n28
human dignity. *See* dignity
human right(s), 4, 5, 36, 98, 123, 133, 138, 141, 144, 145, 177n3
humanitarian(ism), 134, 143
Husserl, Edmund, 32, 58, 91, 137, 163n60
hypothetical imperative, 28, 109, 159n21, 160n38

id, 26. *See also* unconscious
imagination, 21, 27, 33, 106, 158n8, 164n65
imperative. *See* categorical imperative; hypothetical imperative
impossible, the, 34, 35, 53, 60, 91, 111, 112, 121, 132, 137, 147, 164, 176n46
inclination(s), 11, 12, 14, 19, 24, 27–28, 29, 30, 32, 37, 61, 81, 85, 95, 103, 135, 147, 149, 161n41 & n44, 178n14. *See also* drive(s); instinct(s)
inequality, 6–7, 8, 145, 152
instinct(s), 28–29, 37, 110, 122, 160n35, 161n42, 172n21
interest, of reason, 59, 109–10, 111–12, 160n36, 166n17
international law, 17, 58, 126, 127, 133–39, 152
ipseity, 59, 75–76, 77, 78, 82, 108, 137

iterability, 33, 163n62
ius/lex talionis, 55, 104, 115, 116–17, 118, 119, 120, 151, 165n12, 176n37 & n40

Jerusalem, 140–41, 182n71
Jesus (Christ), 30, 32, 163n61
juridical-(cosmo-)political, 132, 144
juridical-political, 112, 130
justice, 2, 4, 7, 9, 17, 35, 37, 58, 59, 85, 97, 113, 114, 118, 123, 136, 137, 138, 140, 145, 146, 147, 151, 152, 153, 157n38, 164n62, 165n10, 175n25, 175n33; criminal/penal, 102, 103, 109, 119; punitive, 13, 108, 118

Kafka, Franz, 20, 22–24, 29, 33, 174n13
khōra, 134, 164n65
Kierkegaard, Søren, 20, 28, 32
Klossowski, Pierre, 128–29
kratos, 79, 80, 137, 149

Lacan, Jacques, 20, 83–84, 92, 96, 157n3, 158n4, 162n56, 171n18
Leibniz, Gottfried Wilhelm, 15, 39, 40–42, 44–46, 47, 49, 51, 54, 55, 147
Levinas, Emmanuel, 20, 27, 34–35, 83, 91, 96, 127, 129, 130–33, 140–41, 142, 144, 166n16, 178–79notes, 181n64 & n66, 182n71
liberty. *See* freedom
logos, 53, 58, 165n6 & n15

maxim(s), 11, 19, 29–30, 33, 69–70, 146, 164n63
means/end-in-itself, 11–12, 70–71, 85–86, 95, 109, 113, 114, 171n6
metaphysics/metaphysical 7, 9, 25, 33, 51, 63, 64, 66, 67, 68, 81, 91, 145–46, 147, 163n62, 174n20

Montesquieu, 1, 3
moral law, 2, 4, 9, 12, 13, 14–15, 19–36, 37, 63, 69–72, 75, 81, 84, 95–96, 97, 114, 125, 146–47, 148, 158–63notes, 167n7, 176n45

Nancy, Jean-Luc, 25–27, 29, 63, 64, 75, 78
nature, state of, 12, 13, 62, 86–87, 92–95, 99, 107, 114, 126, 129–30, 135, 136, 171n9 & n10
Nietzsche, Friedrich, 22, 31, 95, 109–11, 116–17, 151, 162n48 & n51
non-human animal(s), 5, 12, 14, 16, 37, 57, 60, 83–99, 149–50, 152, 170n2, 172n29
noumenon/noumenal, 11, 12, 19, 66, 103, 107, 114

Oedipus/oedipal, 20, 77, 103, 104, 105–106, 107, 151, 157–58n1 & n3, 159n28, 174n16, 176n41

pardon, 104, 112–13, 123, 175n29. *See also* clemency
peace, vii, 1, 2, 4, 9, 13–14, 17, 36, 61, 62–63, 87, 88, 125–44, 145, 147, 148, 151–52, 171n10, 177–78notes, 179n25
perhaps, the, 21, 32, 34, 133, 176n46
personality, 30, 71, 114; legal, 17, 150
perpetual peace. *See* peace
personhood, 68, 71, 85, 86, 89–90, 150, 170n5
Plato, 34, 75, 78–79, 115, 169n29
play, 38, 39, 45, 49, 50, 53, 54, 56, 64, 79, 169n34, 174n21
pleasure, 24, 29, 33, 76–78, 82, 102, 106, 110, 111, 119, 132, 151, 158n8, 161n41 & n42
political, the, 17, 77, 130, 131, 132, 138, 139, 144, 152, 166n18,

178n18 & n19, 182n74. *See also* cosmo-political; juridical-(cosmo-)political; juridical-political
political theology, 17, 77, 102, 115–16, 122, 151
psychoanalysis, 8, 15, 54, 91, 101–102, 103–104, 107, 118, 119, 120, 145, 150–51, 165n13
punishment, 5, 8, 10, 13, 16–17, 20, 36, 55, 101–24 passim, 150–51, 163n58, 173n1 & n8, 174n25, 175notes
prime/first/unmoved mover, 69, 76–77

Rawls, John, 1, 8
reason, vii, 2–17 passim, 19, 27, 28, 30, 35, 37–60, 62, 69, 70, 71–72, 83–96 passim, 109, 114, 115, 126, 133, 135, 136, 145, 147–48, 150, 158n7, 159n19 & n22, 160n36, 162n55, 163n57 & n61, 164–66notes, 170–71n6, 171n11, 173n12, 179n25
regulative idea, 137, 170n37
Reik, Theodor, 17, 102, 103–104, 105, 106, 116–23 passim, 162n48, 173n8, 174n24 & n25
repetition, 32, 34, 76, 77, 163–64n62; compulsion, 80. *See also* iterability; drive(s)
representation: political, 98–99, 173n31; of the 'I', 41–42, 48, 49, 86, 88–90, 96
repression, 16, 22, 54, 96, 159n28, 160n35, 169n31 & n33
republic(an), 12, 13–14, 62–63, 81, 87, 120, 125, 126, 135, 136, 148, 157n35, 169n34, 177n3, 180n44
respect, for the law/persons, 15, 20, 21–22, 23, 24, 27–29, 31, 34–35, 85, 114, 117, 147, 158notes, 159n23, 160n34, 161n41, 176n45

responsibility, vii, 9, 13, 15, 32, 34, 35, 40, 51, 52–53, 54, 57, 59, 60, 65, 69, 71, 75, 84, 90, 97, 113, 140, 148, 152, 162n48, 163n59 & n61, 165n10, 169n29, 179n30; criminal/legal, 16, 17, 95, 97, 98, 101, 102, 103–107, 122, 145, 150
right(s), 3, 4, 5, 12, 14, 17, 36, 37, 55, 64, 80, 82, 87, 95, 97, 98, 114, 118, 121, 123, 127, 133, 138, 139–42, 144, 145, 148, 150, 170n38, 171n9, 172n28, 173n30, 177n3, 178n9, 179n33, 180n44, 181n61 & n66. *See also* human right(s)
right/power to punish. *See* punishment; sovereignty
Rousseau, Jean-Jacques, 1, 170n36

sacrifice, 15, 21, 28, 30, 32–33, 35, 81, 84, 93, 95, 114, 115, 122, 146, 147, 149, 151, 161n42, 162n50, 163n61, 172n25
Schelling, Friedrich Wilhelm Joseph, 168n27
Schmitt, Carl, 2–3, 80, 108, 112, 143–44, 148, 157n35, 168n22, 171n10, 182n74
self-destruction, 2, 38, 58–59, 75, 79, 82, 94, 106, 107, 110, 133, 137, 149, 151, 169n32, 170n35, 172n21, 175n33, 181n56, 182n74. *See also* autoimmune/autoimmunity; death drive
self-government, 1, 17, 62, 145
self-presence, 7, 25, 89–91
separation of powers, 1, 3, 5, 12, 60, 62, 126, 148, 157n35, 177n7
sovereignty, 14, 16, 17, 44, 46, 59, 60, 63, 64, 75–77, 78, 80, 82, 87, 97, 102, 106, 108–13, 114, 122, 123, 129, 131, 132, 134, 135–39, 142, 144, 145, 148, 149, 150,

sovereignty *(continued)*
  151, 152, 167n6, 168n22, 170n35, 172n19, 174n14 & n20, 180n41 & n52
speech/writing opposition, 169n31
state of nature. *See* nature, state of
subject(ivity), 7, 8, 9, 16, 24, 27, 33, 34–35, 39, 45, 48, 49, 54, 59, 60, 64, 75, 78, 82, 85, 88–92, 95, 97, 98, 102, 103, 107, 114, 137, 144, 146, 147–48, 149–51, 161n42, 162n56, 164n62, 172n25, 174n20
subjection, 16, 30, 32, 85, 97, 98, 99, 149, 150, 162n56
sublime, 30, 158n8
superego, 15, 19–20, 24, 103, 157n2 & n3

talionic law/principle. See *ius/lex talionis*
tolerance 139, 181n66
transcendental: apperception 89; force 78; freedom 64, 65–69, 72, 81, 148, 167n8; imagination 27; method, 10, 15, 47, 49, 147

ubuntu, 156n14 & n26

unconscious, vii, 17, 31, 53, 54, 59–60, 76–77, 91, 92, 96, 102, 103, 104, 105, 107, 117, 118, 119, 120, 121, 122, 130, 146, 150–51, 160n35; 164n64; 165n13, 169n33, 173n8 & n11, 175n31, 176n44. See also *id*
university, 42, 50–53, 165n9
utilitarian, 37, 102, 109, 113, 165n11, 175n30

Valery, Paul, 91
virtue(s), 12, 19, 35, 81, 84, 86, 96, 157n36, 158n5 & n6, 166n2

war, 13, 57, 58, 62, 85, 87, 93–94, 96, 97, 126, 127, 128, 129–33, 135, 141, 143, 144, 150, 152, 170n36, 171n9, 172n22 & n26, 178n14 & n16, 179n24 & n25, 181n56, 182n74
welcome, 34–36, 59–60, 65, 80, 82, 127, 129, 132, 142, 143, 144. *See also* hospitality
world state, 14, 134–39, 144, 152, 180n44
world citizenship. *See under* citizen(s)

www.ingramcontent.com/pod-product-compliance
Lightning Source LLC
Chambersburg PA
CBHW030652230426
43665CB00011B/1051